"An excellent analysis of gaming and extremism, which highlights some of the most complex challenges in tackling abuse of a constantly-changing technology space. A perfect introduction for a novice and expert alike."
– **Charley Gleeson,** *Open-Source Intelligence Analyst at Tech Against Terrorism, UK*

"For too long, policy and practice related to gaming and extremism have been based on little more than anecdote and gut feeling. This book is the antidote to that. Full of erudite chapters from world-leading experts, this volume is required reading for policy makers and practitioners alike."
– **Ross Frenett,** *Founder and Co-CEO of Moonshot, UK*

T0372890

GAMING AND EXTREMISM

Charting the increase in the use of games for the dissemination of extremist propaganda, radicalization, recruitment, and mobilization, this book examines the "gamification of extremism."

Editors Linda Schlegel and Rachel Kowert bring together a range of insights from world-leading experts in the field to provide the first comprehensive overview of gaming and extremism. The potential nexus between gaming and extremism has become a key area of concern for researchers, policymakers, and practitioners seeking to prevent and counter radicalization and this book offers insights into key trends and debates, future directions, and potential prevention efforts. This includes the exploration of how games and game adjacent spaces, such as Discord, Twitch, Steam, and DLive, are being leveraged by extremists for the purposes of radicalization, recruitment, and mobilization. Additionally, the book presents the latest counterterrorism techniques, surveys promising preventing/countering violent extremism (P/CVE) measures currently being utilized in the gaming sphere, and examines the ongoing challenges, controversies, and current gaps in knowledge in the field.

This text will be of interest to students and scholars of gaming and gaming culture, as well as an essential resource for researchers and practitioners working in prevention and counter-extremism, professionals working at gaming-related tech companies, and policymakers.

Linda Schlegel is a Research Fellow at modusIzad, a founding member of the Extremism and Gaming Research Network, and an Associate Fellow at the Peace Research Institute Frankfurt. Her research interests include gaming/gamification and radicalization, digital P/CVE, and narrative campaigns against extremism.

Rachel Kowert is a Research Psychologist, the Research Director of *Take This*, and the founder of *Psychgeist*, a multimedia content production studio for the science of games and pop culture. She is a world-renowned researcher on the uses and effects of digital games and currently serves as one of the primary investigators on the first grant-funded project from the Department of Homeland Security about games and extremism. To learn more about Rachel and her work, visit www.rkowert.com.

GAMING AND EXTREMISM

The Radicalization of Digital Playgrounds

Edited by Linda Schlegel and Rachel Kowert

Routledge
Taylor & Francis Group
NEW YORK AND LONDON

Designed cover image: © Andrey Suslov/Getty Images

First published 2024
by Routledge
605 Third Avenue, New York, NY 10158

and by Routledge
4 Park Square, Milton Park, Abingdon, Oxon OX14 4RN

Routledge is an imprint of the Taylor & Francis Group, an informa business

© 2024 selection and editorial matter, Linda Schlegel and Rachel Kowert; individual chapters, the contributors

Library of Congress Cataloging-in-Publication Data
Names: Schlegel, Linda, 1992- editor. | Kowert, Rachel, editor.
Title: Gaming and extremism : the radicalization of digital playgrounds / edited by Linda Schlegel and Rachel Kowert.
Description: New York, NY : Routledge, 2024. | Includes bibliographical references and index.
Identifiers: LCCN 2023042073 (print) | LCCN 2023042074 (ebook) | ISBN 9781032483016 (hardback) | ISBN 9781032482996 (paperback) | ISBN 9781003388371 (ebook)
Subjects: LCSH: Video games--Political aspects. | Video gamers--Political activity. | Radicalization. | Radicalism.
Classification: LCC GV1469.34.P65 G36 2024 (print) | LCC GV1469.34.P65 (ebook) | DDC 794.8--dc23/eng/20231127
LC record available at https://lccn.loc.gov/2023042073
LC ebook record available at https://lccn.loc.gov/2023042074

ISBN: 978-1-032-48301-6 (hbk)
ISBN: 978-1-032-48299-6 (pbk)
ISBN: 978-1-003-38837-1 (ebk)

DOI: 10.4324/9781003388371

Typeset in Sabon
by MPS Limited, Dehradun

An electronic version of this book is freely available, thanks to the support of libraries working with Knowledge Unlatched (KU). KU is a collaborative initiative designed to make high quality books Open Access for the public good. The Open Access ISBN for this book is 9781003388371. More information about the initiative and links to the Open Access version can be found at www.knowledgeunlatched.org.

CONTENTS

CONTRIBUTORS

Dr. Amarnath Amarasingam is an Assistant Professor in the School of Religion, and is cross-appointed to the Department of Political Studies, at Queen's University in Ontario, Canada. His research interests are in terrorism, radicalization and extremism, conspiracy theories, online communities, diaspora politics, post-war reconstruction, and the sociology of religion. He is the author of *Pain, Pride, and Politics: Sri Lankan Tamil Activism in Canada* (2015), and the co-editor of *Stress Tested: The COVID-19 Pandemic and Canadian National Security* (2021) and *Sri Lanka: The Struggle for Peace in the Aftermath of War* (2016). He has also published over 60 peer-reviewed articles and book chapters, has presented papers at over 100 national and international conferences, and has written for the *New York Times, The Monkey Case*, the *Washington Post, CNN, Politico, The Atlantic*, and *Foreign Affairs*. He has been interviewed on *CNN, PBS Newshour, CBC, BBC*, and a variety of other media outlets. He tweets at @AmarAmarasingam.

Jacob Davey is Head of Research & Policy, Counter Hate at the Institute for Strategic Dialogue (ISD). He has led a wide range of projects tracking extremism and hate globally, including a major project of work analyzing ideologically motivated violent extremism in Canada, and work tracking right-wing extremism in the United Kingdom. Jacob regularly advises senior policymakers and has provided evidence to inquiries, including testifying at the UK Intelligence and Security Committee's inquiry into Extreme Right-Wing Terrorism, the UK Home Affairs Committee inquiry into Hate Crime and its Violent Consequences, as well as leading ISD's contribution of written evidence to the United States House Select Committee on the January 6 attack. Jacob sits on the steering board for the Extremism and Gaming Research Network (EGRN). His work has been featured in the *BBC*, the *New York Times*, the *Washington Post*, the *Wall Street Journal*, *Vice*, *Wired*, and *NPR*, among other outlets.

Dr. Nagham El Karhili is the Programs and Partnerships Lead at the Global Internet Forum to Counter Terrorism (GIFCT). She was previously the Program and Research Manager at the Horizon Forum. Dr. El Karhili has developed and coordinated research and programming agendas at think-do tanks focused on countering hate-based extremism. She was a Presidential Fellow at Georgia State University's Transcultural Conflict and Violence Initiative where her research focussed on projects at the intersection of violent extremism, organizational religious identity, and civil society. As a scholar of communication, Dr. El Karhili has authored numerous research articles published in academic peer-reviewed journals such as the *Journal of Media and Religion*, *Dynamics of Asymmetric Conflict*, and *Media, War, & Conflict*, along with sector policy reports. Her academic background also led her to hold teaching positions at Georgia State University and Indiana University Perdue University. Dr. El Karhili is a graduate of the University of Louisiana at Lafayette (BS; MS), and Georgia State University (PhD).

Daniel Kelley (he/him/his) is the Director of Strategy and Operations of the Anti-Defamation League (ADL) Center for Technology and Society (CTS). CTS works through research and advocacy to fight for justice and fair treatment for all in digital social spaces from social media to online games and beyond. For the last five years, Daniel has been the lead author of the first nationally representative survey of hate, harassment and positive social experiences in online games. He is also the co-author of the Disruption and Harms in Online Games Framework (together with members of the Fair Play Alliance), a resource to define harms in online multiplayer games. He also leads CTS' tech accountability research efforts, such as its Antisemitism and Holocaust Denial Report Card, which looks at ways to create research grounded advocacy products to inform the public about the nature of hate and harassment online and to hold tech companies accountable.

Dr. Ashton Kingdon is a lecturer in criminology at the University of Southampton. She is also an Advisory Board Member at the Accelerationism Research Consortium, a research fellow at Vox-POL, a member of the Extremism and Gaming Research Network (EGRN), a member of the steering committee for the British Society of Criminology's Hate Crime Network and former head of Technology and Research Ethics at the Centre for Analysis of the Radical Right. Her research is interdisciplinary, combining criminology, history, and computer science to explore the ways in which extremists utilize technology for recruitment and radicalisation, while giving equal weight to the subcultural elements of the users of this technology. In addition to extremists' use of technology to recruit and radicalize, her expertise lies in analyzing the relationship existing between terrorism and climate change.

Dr. Suraj Lakhani is a Senior Lecturer in the Department of Sociology and Criminology at the University of Sussex. He also holds the roles of Research Fellow at VoxPol, Associate Fellow at the Royal United Services Institute, and part of the Steering Board for the Extremism and Gaming Research Network. His research interests include violent extremism and video gaming, violent extremism and the metaverse, terrorism and the internet, and counterterrorism policy. Suraj has acted as primary investigator on research projects funded by, for example, the Home Office, European Commission, Research England, ESRC, British Academy, and the Leverhulme Trust.

Galen Lamphere-Englund is a senior research and strategic communication professional working at the nexus of violent extremism, conflict, and tech issues. For over 14 years, he has examined how various forms of radicalization can lead to violence and how to foster resilience to societal divides. He has led global research and programming in over 30 countries for United Nations agencies, governments, humanitarian agencies, think tanks, and many of the largest tech platforms. Galen co-founded the Extremism and Gaming Research Network and advises a range of clients on preventing online space exploitation by extremist and terrorist actors. He is an Associate Fellow at the Royal United Services Institute (RUSI), a member of the EU Radicalization Awareness Network (RAN) group of experts, and serves on GIFCT working groups. Galen holds honors degrees, including an MA in Public Policy from CEU, an MA in Development & Public Policy from IBEI, and BA in Global Studies from ASU.

Alex Newhouse is a senior research fellow at the Center on Terrorism, Extremism, and Counterterrorism at Middlebury. He is an expert in far-right extremism, and he specializes in mixed-methods research of how far-right movements exploit technologies such as social media and video games. His work has been published in the *CTC Sentinel* and *GNET*, and he has been cited in media outlets such as the *Washington Post, VICE News*, the *New York Times*, and *The Atlantic*. He holds degrees from the Middlebury Institute of International Studies, Middlebury College, and Georgia Tech.

Mick Prinz is a social scientist from Germany and works at the Amadeu Antonio Foundation in Berlin. His main focus is the extreme right within gaming culture. As project manager of the project "Good Gaming – Well Played Democracy," he analyzes the instrumentalization of gaming culture by right-wing groups. At the same time, he talks to gamers about how more digital courage in gaming can succeed.

Dr. Erin Saltman is the Director of Programs and Partnerships at the Global Internet Forum to Counter Terrorism (GIFCT). She has worked in the technology, NGO, and academic sector building out counterterrorism strategies and counter-extremism programs internationally. Dr Saltman's background and expertise includes both white supremacy and Islamist extremist processes of radicalization within a range of regional and socio-political contexts. Her academic and NGO research and publications have focussed on the evolving nature of violent extremism online, youth radicalization, and the evaluation of counterspeech methodologies. She was formerly Meta's Head of Counterterrorism and Dangerous Organizations Policy across Europe, the Middle East, and Africa. She also spent time as a practitioner working for ISD Global and other CT/CVE NGOs before joining GIFCT. Dr. Saltman is a graduate of Columbia University (BA) and University College London (MA; PhD).

Dr. Constance Steinkuehler is a Professor in the Department of Informatics at the University of California, Irvine where she researches culture, cognition, and learning in the context of multiplayer online videogames. She is an ADL Belfer Fellow, Chair of UCI's Game Design and Interactive Media Program, and Co-Director of the Games+Learning+Society (GLS) Center. Her current projects include investigations of toxicity and extremism in online games, an audit of game company policies related to player-vs-player behavior, reasoning with misinformation, and a literature review of the impact of gaming tech on adjacent and distal fields. Constance formerly served as Senior Policy Analyst under the Obama administration in the White House Office of Science and Technology Policy, advising on videogames and digital media. She is the founder of the Federal Games Guild, a working group across federal agencies using games and simulations as tools for thought, and the

Higher Education Video Games Alliance, an academic non-for-profit organization of game-related programs in higher education. Her research has been funded by the Anti-Defamation League, the Samueli Foundation, the MacArthur Foundation, the Gates Foundation, the National Academy of Education/Spencer Foundation, the National Science Foundation, and the Universities of Cambridge, Wisconsin-Madison, and California-Irvine. She has published over 100 articles and book chapters and worked closely with the National Research Council and National Academy of Education on special reports relate to videogames, and her work has been featured in *Science*, *Wired*, *USA Today*, the *New York Times*, *LA Times*, *ABC*, *CBS*, *CNN NPR*, *BBC* and the *Chronicle of Higher Education*. Constance has a PhD in Literacy Studies, an MS in Educational Psychology, and three Bachelor's Degrees in Mathematics, English, and Religious Studies. Her dissertation was a cognitive ethnography of the MMOs *Lineage I* and *II* where she ran a large siege guild.

Dr. Kurt D. Squire is a professor at The University of California, Irvine, member of the Connected Learning Laboratory, and former director of the Games, Learning & Society Initiative at the University of Wisconsin-Madison, best known for his research into game design for education.

FOREWORD

The landscape of counterterrorism is constantly changing, having to adapt and adjust as the threat itself adapts and adjusts. However, the movement of society towards increasing engagement in and connection to online spaces has challenged counterterrorism frameworks, as they have been imagined and designed over the last two decades. When scanning the future threat horizon, it becomes quickly apparent that increased understanding is needed of online gaming and gaming-adjacent spaces, a gap that this book aims to fill.

As evidence from interventions in the field of preventing and countering violent extremism shows, it is essential that efforts take lessons learned from adjacent fields that can bring complementary and augmenting knowledge in order to better understand and counter the spread of extremism through all media and methods. This book usefully brings together the knowledge and research from experts in the fields of both gaming studies and countering terrorism and violent extremism. As someone who comes from over a decade of experience in countering terrorism, I can attest that there is a lot to learn from one another.

This book compiles a vast amount of knowledge in one place for those seeking to learn about the nexus of online gaming and extremism, in an effort to counter the exploitation of these spaces by extremists.

Without experience of the online gaming world, it is easy to underestimate the mammoth size of the industry – larger by far than the film, music, and television industries combined. There are billions of gamers worldwide – one-third of the global population – and that figure will only keep increasing as access continues to improve globally and more and more opportunities present themselves for online/virtual engagement and reality building. At the same time, concerns of extremism in society continue to grow, as the mainstreaming of extremism across political and social discourse teams with polarization of politics and global crises such as pandemics, climate change, conflicts, etc. These concerns are reflected in the spaces in which people spend their time, including in online gaming and gaming-adjacent spaces. Thus, now is the time to build knowledge of how to prevent and counter the spread of extremism in gaming spaces and to counter the exploitation of these spaces by extremists.

I have had the pleasure and honor of working with the editors of this book, Dr. Rachel Kowert and Linda Schlegel, as well as many of the contributing authors, several of whom are members of the Extremism and Gaming Research Network (EGRN). The authors of these chapters make accessible the world of online gaming and explore the intricacies of how to protect what makes online gaming special while aiming to reinforce its spaces against potential harm.

There are so many avenues to explore within the complexity of what is the online gaming ecosystem. Many of these are investigated with the latest insights presented throughout the chapters of this book. The authors introduce readers to what makes up the ecosystem, how people interact within gaming environments, potential harms and exploitations of these spaces, as well as ways in which gaming is being used to prevent and counter extremism and terrorism. There are fascinating elements to explore throughout, including how people form identities and create communities and the highly gendered and racialized nature of these dynamics. Understanding better how these interactions occur within the transnational spaces of online gaming will only improve our understanding of how to prevent potential harms in these spaces.

Even as potential harms and the prevention of extremism in online gaming spaces are the focus of this book, it remains important to remember that these efforts are made to protect gaming spaces and communities from harm. The authors of this book are seeking to keep gaming spaces as or return them to the positive, interactive environments, and communities that are essential for many. It has certainly been the effort of the Extremism and Gaming Research Network, as well as the authors of this book, to acknowledge, where harms are being perpetrated, not demonization, but encouragement to preventative and protective efforts of online gaming spaces.

This book offers invaluable insights into the nexus of gaming and extremism that will be useful across many fields, including for policymakers working on counterterrorism or countering online harms; practitioners working in the prevention and countering of violent extremism; and, other researchers working to build the evidence base around online gaming in order to help better understand and protect these spaces from exploitation and the spreading of extremism.

Dr. Jessica White
Co-Founder and Co-Convenor of the Extremism and Gaming Research Network (EGRN)

INTRODUCTION

Extremism in Digital Gaming Spaces

Linda Schlegel and Rachel Kowert

Gaming is one of the most popular leisure activities of our time. More people than ever before are playing games and congregating in gaming-related digital spaces. An estimated 3.2 billion people are playing videogames – a whopping one-third of the world's population – and the forecasts predict that this number will continue to grow in the coming years (Statista, 2021a). Today, millions of fans are filling esports arenas (some as big as soccer stadiums) and even more people use gaming (-adjacent) platforms such as *Steam* (www.store.steampowered.com), *Discord* (www.discord.com), *Twitch* (www.twitch.tv), or *DLive* (www.dlive.tv) to talk about gaming, stay informed about their favorite videogames, watch livestreams of popular gaming influencers, and connect with other players. In fact, in the first quarter of 2021, an astonishing 8.8 billion hours of streamed content has been watched on the livestreaming platform *Twitch* alone (Statista, 2021b). Unsurprisingly, the booming gaming industry is expected to continue to increase in size and revenue (World Economic Forum, 2022).

In accordance with the rising popularity of gaming activities across the world, research on videogames, gaming-related content, and digital gaming spaces has also been gaining momentum and is steadily increasing since the 1990s (Kowert & Quandt, 2016). Over the last few decades, a substantial body of research on the social and psychological appeal of games, on gaming communities, gamification, as well as the potential negative and positive effects of gaming and related activities has been amassed (see Hodent, 2021 for an overview). However, until recently, research on the alleged negative impact of playing videogames has largely

DOI: 10.4324/9781003388371-1

focussed on and controversially discussed a potential link between gaming and aggression or gaming addiction. However, a new key area of concern has recently come to the center of attention: A potential connection between gaming and extremism.

On March 15, 2019, a right-wing extremist entered two mosques in Christchurch, New Zealand, and opened fire. He killed 51 and left over 50 others severely injured. Because the perpetrator livestreamed the attack in the style of popular "let's play" videos and mirrored the visual aesthetics of first-person shooter games (Lakhani and Wiedlitzka, 2022), concerns surrounding a potential nexus between gaming culture and extremism arose among governments and policymakers, tech companies, researchers, and actors working in the field of preventing and countering (violent) extremism (P/CVE). From the EU Commission's Radicalisation Awareness Network (RAN, 2020; 2021a; 2021b; 2022) to the United Nations Office of Counter-Terrorism (Schlegel & Amarasingam, 2022) and even the UN Security Council,[1] a range of international actors have displayed a strong interest in gaming and extremism since the Christchurch attack. Even a dedicated research network, the Extremism and Gaming Research Network (EGRN),[2] was founded to examine new questions such as: Was this an isolated incident or could there be a "gamification of terror" (Mackintosh & Mezzofiore, 2019)? Could extremists exploit gaming, gaming-related digital spaces, and gaming culture to facilitate radicalization or even mobilization processes? Is there a link between gaming culture and extremist propaganda? Is gaming only relevant for right-wing extremism or also for jihadism and other extremist ideologies? And how can extremists' exploitation of gaming spaces be countered or prevented? Suddenly, such questions were placed at the top of the agenda and gaming became a "hot topic" in extremism research.

Current Volume

The aim of this edited volume is to shed light on these questions and present the current state of knowledge on gaming and extremism. While much of the existing research is dispersed across think tank reports, policy papers, and academic articles, this volume presents the current state of knowledge and provides a comprehensive discussion on gaming and extremism in a collection of overview articles. Across this book, leading scholars and practitioners currently on the forefront of research efforts in this field showcase their recent empirical and theoretical findings. They examine the theoretical basis of gaming and extremism (Chapters 1 and 2), discuss how extremists are seeking to leverage videogames (Chapters 3 and 4), analyze extremist activity on gaming (-adjacent) platforms (Chapters 5 and 6), investigate the use of gaming cultural references in propaganda (Chapter 7), and examine the gamification of violence (Chapter 8). In addition, gaming-related prevention and counter-extremism efforts are explored (Chapters 9 and 10), addressing how the impact of extremist actors and content in gaming spaces can be mitigated. It is important to note that while most research efforts in this space have focussed on right-wing extremism, we strove to include as much information as possible regarding the use of gaming among other extreme groups such as jihadists.

Before diving in, it is important to provide a context and shared language around gaming and extremism to better understand how these spaces are being leveraged for propaganda dissemination, radicalization, and mobilization by extremist groups.

Although videogames and the appropriation of gaming aesthetics have been used in both right-wing extremist and jihadist propaganda for a substantial amount of time, only the Christchurch attack pulled a potential connection between gaming and extremism to the center of attention and sparked a stark increase in research efforts on this issue. In spite of these efforts, research on gaming and extremism is still in its infancy. At the time of writing, a mere four years have passed since the Christchurch attack – hardly enough time for research and practice to analyze, evaluate, and comprehend all aspects of this issue in their entirety. Consequently, the number of studies on gaming and extremism is still small and our understanding of gaming and extremism must be regarded as limited and in constant flux. As the Extremism and Gaming Research Network postulates, insights on gaming still constitute a large research gap within extremism studies (EGRN, 2021).

Nevertheless, research conducted over the last years has shown that extremists are seeking to use gaming and related content in various ways. The RAN developed a now prominent typology to demonstrate the diverse types of link between gaming and extremism (RAN, 2020). It details five main ways extremists seek to exploit gaming: The production of bespoke games, the use of existing games by developing modifications ("mods")[3] or leveraging in-game chats to communicate with gamers, extremists' presence on gaming (-adjacent) platforms, the use of gaming (cultural) references in propaganda, and gamification. These are briefly described in more detail below:

- **Bespoke games:** Extremist actors have produced bespoke games since the 1980s. This includes both jihadists and right-wing extremists. For example, Hezbollah has developed a whole series of videogames called *Special Forces* (Rose, 2018; see also Lakomy, 2019) and the German-speaking branch of the Identitarian Movement recently developed a jump'n'run game, *Heimatdefender: Rebellion*, in which players fight against the Antifa and shoot politicians (Schlegel, 2020b). Aside from the publicity these games afford extremist actors, it is controversially debated why such games are being produced and whether they are means of "preaching to the (already radicalized) choir" or may also contribute to radicalization processes (Schlegel, 2020a; Robinson & Whittaker, 2021).

- **Existing games:** Existing videogames have been used by extremists in various ways, including the organization of gaming tournaments, the creation of modifications, and the use of in-game communication features. For instance, mods have been developed by extremists and radicalized individuals since the early 2000s when Al Qaeda modified the game *Quest for Saddam* (Petrilla Entertainment) into *Quest for Bush* (Schlegel, 2018). This "tradition" continues until today, exemplified by various modifications of popular video games such as *Minecraft* (Mojang Studios) or *The Sims* (Electronic Arts), which allow players to experience the Christchurch attack in a game format. There is also growing concern that extremist recruiters and radicalized individuals could seek to communicate, build trust, and potentially groom (young) players via in-game communication features such as text- or voice-based chats (RAN, 2021c). While it is currently still unclear in which (types of) games extremists are using in-game communication features, a recent UNOCT study (Schlegel & Amarasingam, 2022, p. 16) suggests that games may be especially prone to the dissemination of violent and hateful content in chats if:

  - "Interacting with others via chat is necessary/useful to coordinate and win
  - It is a popular game with a large player base
  - The game is highly competitive
  - It involves fighting and violence
  - It is an online multiplayer game
  - It is a PvP game[4]
  - Players are assigned into match-based teams with strangers
  - Failure can be attributed to individual team members
  - There is little moderation/regulation
  - There are no real consequences for breaking the rules and using hateful language"

- **Gaming (-adjacent) platforms:** Extremist actors have also established a presence on gaming and gaming-adjacent platforms such as *Twitch*, *DLive*, *Odysee* (www.odysee.com), *Discord*, *Steam*, and *Roblox* (www.roblox.com) (RAN, 2021b). Not only were various attacks and violent acts such as the January 6 storm on the US Capitol livestreamed, these platforms have also been used for internal communication and planning: For instance, the Unite The Right rally in 2017 was planned via *Discord* and the 2016 Munich attack has been linked to communication on *Steam*. While jihadists currently remain largely hidden in these spaces, right-wing extremists are often using these platforms openly and loudly (Davey, 2021).

- **Gaming (cultural) references:** Videogame references, gamer language, and gaming aesthetics have been employed by extremist actors to increase the appeal of their propaganda. This includes, for instance, the use of helmet cameras to mimic first-person shooter games in both jihadist and right-wing extremist videos and livestreams in the style of popular "let's play" videos (Scaife, 2017; Schlegel, 2020a). Other pieces of propaganda have employed direct references to popular videogames or used "gamer language." An ISIS recruiter, for instance, referenced *Call of Duty* (Activision) and tweeted: "You can sit at home and play call of duty or you can come and respond to the real call of duty ... the choice is yours" (Schlegel, 2020c). Other ISIS propaganda included the tag line "This is our Call of Duty and we respawn[5] in *jannah* [paradise]" (Dauber *et al.*, 2019, p. 18). It is currently believed that extremist actors employ gaming references to benefit from the "cool" pop-cultural appeal of gaming content. Recent work has also indicted gamer identities themselves are potentially being leveraged to cultivate stronger in-group identities (Kowert, Martel, & Swann, 2022).
- **Gamification:** Gamification is the "use of game design elements within non-game contexts" (Deterding *et al.*, 2011, p. 1) and describes the process of transferring game components such as points, badges, leaderboards, quests, guilds, etc., to contexts not traditionally regarded as games. There is evidence that gamification has been used both strategically by extremist groups to facilitate engagement with propaganda as well as organically by individuals who are radicalized but not affiliated to a specific group (RAN, 2021a). For example, jihadist groups have employed "radicalization meters" in their online forums to visualize users' degree of radicalization and the far-right Identitarian Movement sought to develop an app, *Patriot Peer*, through which individuals could collect points for attending certain events, participating in demonstrations, or visiting certain historical sites (Schlegel, 2021). Some right-wing extremist attacks too arguably employed gamified elements (Lakhani & Wiedlitzka, 2022).

Before getting started, it is important to note that while this book brings together state-of-the-art research on the issue, it is merely a snapshot of a young and constantly evolving area of research and should be read accordingly. It is also important to remember that many spaces on the internet are being actively utilized by extremist groups. In this respect, digital games and those who play them are just one of the many. Nevertheless, extremists' use of gaming deserves heightened attention as a new digital space such actors are actively involved in. This book provides a valuable starting point for academics, policymakers, journalists, P/CVE practitioners, and students of both game studies and extremism research, who seek to gain and expand their understanding of the potential nexus between gaming and extremism in all its facets.

Notes

1 Open meeting of the Counter-Terrorism Committee on "Countering terrorist narratives and preventing the use of the Internet for terrorist purposes" (2022), https://media.un.org/en/asset/k18/k18xtu7fdl.
2 https://extremismandgaming.org/.
3 Modding "refers to the process of editing or changing the structure, syntax or code of a game. Modification is performed to change the operations of a game in par with the requirements, environment, or end result or experience [and] is performed to allow a gamer to play a game different from its original released version" (Techopedia, 2017).
4 PvP is the abbreviation of player versus player and refers to gaming experiences against other humans rather than opponents being controlled by the game itself (PvE = player versus environment).
5 Respawn is a term used by gamers and refers to restarting a level after failing.

References

Activision (2011). *Call of Duty*. [Videogame]
Dauber, C. Robinson, M., Basilous, J., & Blair, A. (2019). Call of Duty: Jihad – How the Video Game Motif Has Migrated Downstream from Islamic State Propaganda Videos. *Perspectives on Terrorism, 13*(3), 17–31.
Davey, J. (2021). Gamers Who Hate: An Introduction to ISD's Gaming and Extremism Series. https://www.isdglobal.org/isd-publications/gamers-who-hate-an-introduction-to-isds-gamingand-extremism-series/
Deterding, S., Dixon, D., Khaled, R., & Nacke, L. (2011). From Game Design Elements to Gamefulness: Defining Gamification. https://www.researchgate.net/publication/230854710_From_Game_Design_Elements_to_Gamefulness_Defining_Gamification/link/00b7d5315ab1be3c37000000/download.
EGRN (2021). State of Play: Reviewing the Literature on Gaming and Extremism. https://drive.google.com/file/d/1AatJSq8vhXenjnvXHFrsPLmxyH4aONRU/view.
Electronic Arts (2000). *The Sims*. [Videogame]
Hodent, C. (2021). *The Psychology of Video Games*. Routledge.
Kowert, R., Martel, A., & Swann, B. (2022). Not Just a Game: Identity usion and Extremism in Gaming Cultures. *Frontiers in Communication, 7*. 10.3389/fcomm.2022.1007128.

Kowert, R. & Quandt, T. (2016). *The Video Game Debate: Unraveling the physical, social, and psychological effects of digital games.* Routledge.

Lakhani, S. & Wiedlitzka, S. (2022). "Press F to Pay Respects": An Empirical Exploration of the Mechanics of Gamification in Relation to the Christchurch Attack. *Terrorism and Political Violence.* Online First. 10.1080/09546553.2022. 2064746.

Lakomy, M. (2019). Let's Play a Video Game: Jihadi Propaganda in the World of Electronic Entertainment. *Studies in Conflict & Terrorism*, 42(4), 383–406.

Mackintosh, E. & Mezzofiore, G. (2019). How the Extreme-Right Gamified Terror. *CNN* (October 10, 2019). https://edition.cnn.com/2019/10/10/europe/ germany-synagogueattack-extremism-gamified-grm-intl/index.html.

Mojang Studios (2011). *Minecraft.* [Videogame]

Petrilla Entertainment (2003). *Quest for Saddam.* [Videogame]

RAN (2020). Extremists' Use of Video Gaming – Strategies and Narratives. https://home-affairs.ec.europa.eu/system/files/2020-11/ran_cn_conclusion_ paper_videogames_15-17092020_en.pdf.

RAN (2021a). The Gamification of Violent Extremism & Lessons for P/CVE. https://home-affairs.ec.europa.eu/networks/radicalisation-awareness-network-ran/publications/gamification-violent-extremism-lessons-pcve-2021_en.

RAN (2021b). Extremists' Use of Gaming (-Adjacent) Platforms – Insights Regarding Primary and Secondary Prevention Measures. https://home-affairs. ec.europa.eu/networks/radicalisation-awareness-network-ran/publications/ extremists-use-gaming-adjacent-platforms-insights-regarding-primary-and-secondary-prevention_en.

RAN (2021c). Digital Grooming Tactics on Video Gaming & Video Gaming Adjacent Platforms: Threats and Opportunities. https://ec.europa.eu/home-affairs/system/files/2021-05/ran_cn_conclusion_paper_grooming_through_ gaming_15-16032021_en.pdf.

RAN (2022). Countering the Misuse of Gaming-Related Content & Spaces: Inspiring practices and opportunities for cooperation with tech companies. https://home-affairs.ec.europa.eu/whats-new/publications/countering-misuse-gaming-relatedcontent-spaces-inspiring-practices-and-opportunities-cooperation_en.

Robinson, N. & Whittaker, J. (2021). Playing for Hate? Extremism, Terrorism, and Videogames. *Studies in Conflict & Terrorism.* Online First. 10.1080/ 105 7610X.2020.1866740

Rose, S. (2018). "Holy Defence": Hezbollah Issues Call of Duty to Video Gamers. https://www.middleeasteye.net/news/holy-defence-hezbollah-issues-call-duty-videogamers.

Scaife, L. (2017). *Social Networks as the New Frontier of Terrorism: #Terror.* Routledge.

Schlegel, L. (2018). Playing Jihad: The Gamification of Radicalization. https:// www.thedefensepost.com/2018/07/05/gamification-of-radicalization-opinion/.

Schlegel, L. (2020a). Jumanji Extremism? How Games and Gamification Could Facilitate Radicalization Processes. *Journal for Deradicalization*, 23, 1–44.

Schlegel, L. (2020b). No Child's Play: The Identitarian Movement's "Patriotic" Video Game. https://gnet-research.org/2020/09/17/no-childs-play-the-identitarian-movements-patriotic-videogame/.

Schlegel, L. (2020c). Can You Hear Your Call of Duty? The Gamification of Radicalization and Extremist Violence. https://eeradicalization.com/can-you-hear-your-call-of-duty-the-gamificationof-radicalization-and-extremist-violence/.

Schlegel, L. (2021). Working Paper 1/2021: The Role of Gamification in Radicalization Processes. https://modus-zad.de/wp-content/uploads/2021/01/modus-working-paper12021.pdf.

Schlegel, L. (2022). Playing Against Radicalization: Why Extremists Are Gaming and How P/CVE Can Leverage the Positive Effects of Video Games to Prevent Radicalization. https://www.scenor.at/_files/ugd/ff9c7a_9f5f3687937b4f3384e2b0a7eac8c33f.pdf.

Schlegel, L. & Amarasingam, A. (2022). Examining the Intersection Between Gaming and Violent Extremism. UNOCT *Action Research*. https://www.un.org/counterterrorism/sites/www.un.org.counterterrorism/files/221005_research_launch_on_gaming_ve.pdf.

Statista (2021a). Number of Video Gamers Worldwide in 2021, by Region. https://www.statista.com/statistics/293304/number-video-gamers/.

Statista (2021b). Number of Hours of Video Game Live Streams Watched on Streaming Platforms Worldwide in Q1 2019 to Q1 2021. https://www.statista.com/statistics/1125469/video-gamestream-hourswatched/#:~:text=Video%20game%20live%20streaming%20hours%20watched%202019%2D2021&text=In%20the%20first%20quarter%20of,billion%20hours%20two%20years%20previously.

Techopedia (2017). Modification (Mod). https://www.techopedia.com/definition/3841/modification-mod#:~:text=In%20gaming%2C%20modification%20(mod),or%20end%20result%20or%20experience.

World Economic Forum (2022). Gaming Is Booming and Is Expected to Keep Growing. This Chart Tells You All You Need to Know. https://www.weforum.org/agenda/2022/07/gaming-pandemic-lockdowns-pwc-growth/.

1

INTRODUCTION TO VIDEOGAMES AND THE EXTREMIST ECOSYSTEM

Constance Steinkuehler and Kurt Squire

In February 2023, two young men were arrested in Singapore for plotting violent jihadist terrorist attacks including bombings, beheadings, and knife attacks on public spaces (Dass, 2023). At 15 and 16 years of age, they were the youngest individuals ever arrested for terrorist activity in the country. Both had been radicalized through an Islamic State (IS)-themed server on the gaming platform *Roblox* (Roblox Corporation, 2006) and game-adjacent platform *Discord* (Discord, Incorporated, 2015).

Such cases have raised significant concern among researchers, policy-makers, and the public. According to the Global Terrorism Index 2022 (Institute for Economics and Peace, 2022), while the global number of deaths from terrorism fell to only-one third of its 2015 peak, the number of attacks has increased by 17% to 5,226. In the report, videogames and game-adjacent platforms such as *Discord*, *Twitch* (Twitch Interactive, 2011) and the like were pronounced the new "'hotbeds' for radicalisation" (p. 74). Given their global dominance as an entertainment medium of choice, particularly among younger adults, such declarations indeed raise the alarm.

The global entertainment industry complex is worth an estimated \$207.06 billion in 2023 ("Global Video Game Market Value", 2023) with revenues growing at a rate of 7.17% annually. Today's game marketplace is predominantly online and notably long tailed with the top ten computer and console games representing around 10% of total industry revenues while, at the other end of the distribution, the entire indie games market represents about 4.3% (Bruce, 2022). Moreover, the social impact of the medium is hard to deny, particularly in a post-pandemic world during which games provided one of the few spaces in which players could

DOI: 10.4324/9781003388371-2

socialize and engage in joint activity. Today, games are among the most common platforms for socializing with friends, acquaintances, and strangers – in both the digital playground of *Roblox* (Roblox Corporation, 2006), *Fortnite* (Epic Games, 2017) and similar titles and on physical playgrounds and hangouts of old, "what game you're into" may well determine the social groups in which you participate (Kutner & Olson, 2008). Whether joining friends after school to play *Minecraft* online (Mojang Studios, 2011) or buying Robux (the in-game currency in *Roblox*) to purchase new skins or piling onto *Discord* to voice chat with friends, game and game-related on- and offline fandom spaces serve as a vital platform for the creation and maintenance of informal social networks of affiliation and disaffiliation, loosely tied together through online technologies in spaces "corporate owned but player constituted" (Steinkuehler, 2006).

This chapter provides a broad overview of videogames and their player communities with an eye toward those aspects that bear on the patterns of extremist activity we see today. We provide an introduction to videogames, their definition and defining elements, the issue of violence, key industry stakeholders in their development, and discuss the centrality of rules and systems to games, on the one hand, and player action, reaction, and interpretation, on the other. We then discuss the nature of game communities, including what we know about player demographics, their varying motivations for play, the structural features that game communities have in common, and how extremists exploit them. We then consider games as social platforms, including both online game titles (and specialized content creation servers within them) and online game-adjacent platforms, and compare and contrast them to other traditional social platforms. We conclude with a discussion of the vulnerabilities in the current gaming ecosystem.

Understanding Videogames

Videogames are not monolithic. Originally the entertainment medium of the computer, they now span numerous platforms including computer, console, tablet, smart phone, and augmented reality/virtual reality headsets, enabling a breathtaking range of gameplay from tiny button-mashing arcade experiences lasting only a few seconds as in *Flappy Bird* (Nguyen, 2013) to sprawling persistent virtual worlds, for example, *World of Warcraft* (Blizzard, 2004) to multiplayer online battle arenas including *League of Legends* (Riot Games, 2013), the world's largest esport played by 150 million players ("League of Legends Live Player Count", 2023) and drawing over 100 million unique viewers to its championship events (Webb, 2019). Dominant brands around the globe include a broad range of genres and familiar titles from *Minecraft, Pokemon* (Nintendo, 1996) and *Candy Crush* (King, 2012) to *Call of Duty* (Activision, 2003), *Grand Theft Auto* (Rockstar Games, 1997), and *League of Legends*, yet games are more than just these top sellers. Rapidly evolving genres and sub-genres, from first- person shooters to bird flying simulators, means that almost any audience can find almost any activity of their liking remediated as a game, and there is a game for nearly any market segment imaginable. We know relatively little about how the range of specific game genres and mechanics are leveraged by varying extremist groups (Schlegel & Amarasingam, 2022). Still, all games have some key elements in common.

Systems and Rules

A game is a "system in which players engage in an artificial conflict defined by rules that results in a quantifiable outcome" (Salen & Zimmerman, 2004, p. 11). Games are essentially systems, constituted by the interactions among their elements and their player(s). From this perspective, we can think of games as a kind of computational model or simulation of some system or dynamic, either real or imagined. In this way, games are a kind of argument about how the world (again, real or imagined) works; they have a *procedural rhetoric* (Bogost, 2007). Indeed, the earliest video-games, such as *Pong* (Alcorn, 1972), originally a game designed for an oscilloscope entitled *Tennis for Two* (Higinbotham, 1958), were models of well-known physical and social activities.

Game *systems* are defined by rules or mechanics, which, simply put, are statements or directives that govern behavior within the system. Rules determine both what players can and cannot do as well as how the game system processes and responds to players' actions. These cycles of game stimuli, player action, game system processing and then feedback are re-ferred to as *game loops*, and they are key to understanding how games operate (Cook, 2012). From the player's perspective, these loops *are* the game play, and good game play is simply "a series of interesting choices" (Meier, as cited on Rollings & Morris, 2000, p. 38). Artificial conflict is core to games; games are goal-directed activities in which the rules of the game pose an unnecessary or "unnatural" challenge to obtaining the goal (Suits, 2004). Indeed, it is just this challenge, resulting from the artificial conflict, that gives games their stickiness. Together, these elements func-tion to create a designed experience for the player (Squire, 2006).

Violence in Games

But if games are arguments or models of how systems work, then are games essentially arguments for conflict, since conflict is at the heart of gameplay? Links between games and violent extremism renew concerns that videogame play might cause aggression and violence. Shooters in both the 2019 terrorist attacks in Christchurch, New Zealand, and in El Paso, Texas, for example, made explicit references to first-person shooter games and games culture more broadly (Robinson & Whitaker, 2021). However, case studies of violent behavior reveal the role of prior exposure to abuse, violence in the home, bullying, social ostracization, and other social factors (Ferguson & Wang, 2019), leading the American Psychological Association (2020) to conclude that, "violence is a complex social problem that likely stems from many factors that warrant attention from researchers, policy makers and the public. Attributing violence to violent video gaming is not scientifically sound and draws attention away from other factors" (p. 1). Indeed, the rise of videogame play, including violent videogame play, has coincided with an overall *decline* in violence in society, supporting a kind of "catharsis effect" from videogames (Ferguson, 2015). This is not to posit that cultural references to games among violent extremists are harmless; rather, it is to point to the proliferation of games and pervasiveness of game culture globally in how we communicate, network, and socialize.

Research on violence and aggression in games, like much of the media effects research, employs an exposure model whereby players' intentions, experiences, goals, and interpretations of an experience are largely irrelevant. Such an approach discards context (such as why would one choose to play a game) and ascribes agency to *media*, rather than to *players*, which has been called an *active media* approach (Egenfeldt-Nielsen & Smith, 2004). In contrast, an active *player* (or user) approach, assumes that people are active sense-making organisms, with interests, goals, reasons for choosing and participating in the media that they do. The role of researchers in this context is to understand the choices that people make, the impact that it has on their lives, and the contexts in which they consume media. These dynamics are true to any media, but are especially important in games, where, for example, one player might play *Grand Theft Auto* to connect with friends whereas another plays out of an interest in car culture, and a third player enjoys its transgressive elements (DeVane & Squire, 2008). The interactive elements of games require us to account for users' intentions and actions to understand play. This shift in focus from the active media to active player problematizes theories of radicalization via games (and other forms) in which extremists create games that radicalize unwitting players into their ideologies in some straightforward way. As Robinson and Whittaker (2021) argue: "[P]layers retain independent thought and judgment and bring their critical faculties into their engagement with games. They are not brainwashed by their engagement with games, but are thinking 'player subjects,' exercising a particular type of subjectivity when they play games, which has minimal implications for their broader subjectivity" (p. 15).

Narrative

Games typically have a narrative or at least a narrative premise that frames play. Like written literary works, games use standard narrative devices including characters, context, plot structure, pacing, dialog, and, in some cases, cutscenes. Game narratives are more often complicated branching structures rather than standard linear plot structures. They are what Jenkins (2002) calls "narrative architectures." Unlike written literary works, games also use spatiality as a key means for storytelling in games: The internal world or geography of the game is often designed for narrative potential such as characters with backstories that help shape the action and its meaning or props and resources that convey context. Because games are interactive, the stories they tell must be collaboratively accomplished, often with the player situated as the main protagonist as in Campbell's (1949) hero's journey, with the game serving as a kind of authoring environment for the player to then write within.

Indeed, one common way that extremists leverage game narratives is by positioning violent extremists as protagonists who battle ideologically opposed forces (Selepak, 2010). For example, pro-IS mods of *ARMA 3* (Bohemia Interactive, 2013) depict IS fighters in victorious combat against the Syrian Arab Army and Iraqi forces as seen in the series of *YouTube* (www.youtube.com) videos posted by Jihadi Mark (Lakomy, 2019).[1] Similar games can be found across the political spectrum; Osama bin Laden and George Bush were featured in Flash shooting games in the 2000s; similar games were subsequently developed involving Presidents Obama and Trump and presidential candidate Hillary Clinton (Fiadotau, 2020; Neys & Jansz, 2010).

Treatment

A game's treatment is "the cohesive whole formed by visual art, visual effects, sound effects, tactile effects and music" (Swink, 2008, p. 189). It determines a game's *feel*, signaling the presumed audience for the game and setting player expectations about how the system will behave. Does the game treatment consist of vivid primary colors and geometric shapes with forgiving touchscreen sensitivity for children under six? High fidelity graphics in sepia tones with a complex user interface overlaying a sweeping landscape shot for dads who love historical simulations? Pastel 2D rounded squares tucked snugly together on a 6.06-inch diagonal rectangle just aching to be moved into arrays of three by two thumbs in a slow checkout line at the grocer? A game's treatment may be abstract, as the objects falling in space in *Tetris* (Pajitnov, 1984) or iconic, as in the pie-shaped character gobbling up pellets while dodging three hungry ghosts trying to eat him in *Pac-Man* (Namco, 1980) or representational, as in the high fidelity battle-torn French and German territories whose fascist Nazi occupiers you must push back in *Call of Duty: World War II* (Sledgehammer Games, 2017). In each case, the game's treatment is not merely eye candy or visual wrapping; it fundamentally helps constitute the game experience and meanings conveyed. In a well-polished game, the game treatment, narrative, and core game mechanics (system) cohere, which takes time and resources, design expertise, and typically teams of individuals in specialized roles.

Game Development

Game development is a rapidly evolving ecosystem transitioning from a *physical* distribution system (where games were distributed via physical media such as cartridges, discs) to a *digital* distribution system, wherein games are developed and distributed digitally. This transition, when combined with a democratization of game development tools, has led to the proliferation of game titles and content. Whereas previously, developers needed to meet content standards to be placed on a console or compete for shelf space at a store, today, almost anyone can assemble a team, make a game (of uncertain quality), and attempt to sell it online. This leveling of the ecosystem is often considered good for the industry in that it diversifies the marketplace in healthy ways, but the loss of content gatekeeping structures leaves the industry open to extremist actors and other abuses. Likewise, the development of online games (particularly "software-as-a service" models) means that game content is not wholly defined by developers; rather, more and more game systems include online modes or other ways for users to generate and share content, which creates additional openings within the game ecosystem to extremism and other dangerous content.

Game Developers

Game developers are the artists, programmers, writers, designers, sound engineers, and producers who create game software working together at a *game studio*. Game studios can be *independent* (indie), meaning that they are *not* owned by a *game publisher*, or they might be *AAA* (triple A, a term borrowed from the credit industry) meaning they are owned by a publisher. The size of game development teams varies by orders of magnitude. Whereas the original *Minecraft* was made primarily by the single developer

Notch and *Call of Duty* teams are the size of small villages, most development teams fall somewhere in between these two extremes. Indie teams often feature around a dozen developers, including both artists and programmers, whereas smaller AAA teams may only have a few hundred developers.

Game Engines and Mods

Game developers use a variety of tools and engines to make games. While specialized genres may require custom game tools to optimize game performance, general purpose game development platforms lower the bar to entry for development. *Unity* (Unity Technologies, 2005) and *Unreal Engine* (Epic Games, 1998) are powerful tools for game making, requiring only basic programming skills and offering extensive tutorials and blueprints to aid independent development. Today, many commercial games also provide users access to the tools they themselves used such that creating new content and levels or modifying (or "modding") existing ones is relatively easy even for novices. The combination of accessible game development engines, modding capabilities within commercial titles, and digital distribution platforms (described later) has democratized game development, allowing a much wider range of people to design and share their work, largely free from institutional (and perhaps even financial) constraints. As a result, there are more and more varied games available today than ever before.

Game Publishers

Game publishers fund game projects, market games, handle distribution, and provide legal and business support. In the retail era, publishers were a necessity. They ensured that games were accepted by console manufacturers (which exercised their own authority), negotiated deals to place games in retail stores, and promoted games in the press. With respect to extremism, publishers played a critical role in shaping and gatekeeping – although publishers were hardly a purely benevolent force, neither were they all equal. *Rockstar Games*, for example, tolerated (if not cultivated) sexist themes and questionably violent content in many titles while *Nintendo* maintained some of the strictest of content standards. Still, publishers added accountability with respect to game content and themes.

Game Distribution Platforms

Game distribution platforms such as *Steam* (https://steamcommunity.com), *Google Play* (https://play.google.com/store/games) and *Itchi.io* (https://itch.io) allow game developers to market straight to game audiences globally.

Anyone can make a game, upload it to one of these services, and, if approved, sell their game online. As a result, millions of games are now available: roughly 500,000 on both *Apple iOS* and *Google Play* ("Number of Available Gaming Apps", 2023), 700,000 on itch.io ("Top Games", 2023), 40,000 on console (Kowalcyzk, 2021), and 50,000 games on *Steam* (Bailey, 2023) with 10,000 new ones added annually. Apart from perhaps *Itch.io*, online distributors generally exercise some degree of content curation and quality control, filtering content and providing some minimal level of developer and player customer support. The question is whether this is enough.

Extremist Games

Early extremist games were mostly awkward combinations of popular game mechanics (e.g., *Pac-Man*) with a new hate-based narrative premise and treatment applied – essentially, abstract or symbolic games rebranded with extremist imagery and symbols. Examples include white nationalist computer games posted online by American neo-Nazi Gerhard Rex Lauck (the Farmbelt Fuehrer) such as *SA-Mann*, *Aryan 3*, *Shoot the Blacks*, *NSDoom*, *WPDoom* (Anti-Defamation League, 2002), *KZ Manager Millennium: Hamburg Edition*, and *Watch Out Behind You Hunter!* (White Aryan Resistance, n.d.a, n.d.b). Here, game mechanics with thin to no relationship to the revised narrative premise and treatments result in a notably amateur final product allowing players to interact with extremist content but in mostly irrelevant ways. Such games are generally poor in quality (Selepak, 2010) due to lack of design experience and skills (Schlegel & Amarasingam, 2022); as a result, made-from-scratch games by extremists are largely on the wane (Robinson & Whittaker, 2021).

Extremist titles beginning in the early 2000s took playing hate to a new level, moving beyond unpolished reskins of popular game mechanics to games whose narrative and treatment align and amplify their procedural rhetoric (Bogost, 2007). One key enabling factor was the availability of open-source game engines such as *Genesis3D* (Eclipse Entertainment, 1997), an early predecessor of today's *Unity* and *Unreal Engines*, and the capacity to mod commercially produced titles (Selepak, 2010; Lakomy, 2019). Examples include Hezbollah's *Special Force* (2003) and *Special Force 2: Tale of the Truthful Pledge* (2007), and the National Alliance's (2002) *Ethnic Cleansing*. With such tools, a new generation of extremist games emerged, one that raised the bar to better match consumer expectations on the open game market.

Consensus, however, is that extremist games are less effective for recruitment of new members than they are for solidifying the already existing base. As Robinson and Whittaker (2021) describe: "[T]he games contain iconography and specialist knowledge that is clearly intended for audiences that are already invested in the underlying ideology" (pp. 2–3). As a result, only those with some prior recognition of the game's treatment and narrative are likely to seek it out. Rather, extremist communities on *Steam* and similar platforms appear to use their games "to promote political affiliation, as a means of roleplaying extremist fantasies, or as a means of building communities" (Vaux, Gallagher, & Davey, 2021).

Active Media vs Active Player

Yet, it is worth noting that even games intended overtly to inculcate players with specific knowledge, skills, and dispositions only do so under specific conditions, including a willing player. Players draw interpretations from gameplay based on their own gameplay intentions, experiences, models of the world, and ideologies. For example, an historian playing *Civilization* (Meier, 1991) might play to test materialist theories of world history and generate new insights about comparative world history, whereas a younger player might play the game for escape. Similarly, an African American male might play *Grand Theft Auto: San Andreas* (Rockstar North, 2004) and reflect on the nature of structural racism in American cities, whereas a feminist player may identify structural gender inequities encoded in the game (DeVane & Squire, 2008). Although most contemporary theories of media emphasize how audiences shape meanings, in games, such differences can be profound. As a thoroughly interactive medium, by definition, different players taking different sequences of actions in the same game title results in vastly different play experiences.

Understanding Game Communities

If videogames are diverse, then so too are the communities that form in relation to them. Different designs appeal to different audiences and generate different gameplay cultures as a result. Nintendo's *Animal Crossing* (Eguchi & Nogami, 2001) in which players collect and design items in a cartoon world of cute animals is designed to be a cozy game; as a result, its game community has remarkably caring cultural ethos (Zhu, 2021). In contrast, *Player Unknown Battleground* (PUBG Studios, 2017), is a "king of the mountain" style survival game in which players parachute onto an island, scavenge for equipment, and then fight to be the last one standing in a dark world of industrial decay. Perhaps not surprisingly then, its game community has a reputation for being hostile and humiliating; in fact, one study suggests that amount of PUBG gameplay is significantly (albeit weakly) associated with feelings of aggression and underachievement

(Ohno, 2022). In this way, different games draw different player bases and broad generalizations across them are as suspect as broad generalizations about the medium of "games" as a whole. Still, their communities do share some common structural features salient to the study of extremism within them. Here we review the basics on who plays and then describe these community structures and norms.

Demographics

Game communities are broad, networked, diverse and global, drawing and connecting players from disparate backgrounds. Gone are the days when gaming was purely the domain of adolescent males; now more than 3.2 billion people of all ages (roughly 40%) from around the world play games (Newzoo, 2022). The largest growth regions continue to be Latin America, the Middle East, and Africa, spurred by improving mobile internet infrastructure, a growing number of smartphone users, free-to-play gaming models, and a growing middle class. Public reports on global player demographics are inconsistent; however, industry reports from the United States (Entertainment Software Association, 2022) suggest a few notable trends: Today, 48% of female-identifying individuals and 52% of male-identifying individuals' game. Three-fourths of the player base are adults over the age of 18 and the average age of players is 33, a number that continues to rise each year. Of the 13 hours a week on average players spend gaming, 41% is spent playing with others (25% online, 16% in-person).

Play Motivations

Colloquially, people think of gaming as escapist diversion, but under closer scrutiny, gaming is a multifaceted activity that draws different people for different reasons, and games researchers have long sought to tease out just what those motivations may be. Early research focused on how games leverage fantasy, control, challenge, curiosity, competition, and cooperation to engage players (Malone & Lepper, 1987). Studies of players in virtual worlds distinguish between those who orient to games as achievers, explorers, socializers, and "player killers" (actors on other players; Bartle, 2003). Yee's gamer motivation model (Quantic Foundry, 2023) is the most comprehensive approach to understanding player motivations, and it describes six key motivations: Action, social connection, mastery, achievement, immersion, and creativity. For the purposes of understanding extremism and games, it may be less important to distinguish between these motivations than to realize that people game for different reasons at different times – and that those motivations shape their gameplay and the meanings they draw from it.

Structural Features of Game Communities

Despite their variations by game title and region, game communities do still generally share some common structural features. Online game communities function as *third places* for social interaction (Steinkuehler & Williams, 2006): spaces that are neither home nor work, allow social engagement, and provide a sense of shared place. As third places, the bridging social networks created within them are typically more *diverse* than on online social platforms where we choose the content and people we connect with, typically in ways that reify our own worldview. Discovering that your closest clan member has political views contrary to your own can be a source of joy or consternation or both. Game communities are notably *flat in organizational structure*, at least compared to other social institutions, whereby anyone interested can participate (Gee, 2004). Games communities typically applaud *meritocracy* and believe that skill alone should determine who wins (Steinkuehler, 2005), but often ignore the forms of social, cultural, and material capital beyond the game that advantage some while excluding others, resulting is a kind of *toxic meritocracy* (Paul, 2018) in which structural inequities are ignored and those who cannot compete equally are seen as less competent rather than differently advantaged.

Extremist Exploitation

Extremists take advantage of these common game community characteristics in myriad ways. While there is little evidence of overt large-scale recruitment in game communities, extremist subgroups do use game contexts to build community and bonds among peers (Koehler, Fiebig, & Jugl, 2023). Among individuals who already agree, sharing one's political or social views in the context of a shared game may "[metamorphosize] into an echo chamber where the existing beliefs of members of these small groups are amplified, facilitating their psychological pathway further into extremism" (Dass, 2023). Case studies of individuals who have been radicalized in game communities show that gaming together in shared spaces creates opportunities for radicalization to occur, particularly among individuals seeking a sense of belonging and group membership (Koehler, Fiebig, & Jugl, 2023). Indeed, the *relationships* formed online through games may be virtual, but they are no less real; indeed, joint activity in multiplayer and online games may engender "band of brothers" effects (Whitehouse *et al.*, 2014) even though the conflict players share is artificial. Understanding how these dynamics of trust among networks of high diversity may contribute to radicalization (Schlegel & Amarasingam, 2022) requires additional research. One important means for player development is the in-game enculturation of lower level players into more advanced skills and practices by higher level ones, but these forms of mentoring can also serve to *enculturate players into particular ideologies* related to the game and perhaps even beyond it (Steinkuehler & Oh, 2012); more detailed analyses of the dynamics of radicalization is needed.

Understanding Games as Social Platforms

Although not all games themselves are multiplayer and online, the prevalence of gaming-adjacent platforms – online digital platforms that are commonly used simultaneously or consecutively to support and enhance gameplay – means that most game players are, at some point in their activity, participating online in game communities and cultures. Thus, game communities manifest online and across multiple online platforms, even when the game is single player.

Online Games

Online games are 2- or 3D virtual spaces hosted on servers, typically divided by continental region to reduce latencies, that enable multiplayer gameplay. Such games offer a wide range of experiences, from parallel gameplay with lightweight chat and resource-sharing functions such as *Candy Crush Saga* to the formation of complex virtual communities in persistent online worlds (Koster, 2011) including *World of Warcraft* and *Eve Online* (Simon & Schuster Interactive, 2003) to team-based competition and esports on multiplayer online battle arenas (MOBAs), for example, *League of Legends*, notorious for their toxicity toward new or unskilled players, including the common use of racial, ethnic, or gender-based slurs.

Online gameplay is pervasive, with the number of players projected to reach 1.25 billion by 2027 or more than half of the global game players, roughly one-fifth of the human population ("Online Games Worldwide," 2023). They are unique as social platforms because they position players in *joint activity* whereby they are engaged in common tasks. Playing together requires developing shared perspectives as they make game preparations, discuss the state of the game world, coordinate action, make sense of feedback given from the game world, and then repeat. In short, players engage in the same *game loop*. During each phase, players must communicate to coordinate; thus, online game titles feature in-game text chat systems and occasionally voice chat. Perhaps not surprisingly then, hate-based harassment extremism tends to flourish in such spaces since interaction cannot easily be avoided (Schlegel & Amarasingam, 2022). As players communicate, opportunities to introduce extremist, derogatory ideas (often under the guise of humor) constantly arise. One key related concern is that extremist ideology may spread virally as a byproduct of the need for players to achieve intersubjectivity in order to coordinate play.

Online games are a key site for extremist activity. According to the latest Anti-Defamation League (2022b) report, 20% of adult online players and 15% of youth aged 13–17 in the United States are exposed to white supremacist ideology, more than double the number three years ago. Identity-based harassment in online games is on the rise, with Jewish (34%), Latino (31%) and Muslim players (30%) reporting the highest rates of targeted hate. Team-based competition games, such as those enabled by MOBAs, show by far the highest rates of in-game toxicity and harassment than other forms. Indeed, one might argue that it is here, in the deeply interactive spaces of online games and their adjacent communicative platform, that extremists currently seem to thrive most.

Specialized Content Creation Servers

Specialized content creation servers with their own unique gameplay modes within larger online games such as *Minecraft* and *Roblox* deserve special mention given the number of young players they attract and high-profile cases of radicalization and extremism (see the introduction). *Hypixel* (https://hypixel.net), for example, is a Minecraft mini-game server serving ten million players and with an average of 150,000 concurrent users. Using the *Minecraft* engine, Hypixel games are mostly remediations of classic games, such as *Capture the Flag* or *Building with Blocks*. Hypixel servers support general chat and direct messaging, which is moderated by the company Hypixel, Incorporated and *not* Microsoft, the developers and publishers of *Minecraft*, who have little control over what communication and activities on their teeming servers. *Roblox* is another, similar game property featuring specialized game servers. With a market capitalization of $22 billion as of this writing, *Roblox* is its own behemoth, boasting almost 60 million active users daily (Ruby, 2023). Using their building tool *Roblox Studio*, over 9.5 million developers have created over 50 million games for players, earning millions of dollars in profit as players buy their wares using the "Robux" virtual currency.

Today, such game creation servers are the latest game spaces to be taken up by extremists (Schlegel & Amarasingam, 2022). Because such spaces are hybridized amalgamations of game creation and distribution mixed with both corporatized (e.g., *Hypixel*) and amateur/indie games for consumers to play, they are particularly susceptible to extremist content. Both *Roblox* and *Minecraft* are behemoths on the current market, with 202 million (Ruby, 2023) and 93 million (Curry, 2023) active monthly users respectively; the sheet scale of the platforms and its pro-am developer communities make the enforcement of content standards challenging. Both are under constant threat of inadvertently hosting wildly problematic content including several high-profile examples of games with extremist ideologies (Farivar, 2019; D'Anastasio, 2021; Miller & Silva, 2021; Anti-Defamation League, 2022a; Dass, 2023).

Gaming-Adjacent Platforms

The game ecosystem is increasingly overlapped and integrated through cross-platform games and third-party services offering gaming-adjacent platforms (Newzoo, 2022) used to share information, build the meta, search for FAQs and walk-thrus, and find friends. Common examples include text and voice communication platforms including *Discord*, *TeamSpeak* (Teamspeak Systems, Inc., 2002), *D-Live* (https://community. dlive.tv) and *Slack* (Slack Technologies, 2013); game distribution platforms with community functions such as *Steam* and the *Epic Games Store* (https://store.epicgames.com), streaming platforms such as *Twitch* and *YouTube Gaming* (https://www.youtube.com/gaming), and even other more prototypical social platforms, most notably *Facebook* (Meta Platforms, 2004) and *Twitter* (Twitter Incorporated, 2006). Gaming-adjacent platforms can be thought of as an ecosystem that participants engage across and within. A recent study by Schlegel and Amarasingam (2022) found the follow respective rates of use by players: *Discord* (83%), *Twitch* (45%), *YouTube* (39%), and *Reddit* (24%), with *Twitter*, *Steam*, *Facebook*, and general internet forums also mentioned.

Today, many games rely on just such out-of-game platforms to enable gameplay. Take, for example, the popular multiplayer game *Among Us* (Inner Sloth, 2018) which is designed to be played in groups of four to 15 but features no real matchmaking services for group formation or integrated voice communication for coordination and discussion. Here, game design just assumes the use of external chat platforms such as *Discord* as part and parcel of gameplay. Today, *Discord* (founded in 2015) is used by hundreds of millions for gaming and other activities, and has become the de facto voice over internet protocol (VoIP) service for most gamers, allowing users to host their own "servers" that enable individuals to communicate by text, voice, and files. Such servers might be hosted and administered by formal groups such as schools or clubs or informal groups of friends and fellow players.

Fully monitoring such communication is outside the purview of games companies. Indeed, moderation at all is fraught with technical, social, privacy, and province challenges well beyond the scope of this chapter. To illustrate the dynamics, imagine a scenario in which a group of long-standing friends sets up their own *Discord* server to communicate while playing *World of Warcraft*, reasonably expecting privacy from uninvited guests and surveillance. The same group could become politically engaged, start using *Discord* for political organizing, and soon find themselves fomenting increasingly radical positions. Or not. By contrast, a teenager might purchase the Western game *Red Dead Redemption 2* (Rockstar Games, 2018), open multiplayer on their *Xbox*, and be surprised to hear racial epithets spewed by complete strangers over voice chat and wonder how or why this is allowed. Providers such as Sony enable voice recording for moderation purposes, but most require users to opt in for legal and privacy concerns.

Game-adjacent platforms play an integral role in gameplay and how teens meet and interact with friends (Lenhart *et al.*, 2015). Together, they constitute a kind of affinity space, "a place or set of places where people affiliate with others based primarily on shared activities, interests, and goals, not shared race, class culture, ethnicity, or gender" (Gee, 2004, p. 67). Yet platforms such as *Discord* and *Twitch* have garnered much attention as sites on which extremist, racist, toxic, or otherwise antisocial *content* and *behaviors* can proliferate. Such servers are often moderated, either by administrators or users themselves. However, the porous nature of game communities inevitably means that people – including youth – encounter people with ideas and agendas that would not flourish in less supervised spaces. For example, Koehler, Fiebig, and Jugl (2023), report on a study by Gallagher and colleagues (2021) in which:

> Discord users who were active in the extreme-right groups were generally very young (average age of 15). In those groups, discussing ideologically framed online social activities such as in-game raids against perceived enemies was one of the most common themes. Furthermore, 13 of the 24 far-right Discord servers used forms of ideological vetting to assure only those with some level of ideology-specific knowledge and already present degree of radicalization entered. This shows that according to this ISD report, Discord as well does not appear to be used strategically by extreme-right groups beyond the building of a virtual community for insiders. (Gallagher *et al.*, 2021, p. 423)

While recent news stories of recruitment and radicalization on game platforms have captured public attention, recent studies indicate that game-adjacent platforms are largely used for "social interaction and community building within a comparatively safe and private space" (Koehler, Fiebig, & Jugl, 2023, p. 423) rather than *recruitment* of new members. In a survey conducted by Schlegel and Amarasingam (2022), 30% of participants reported encountering "toxic, hateful or violent content predominantly in in-game chat" while 41% reported encountering it "across all platforms listed, which included in-game chats, live audio conversations and streams, as well as Discord servers" (p. 16). A study by Vaux and colleagues (2021) found that *Steam* had the largest and active extremist activity among the platform studied, while later work by Davey (2022) documented higher numbers elsewhere: "45 public groups associated with the extreme right on *Steam*, 24 extreme right chat servers on *Discord*, 100 extreme right channels on *DLive* and 91 channels on *Twitch*" (Davey, 2022, p. 8).

Games versus Other Social Platforms

The claim that games are social platforms is contested within the industry, largely in response to recent efforts at regulation to tamp down the spread of extremism, misinformation, and privacy concerns (e.g., "Social Media Companies," 2022). Yet, online games and gaming-adjacent spaces do indeed meet the definition: They offer "public or semipublic internet-based services in which one substantial function is to connect players so they may interact socially within the game, and players (1) create public or semipublic profiles, (2) populate a list of other players to whom they are connected in the system, and (3) post content shared with others (in the form of chatroom style messages) that includes content generated by other players" (Steinkuehler, 2023, p. 8). Table 1.1 broadly compares basic features of the two.

We know relatively little about the overall rates of extremist activity across social platforms. Such activity is rarely shared in public, and companies do not release data on– private communications. Further, the majority of such content most certainly would occur on private channels, through direct messages, and on private servers (see Lavin, 2020, for a description of the processes involved in penetrating such servers).

Vulnerabilities in the Gaming Ecosystem

Although every sector of society is vulnerable to extremism (and most have undergone elements of it), videogames and associated platforms have their own vulnerabilities. *Transgressive play* is common – even honored – within gaming culture and communities, where the so-called "magic circle" (Huizinga, 1955) deters in-game actions from having beyond-game consequences (Jorgensen & Karlsen, 2018). Players can introduce "softer" extremist content under the rubric of joking (j/k) as generally toxic, racist, or misogynistic behavior, which can normalize such ideas as well as recruit others to their cause. On North American and European servers, there is a

TABLE 1.1 Comparison of games and prototypical social platforms

Online games and game-adjacent spaces	*Social platforms*
Primary purpose: Entertainment through interactive gameplay, typically featuring multiplayer modes that enable joint activity	**Primary purpose:** Communication, connection, and content sharing, enabling users to form and maintain social relationships, communities
Secondary purpose: Communication, connection, and content sharing, enabling users to form and maintain social relationships, communities	**Secondary purpose:** Entertainment through social interaction
Interactivity: Players interact with the game environment and other players, make decisions, and take actions to progress through the content	**Interactivity:** Users interact with other people through shared text, images, videos, or other multimedia content
Focus on gameplay: Main objective is to achieve specific goals or objectives requiring the development of skills and strategies	**Focus on communication:** Primary focus is social networking through communication with connected individuals
Designed treatment: Art, animations, and sound combine to create an immersive environment for gameplay	**Emergent aesthetic:** Visual and auditory elements are user, rather than designer, generated, with emergent aesthetics
Storytelling: Typically include narratives or narrative premises to contextualize gameplay	**Storytelling:** Storytelling may emerge through shared content, but personal and less structured
Competition and collaboration: Often include competitive or collaborative elements	**Competition and collaboration:** Focus is connection and collaboration, with competition (e.g., for "likes") possible but less common
In-game tools: Reporting, blocking, banning, in-game moderation tools, code of conduct, parental controls, private servers or groups, community engagement	**Platform tools:** Reporting, blocking and muting, privacy settings, content filters, community guidelines and moderation, educational resources

pervasive *hardcore gamer identity* in games that is coded as male, white (or Asian), and heterosexual (Parkin, 2013), and this identity has become increasingly defined in opposition to the politically correct (read: socially sensitive) mainstream. Recent research by Kowert, Martel, and Swann (2022) provides some of our first insights into how identity fusion with gamer culture acts as a mechanism through which extremist ideologies can take root.

Current in-game tools and tactics (muting, blocking, reporting,) for victims of hate-based harassment and extremism often fail to adequately address the issues, leave the dynamic of the interaction in place, lack follow up with the originator of the complaint so that the information loop is closed, do nothing to repair the breach of social contract, and are implemented inconsistently or not at all. As previously discussed, moderation across both text and voice communications across the multitude of platforms in which gameplay arises is exceedingly difficult to implement. Game companies' policies against extremism and hate speech on their platforms (and few do) end up burying those policies deep in their online annual of legal documents that players do not access when, instead, they might swap out their mandatory click-through EULA for a clear and concise code of conduct in plain language to make the corporate and community norms explicit and therefore enforceable. Together, these vulnerabilities in the current gaming ecosystem leave the medium and its players easy targets.

Concluding Thoughts

Videogame playing communities are garnering increased interest for their potential role as platforms on which extremists can radicalize and recruit. Understanding the videogame industry, the content and mechanics of games, and the other aspects of their ecosystem are critical in understanding the potential role that videogames may, and may not, play in this space. Research has identified vulnerabilities in the structural and social features of games, and gaming- adjacent platforms, indicating greater attention should be placed on examining and understanding these *social spaces*.

Note

1 A "mod" is a modification of an existing game.

References

Activision (2003). *Call of Duty*. [Videogame]

Alcorn, A. (1972). *Pong*. [Videogame]

American Psychological Association (2020). APA RESOLUTION on Violent Video Games. https://www.apa.org/about/policy/resolution-violent-video-games.pdf.

Anti-Defamation League (2002). Racist Groups Use Computer Gaming to Promote Hate. https://www.adl.org/sites/default/files/documents/assets/pdf/combating-hate/Racist-groups-use-computer-gaming.pdf.

Anti-Defamation League (2022a). Breaking the Building Blocks of Hate: A Case Study of Minecraft Servers. https://www.adl.org/resources/report/breaking-building-blocks-hate-case-study-minecraft-servers.

Anti-Defamation League (2022b). Hate Is no Game: Hate and Harassment in Online Games 2022. https://www.adl.org/resources/report/hate-no-game-hate-and-harassment-online-games-2022.

Anti-Defamation League (2022c). Deplatform Tucker Carlson and the "Great Replacement" Theory. https://www.adl.org/resources/blog/deplatform-tucker-carlson-and-great-replacement-theory.

Bailey, D. (2023). Steam just Reached 50,000 Total Games Listed. *PCGamesN*. https://www.pcgamesn.com/steam/total-games.

Bartle, R. (2003). *Designing Virtual Worlds*. New Riders.

Blizzard (2004). *World of Warcraft*. [Videogame]

Bogost, I (2007). *Persuasive Games: The expressive power of videogames*. MIT Press.

Bohemia Interactive (2013). *ARMA 3*. [Videogame]

Bruce, G. (2022). Charting the Rise of Indie Video Games. *YouGov*. https://business.yougov.com/content/41600-us-charting-rise-indie-video-games.

Campbell, J. (1949). *The Hero with a Thousand Faces*. Princeton University Press.

Cook, D. (2012). Loops and Arcs. *Lost Garden*. https://lostgarden.home.blog/2012/04/30/loops-and-arcs/.

Curry, D. (2023, January 9). Minecraft Revenue and Usage Statistics Business of Apps. https://www.businessofapps.com/data/minecraft-statistics/.

D'Anastasio, C. (2021, June 10). How "Roblox" Became a Playground for Virtual Fascists. *Wired*. https://www.wired.com/story/roblox-online-games-irl-fascism-roman-empire/.

Dass, R. (2023, March 8). The Link Between Gaming and Violent Extremism. *The Diplomat*. https://thediplomat.com/2023/03/the-link-between-gaming-and-violent-extremism/.

DeVane, B. & Squire, K.D. (2008). The Meaning of Race and Violence in Grand Theft Auto: San Andreas. *Games and Culture*, 3(3–4), 264–285. 10.1177/1555412 00831730.

Davey, J. (2021). Gamers Who Hate: An Introduction to ISD's Gaming and Extremism Series. *Institute for Strategic Dialogue*. https://www.isdglobal.org/isd-publications/gamers-who-hate-an-introduction-to-isds-gaming-and-extremism-series/.

Davey, J. (2022, March 31). Radicalization and the Role of Video Games. *Fair Observer*. https://www.fairobserver.com/politics/extremism/jacob-davey-right-wing-extremism-radical-right-video-games-radicalization-32902/.

Discord, Incorporated (2015). Discord. [Computer software]

Eclipse Entertainment (1997). Genesis3D. [Computer software]

Egenfeldt-Nielsen, S. & Smith, J.H. (2004). *Playing with Fire: How do computer games influence the player?* University of Gothenburg Press.

Eguchi, K. & Nogami, H. (2001). *Animal Crossing*. [Videogame]

Entertainment Software Association (2022). Essential Facts about the Video Game Industry. https://www.theesa.com/resource/2022-essential-facts-about-the-video-game-industry/.

Epic Games (1998). *Unreal Game Engine*. [Computer software]

Epic Games (2017). *Fortnite*. [Videogame]

Farivar, C. (2019, August 21). Extremists Creep into Roblox, an Online Game Popular with Children. *NBC news*. https://www.nbcnews.com/tech/tech-news/extremists-%20creep-roblox-online-game-popular-children-n1045056.

Ferguson, C.J. (2015). Do Angry Birds Make for Angry Children? A Meta-Analysis of Video Game Influences on Children's and Adolescents' Aggression, Mental Health, Prosocial Behavior, and Academic Performance. *Perspectives on Psychological Science, 10*(5), 646–666.

Ferguson, C. & Wang, J. (2019). Aggressive Video Games Are not a Risk Factor for Future Aggression in Youth: A Longitudinal Study. *Journal of Youth and Adolescence, 48*(1), 439–451. https://link.springer.com/article/10.1007/s10964-019-01069-0.

Fiadotau, M. (2020). Growing Old on Newgrounds: The Hopes and Quandaries of Flash Game Preservation. *First Monday, 25*(8). 10.5210/fm.v25i8.10306.

Gallagher, A., O'Connor, C., Vaux, P., Thomas, E., & Davey, J. (2021). The Extreme Right on Discord. Institute for Strategic Dialogue (ISD). https://www.isdglobal.org/isd-publications/gaming-and-extremism-the-extreme-right-on-discord/.

Gee, J.P. (2004). *Situated Language and Learning: A critique of traditional schooling.* Routledge.

"Global Video Game Market Value from 2020 to 2025" (2023). Statista. https://www.statista.com/statistics/292056/video-game-market-value-worldwide/.

Hezbollah (2003). *Special Force.* [Videogame]

Hezbollah (2007). *Special Force 2: Tale of the Truthful Pledge.* [Videogame]

Higinbotham, W. (1958). *Tennis for Two.* [VideoGame]

Huizinga, J. (1955). *Homo Ludens: A study of the play-element in culture.* Beacon Press.

Inner Sloth (2018). *Among Us.* [Videogame]

Institute for Economics and Peace (2022). Global Terrorism Index 2022: Measuring the Impact of Terrorism. https://www.visionofhumanity.org/wp-content/uploads/2022/03/GTI-2022-web.pdf.

Jenkins, H. (2002). Game Design as Narrative Architecture. In P. Harrington & N. Frup-Waldrop (Eds.). *First person.* MIT Press. http://www.anabiosispress.org/VM606/1stPerson_hjenkins.pdf.

Jenkins, H., Ito, M., & Boyd, D. (2015). *Participatory Culture in a Networked Era: A conversation on youth, learning, commerce, and politics.* Polity Press.

Jorgensen, K. & Karlsen, F. (2018). *Transgression in Games and Play.* MIT Press.

King (2012). *Candy Crush Saga.* [Videogame]

Koehler, D., Fiebig, V., & Jugl, I. (2023). From Gaming to Hating: Extreme-Right Ideological Indoctrination and Mobilization for Violence of Children on Online Gaming Platforms. *Political Psychology, 44*(2), 419–434. 10.1111/pops.12855.

Kowert, R., Martel, A., & Swann, B. (2022). Not Just a Game: Identity Fusion and Extremism in Gaming Cultures. *Frontiers in Communication.* 10.3389/fcomm.2022.1007128.

Koster, R. (2011). Social Mechanics: The Engines Behind Everything Multiplayer. Lecture presented at the Game Developers Conference, San Francisco, CA. https://www.raphkoster.com/wp-content/uploads/2011/02/Koster_Social_Social-mechanics_GDC2011.pdf.

Kowalcyzk, S. (2021, April 24). How Many Games? How Are the Number of Aames on Consoles? ISGamer. https://www.isgamers.com/news/how-many-games-how-are-the-number-of-games-on-consoles/.

Kutner, L. & Olson, C. (2008). *Grand Theft Childhood: The surprising truth about violent video games and what parents can do.* Simon & Schuster.
Lakomy, M. (2019). Let's Play a Video Game: Jihadi Propaganda in the World of Electronic Entertainment. *Studies in Conflict & Terrorism*, 42(4), 383–406.
Lavin, T. (2020). *Culture Warlords: My journey into the dark web of white supremacy.* Legacy Lit.
"League of Legends Live Player Count and Statistics" (2023). Active Player. https://activeplayer.io/league-of-legends/.
Lenhart, A., Smith, A., Anderson, M., Duggan, M., & Perrin, A. (2015). Teens, Technology, and Friendships. Pew Research Center, 1-60. https://www.pewresearch.org/internet/2015/08/06/teens-technology-and-friendships/.
Malone, T.W. & Lepper, M.R. (1987). Making Learning Fun: A Taxonomy of Intrinsic Motivations for Learning. In R.E. Snow & M.J. Farr (Eds.), *Aptitude, Learning, and Instruction: Vol. 3. Cognitive and affective process analysis* (pp. 223–253). Erlbaum.
Meier, S. (1991). *Civilization.* [Videogame]
Meta Platforms (2004). *Facebook.* [Online social platform]
Miller, C. & Silva, S. (2021, September 23). Extremists Using Video-Game Chats to Spread Hate. *BBC News.* https://www.bbc.com/news/technology-58600181.
Mojang Studios (2011). *Minecraft.* [Videogame]
Namco (1980). *Pac–Man.* [Videogame]
National Alliance (2002). *Ethnic Cleansing.* [Videogame]
Newzoo (2022). Global Games Market Report 2022. https://newzoo.com/insights/trend-reports/newzoo-global-games-market-report-2022-free-version.
Neys, J. & Jansz, J. (2010). Political Internet games: Engaging an Audience. *European Journal of Communication*, 25(3), 227–241.
Nintendo (1996). *Pokémon.* [Videogame]
Nguyen, D. (2013). *Flappy Bird.* [Videogame]
"Number of Available Gaming Apps in the Google Play Store from 1st Quarter 2015 to 3rd Quarter 2022" (2023). Statista. https://www.statista.com/statistics/780229/number-of-available-gaming-apps-in-the-google-play-store-quarter/.
Ohno, S. (2022). The Link Between Battle Royale Games and Aggressive Feelings, Addiction, and Sense of Underachievement: Exploring eSports-Related Genres. *International Journal of Mental Health & Addiction*, 20, 1873–1881. 10.1007/s11469-021-00488-0.
"Online Games Worldwide" (2023). Statista. https://www.statista.com/outlook/dmo/digital-media/video-games/online-games/worldwide.
Pajitnov, A. (1984). *Tetris.* [Videogame]
Parkin, S. (2013, December 9). If You Love Games, You Should Refuse to be Called a Gamer. *New Statesman.* Retrieved from http://www.newstatesman.com/if-you-love-games-you-are-not-a-gamer.
Paul, C.A. (2018). *The Toxic Meritocracy of Video Games: Why gaming culture is the worst.* University of Minnesota Press.
PUBG Studios (2017). *Player Unknown Battleground.* [Videogame]
Quantic Foundry (2023). Gamer Motivation Model. https://quanticfoundry.com/blog/.
Riot Games (2013). *League of Legends.* [Videogame]

Robinson, N. & Whittaker, J. (2021). Playing for Hate? Extremism, Terrorism, and Videogames. *Studies in Conflict & Terrorism*, 1–36. 10.1080/1057610X.2 020.1866740.

Roblox Corporation (2006). *Roblox*. [Videogame]

Rockstar Games (1997). *Grand Theft Auto*. [Videogame]

Rockstar Games (2018). *Red Dead Redemption 2*. [Videogame]

Rockstar North (2004). *Grand Theft Auto: San Andreas*. [Videogame]

Rollings, A. & Morris, D. (2000). *Game Architecture and Design*. New Riders.

Ruby, D. (2023, January 3). Roblox Statistics: How Many People play Roblox. *Demand Sage*. https://www.demandsage.com/how-many-people-play-roblox/.

Ruby, D. (2023, March 20). Social Media Users in the World: 2023 Demographics. *Demand Sage*. https://www.demandsage.com/social-media-users/.

Salen, K. & Zimmerman, E. (2004). *Rules of Play: Game design fundamentals*. MIT Press.

Schlegel, L. (2021). *Extremists' Use of Gaming (-Adjacent) Platforms: Insights Regarding Primary and Secondary Prevention Measures*. Luxembourg: Publications Office of the European Union. https://home-affairs.ec.europa.eu/networks/ radicalisation-awareness-network-ran/publications/extremists-use-gaming-adjacent-platforms-insights-regarding-primary-and-secondary-prevention_en.

Schlegel, L. & Amarasingam, A. (2022). Examining the Intersection Between Gaming and Violent Extremism. *United Nations Office of Counter-Terrorism*. https://www.un.org/counterterrorism/sites/www.un.org.counterterrorism/files/ 221005_research_launch_on_gaming_ve.pdf.

Selepak, A. (2010). Skinhead Super Mario Brothers: An Examination of Racist and Violent Games on White Supremacist Web Sites. *Journal of Criminal Justice and Popular Culture*, 17(1), 1–47.

Simon & Schuster Interactive (2003). *Eve Online*. [Videogame]

Slack Technologies (2013). *Slack*. [Computer software]

Sledgehammer Games (2017). *Call of Duty: World War II*. [Videogame]

Social Media Companies: Terms of Service, A.B. 587, § 22.8 (2022). https:// trackbill.com/bill/california-assembly-bill-587-social-media-companies-terms-of-service/2030857/.

Squire, K. (2006). From Content to Context: Videogames as Designed Experience. *Educational Researcher*, 35(8), 19–29.

Steinkuehler, C.A. (2005). *Cognition & Learning in Massively Multiplayer Online Games: A Critical Approach*. [Unpublished doctoral dissertation]. University of Wisconsin-Madison.

Steinkuehler, C. (2006). The Mangle of Play. *Games & Culture*, 1(3), 1–14.

Steinkuehler, C. (2023). Games as Social Platforms. *Games: Research and Practice*, 1(1), 7–8.

Steinkuehler, C. & Oh, Y. (2012). Apprenticeship in Massively Multiplayer Online Games. In C. Steinkuehler, K. Squire, & S. Barab (Eds.), *Games, Learning, and Society: Learning and meaning in the digital age* (pp. 154–184). Cambridge University Press.

Steinkuehler, C. & Williams, D. (2006). Where Everybody Knows Your (Screen) Name: Online Games as "Third Places." *Journal of Computer-Mediated Communication*, 11(4), article 1.

Suits, B. (2004). Construction of a Definition. In K. Salen & E. Zimmerman (Eds.), *Rules of Play: Game design fundamentals* (pp. 172–191). MIT Press.

Swink, S. (2008). *Game Feel: A game designer's guide to virtual sensation.* Taylor & Francis.

Teamspeak Systems, Inc. (2002). *TeamSpeak.* [Computer software]

Twitch Interactive (2011). *Twitch.* [Computer software]

Twitter Incorporated (2006). *Twitter.* [Online social platform]

"Top Games" (2023). Itch.io. https://itch.io/games.

Unity Technologies (2005). *Unity Game Engine.* [Computer software]

Vaux, P., Gallagher, A., & Davey, J. (2021). *The Extreme Right on Steam.* Institute for Strategic Dialogue. https://www.isdglobal.org/wp-content/uploads/2021/08/02-revised-gaming-report-steam.pdf.

Webb, K. (2019). More than 100 Million People Watched the "League of Legends" World Championship, Cementing its Place as the Most Popular Esport. Business Insider: India. https://www.businessinsider.in/tech/news/more-than-100-million-people-watched-the-league-of-legends-world-championship-cementing-its-place-as-the-most-popular-esport/articleshow/72875445.cms.

White Aryan Resistance (n.d.a). *KZ Manager Millenmium: Hamburg Edition.* [Videogame]

White Aryan Resistance (n.d.b). *Watch Out Behind You Hunter!* [Videogame]

Whitehouse, H., McQuinn, B., Buhrmester, M., & Swann, W.B. (2014). Brothers in Arms: Libyan Revolutionaries Bond like Family. *PNAS, 111*(50), 17783–17785.

Zhu, L. (2021). The Psychology Behind Video Games during COVID-19 Pandemic: A Case Study of Animal Crossing: New Horizons. *Human Behavior & Emerging Technology, 3,* 157–159.

2
THEORIES OF DIGITAL GAMES AND RADICALIZATION

Galen Lamphere-Englund

Gaming is big business: above music, film, and TV, gaming is the most profitable and expansive entertainment sector. Revenues for 2022 are estimated to be $196.8 billion (WePC, 2022). While their level of commitment to gaming varies, nearly three billion people, or around one in four humans, play videogames. Nearly 50% are women. Half the world's gamers are in the Asia-Pacific region, while the fastest growing audiences are in the Middle East, Africa, and Latin America (Newzoo, 2022b). For many gamers and across the multitude of sub-communities inside that broad group, life in and out of game (sometimes referred to as "in real life' or IRL) are equally valuable. Recent philosophical discourse increasingly points to the fallacy of viewing virtual realities, like games, as less "real" than physical experiences (Chalmers, 2022). Online games and the adjacent platforms around them, like live streaming and messaging apps, are social ecosystems. They show us how virtual worlds – the metaverse or metaverses – are already coming into form. They mirror elements of, and in turn shape, the physical world.

Nearly three decades of research have not shown violence in videogames definitely to be connected to violence in the physical world (APA Task Force on Violent Media, 2015). On the contrary, games can actually have substantial positive effects and facilitate prosocial outcomes for many players (Bateson & Martin, 2013; Kowert *et al.*, 2014). However, the social worlds on gaming platforms may also bring risks for other social harms, including the exploitation of games and gaming-adjacent spaces by violent extremist and terrorist actors. Far-right actors in the USA, EU, Australia, and New Zealand have created standalone anti-Semitic games

DOI: 10.4324/9781003388371-3

for propaganda (Robinson & Whittaker, 2021; Anti-Defamation League, 2022), livestreamed terror attacks on gamer-targeted platforms (Lakhani & Wiedlitzka, 2022), and created strong social networks on gaming-adjacent platforms to recruit and mobilize real-world violence (Davey, 2021; Koehler *et al.*, 2022; Kowert *et al.*, 2022). Similarly, violent jihadist actors have also created their own bespoke games and modifications, as well as specific game servers (Schlegel, 2020); developed propaganda with video game motifs (Dauber *et al.*, 2019; Mahmoud, 2022); and sought to recruit through gaming-adjacent platforms (Singapore Ministry of Home Affairs, 2023).

After a spike in research from 2010–2012, gaming and extremism study was less popular for much of the last decade. Yet since 2020, perhaps spurred by livestreaming of the Christchurch attack in 2019 followed by the vast increase in gaming during COVID-19 lockdowns, interest in the topic has surged (Lamphere-Englund & Bunmathong, 2021). Security and law enforcement professionals regularly document cases of violent extremist exploitation of gaming, while researchers are shedding new light on the scale of exposure to extremist content in gaming spaces (ADL, 2022; Schlegel & Amarasingam, 2022). Accordingly, thinkers on the subject have developed a range of theories attempting to explain why extremists exploit gaming, what makes gamer (sub-)communities attractive to extremists, and what implications their exploitation has on broader processes of radicalization.

Typologies of Harm

As researchers and practitioners have sought to explain violent extremists' increased use of games and gamified approaches over the last years, several groups have sought to codify and enumerate types of exploit. In particular, the Radicalisation Awareness Network (RAN), an EU advisory network of researchers and counter-extremism practitioners, has developed a six-part typology of "video games and gaming adjacent communication platforms and gaming imagery [used] by violent extremists" (2020). Subsequently, the Extremism and Gaming Research Network (EGRN), which includes some of the original RAN typology authors, has iterated a refined version of that typology of harms (Lamphere-Englund & White, 2023). In addition, tech platform trust and safety teams responsible for violent extremism responses through specific platforms have sought to explain harmful user behavior through various definitions and behavioral hierarchies that help to define the field (Davey *et al.*, 2021; GIFCT, 2021). While many of these trust and safety responses constitute the frontline of defense online, most are kept internal to each company, so public access to their knowledge is decidedly more limited.

The revised six-part RAN/EGRN typology (Lamphere-Englund & Bunmathong, 2021, based on RAN, 2020) (below) covers most of the current cases of extremist and terrorist uses of games and gaming-adjacent platforms. These distinctions often blur together when discussing specific cases, yet are still a helpful heuristic device for researchers and practitioners to distinguish between different extremist tactic, strategy, and types of harm.

The Development of New Videogames and Modifications

Perhaps the most obvious of exploits is the creation of video games by terrorists and extremists. Since as early as 2002, when the National Alliance, a US-based white supremacist hate group, created *Ethnic Cleansing* as a standalone racist and anti-Semitic game, a slate of provocative and extremist games across the ideological spectrum have trickled into existence. Some of these, including *Ethnic Cleansing*, were built as simple standalone games requiring users to seek them out online from corners of the internet, install them, and suffer through clunky game mechanics. Others act as modifications, or "mods," to existing games, allowing users to keep playing their favorite titles but with graphic extremist content and narratives. These include, for example, various white supremacist *Deus Vult* mods for popular games ranging from old school titles such as *Doom* (id Software), to more recent strategy titles such as *Hearts of Iron IV* (Paradox) and *Medieval II* (Creative Assembly). Similar titles with racist epithets for names include *Muslim Massacre* (Eric "Sigvatr" Vaughn, 2007), *Stormer Doom* ("StormerDoom," 2015), and *Angry Goy I* and *II* (Wheel Maker Studios, 2017, 2018).

Similarly, jihadist actors such as Hezbollah have built a range of titles, including *Special Forces* (2003) and *Holy Defense* (2018), where players can fight Israeli armed forces and the so-called Islamic State (ISIS). Meanwhile, ISIS sympathizers and designers, apathetic to the use of their creations for propaganda, have built mods for the popular first-person shooter (FPS) title *Arma 3* (Bohemia Interactive), including *Dawn of ISIS* (2017) and *Islamic State* (2017–2021). Other mods to *Grand Theft Auto* (GTA, Rockstar Games) feature in propaganda by ISIS, with titles such as *Salil al-Sawarem* (Al-Rawi, 2016), yet these appear to mainly be reappropriations of existing mods not made by the terrorist group (Reddit, r/GrandTheftAuto, 2016). More recently, extremist actors have made worrisome models, such as recreations of internment camps, ISIS battles, and far-right shootings, through minigames in sandbox games where users can build their own worlds such as *Roblox* (Roblox) and *Minecraft* (Microsoft) (D'Anastasio, 2021; Kowert *et al.*, 2022; Seng, 2023; Singapore MHA, 2023). However worrying these games and mods may appear, the primary audience seems to be sympathizers and radicalized individuals seeking ideological affirmation. Additionally, many violent extremist organizations (VEOs) are extremely media savvy and may seek to use public reactions to shocking gaming content to gain additional attention. Users must seek out mods in specific online forums and then install them, which creates a barrier to access and a clear selection bias among those who play them. As such, bespoke games may be among the less threatening tactics deployed by violent extremists in the gaming sphere. Still, these games can be helpful in propagandizing, radicalizing, and retaining supporters of violent extremism.

Gamification as a Radicalization Tool

In its simplest form, gamification refers to using elements from games repurposed in nongame settings (Deterding *et al.*, 2011). Marketers have popularized gamification to impressive behavioral effect: Have you ever tried to reach a higher tier of reward with your airline frequent flyer club? Then you have engaged in a gamified scheme. Gamified systems give us roles, rules, and ways to win, setting boundaries and mechanics for that experience (Hunicke *et al.*, 2004). Some mechanics deal with the setup of the game (you can only join the frequent flyer club as an individual), others with the rules (you need to fly, not drive, to advance), and others with progression (you get a higher level, with more perks, the more you fly). Similarly, to optimize the time users spend online for revenue generation, platforms optimize their algorithms to retain users through minigame-like engagements: *Pokemon GO* (Niantic), for example, gamifies fitness by rewarding users with higher level Pokemon for walking more. Garmin, Strava, and Nike all use ranking systems, badges, and awards in their apps to reward and incentivize users to reach fitness goals.

Nefarious actors use similarly addictive and effective approaches to reach and engage others in their cause. Gamification is discussed in more depth later in this chapter, but it is worth noting we have seen this taking the form of using leaderboard rankings and award badges to rank terrorist acts (Schlegel, 2020); and meme-based (or "memetic") imagery used to depict terrorists leveling up based on their atrocities (Thorleifsson & Düker, 2021). Specific apps developed by ISIS have also been gamified to teach Arabic alongside ideological indoctrination to better research young children (Lakhani, 2022).

At a meta-analytical level, we can see how gamifying terrorism blurs the lines between real and virtual worlds (Schlegel, 2022) as acts of terrorism are livestreamed by perpetrators seeming to follow virtual "cultural scripts"' developed in prior attacks (Macklin, 2022). We also find it helpful to distinguish between top-down gamification, or the "strategic use of gamified elements by extremist organizations to facilitate engagement with their content" (Schlegel, 2021c, p. 4), and bottom-up gamification, which percolates organically from small groups or individuals using similar elements. These approaches may prove to be effective tools – building on the consumer marketing successes of your airlines, credit card companies, and fitness apps – for the full lifecycle of recruiting, radicalizing, and retaining existing members in violent extremist organizations. Additional research is needed to fully determine the impact of these approaches.

Using Gaming Pop Culture References

Games and the iconographic styles in them, beyond allowing for the active gamifying of specific elements, hold undeniable pop cultural appeal. First-person shooters (FPS) such as *Call of Duty* (Activision), *Halo* (343 Industries), *CounterStrike* (Valve), and more recent FPS games such as *Valorant* (Riot) and *Fortnite* (Epic), all reference distinct graphic gameplay styles where the player is immersed in the game through the eyes of the protagonist. From millennials to younger generations, video game references are eminently pop. Extremists exploit this visual familiarity, such as through helmet-cam footage of attacks, starting, notably, with the Christchurch attack in 2019, to popularize their attacks. Livestreaming video footage directly mirrors FPS style to engage viewers and invite them into side chats during actual terrorist attacks. This practice echoes "Let's Play" videos, in which livestreaming gamers interact with their virtual audiences in real time (Lakhani & Wiedlitzka, 2022). Analysis of the attackers' weapons and subtle iconography used in the attacks also shows parallels to "Easter eggs'" embedded in video games that players are encouraged to find by paying close attention (Amarasingam *et al.*, 2022; Lamphere-Englund & White, 2022).

Apart from livestreaming, extremist groups have worked gaming cultural references into many propaganda formats. ISIS, for example, infamously used a *Grand Theft Auto V* (GTA) mod to create propaganda videos that gave the illusion of having the ability to produce top-quality games (Dauber *et al.*, 2019; Garcia, 2022). Similar propaganda videos using ISIS-inspired mods for *Arma 3*, another FPS game, have been identified (Garcia, 2022; Mahmoud, 2022). More recently, two youths were arrested in Singapore after making ISIS games and content in *Roblox* (Singapore MHA, 2023). Meanwhile, far-right actors have developed more content "related to historical simulation and strategic videogames such as Europa Universalis IV, Hearts of Iron IV, and Stellaris" (Garcia, 2022, p. 23). Game-based memes and dark humor, especially those drawing on Viking-themed video games, are also actively used by the far right as a form of memetic warfare to weaponize video game aesthetics for effective propaganda among their target audience (Kingdon, 2023). Drawing on the pop cultural power of gaming is good marketing and helps violent extremists to promote, propagandize, and recruit effectively.

Using Online Games for Communication

We have also found that extremists and violent extremist organizations use in-game chat functions – both text and voice based – as channels for grooming and recruitment efforts as well as intragroup conversations (RAN, 2021). Specific tactics include using racist or discriminatory language and humor through game chats to find like-minded individuals (ADL, 2020; Davey, 2021), and facilitating conversations with them to garner more interest in the recruiting organization's ideology. Frequently, in-game chats are less moderated – or are at least perceived to be so – compared to other unencrypted messaging platforms. In-game chats also allow users to reach an array of people in the same game server, facilitating open group conversations with nonmembers. Often these preliminary, humorous conversations can help facilitate a "cognitive opening" (Trip *et al.*, 2019) that can be leveraged into a conversion funnel that draws users from gaming spaces into private conversations in group-run chat servers (such as specific servers on Discord), semi-encrypted chatrooms (Telegram groups, for example), or onto websites controlled by the organization. Additionally, these "gaming-adjacent platforms have also been exploited by far-right ... networks to vet applicants" and disseminate propaganda that would likely be moderated elsewhere (Tech Against Terrorism, 2022). In short, exploiting in-game chat functionalities may further recruitment and potentially aid internal communication efforts.

Using Gaming-Adjacent Platforms and Ecosystems

Online gaming is not just about the game: gamers and their many subcommunities use a broader ecosystem of online spaces crafted, or developed, along similar cultural norms (Baele *et al.*, 2020). Research commissioned by the EU Radicalisation Awareness Network has noted that "video gaming can be an entry point where, once trust is established, there is the possibility that recruiters are able to guide people to alternative, less monitored, spaces" (Lakhani, 2022, p. 15). Gaming-adjacent platforms include, but are not limited to:

- Game distribution and purchase platforms such as *Steam* (store. steampowered.com), which includes social networking functionalities, and *Epic Games* (www.epicgames.com)
- Livestreaming sites (including the popular *Twitch* (twitch.com) and more fringe *DLive* (dlive.tv))
- Gaming forums, including many *Discord* (discord.com) servers, sections on imageboards such as *4Chan*, sub-Reddits on *Reddit* (www.reddit.com), and dedicated gaming corners on forms popular with extremists such as *Kiwifarms*)
- Video content, such as "Let's Play" content on *YouTube* (www.youtube.com), *Odysee* (odysee.com), and other video-sharing platforms

In particular, livestreaming platforms have been popularized by gamers and esports stars who draw millions of viewers while narrating their gameplay, tournaments, or other content (Twitch Tracker, 2023). Multiple far-right attackers have exploited this vast viewership to broadcast their acts of terrorism. The Christchurch (New Zealand), Halle (Germany), and Buffalo (United States) far-right terror attacks were all livestreamed but platform response times have improved, leading to the swift removal of content from the original platform. However, rapid archiving by sympathizers and out-linking has enabled millions of subsequent views of the atrocities (Koehler, 2019; Macklin, 2019; Amarasingam *et al.*, 2022). Similarly, during the US Capitol riots, *DLive*, a blockchain-based platform with many gaming streamers, was used to host videos of rioters storming the area. As perpetrators broadcast their crimes and misinformation, spectators could engage directly with the streamers and donate to their attacks (SPLC, 2021). Meanwhile, the use of semi-closed chat servers such as *Discord*, a service originally designed to run alongside online games to allow voice and text chat, has been exploited by violent extremists to mobilize, including during the deadly 2017 Unite the Right rally in Charlottesville, USA, and the far-right terrorist attack in Buffalo, USA, in 2022 (Discord, 2021; Tech Against Terrorism, 2022). Such gaming-adjacent ecosystem platforms can be exploited to propagandize, recruit, and mobilize extremist actors.

Financing and Money Laundering through Gaming Platforms

Lastly, as the research and evidence base has expanded over the last years, researchers have seen worrying indications of potential terrorism-related financing and money laundering via gaming-related platforms. So far, exploitation of gaming-related marketplaces by terrorists and violent extremists appears to be small scale. However, comprehensive data is elusive, and the potential to sell in-game items, game keys, and other products in exchange for crypto currencies (distributed and typically not governmentally controlled) or fiat currency (issued by governments) provides potential regulatory and platform policy loopholes that can be exploited. The Financial Action Task Force (FATF), an intergovernmental organization that combats financial crime, has issued warnings since 2018 to regulate virtual currency exchanges with anti-money laundering (AML) requirements (Kelly, 2021).

However, most agencies globally do not yet require AML regulation in virtual worlds or gaming spaces (ibid). This is despite the fact that one firm alone (*Roblox*) took in over $2.2 billion in revenue in 2022, with a significant share (between 24.5–29.6%) of each dollar spent in-game going to individual developers via an in-game currency, Robux, that can be converted to real currency (Roblox, 2023a; 2023b). Meanwhile, *Fortnite*, a global blockbuster game produced by Epic Games, generated an estimated $5.8 billion in revenue in 2021 (Iqbal, 2023). The game uses "loot boxes," which randomly generate prizes in exchange for cash paid via the in-game currency: billions are spent this way annually, and money-laundering schemes exploiting them have been uncovered (Mistry, 2018; Conneller, 2019). Globally, microtransactions such as those in *Roblox*, *Fortnite*, and across other platforms are forecasted to reach nearly $67.66 billion by 2023 (Business Research Company, 2023). Notably, not all in-game currencies are designed to be converted to real money: some are non-convertible and are designed to stay in-game, while others can be easily converted to real and crypto funds. Yet some third-party marketplaces facilitate in-game currency conversion to both types (Kelly, 2021).

Livestreaming, too, provides tremendous monetization prospects for the most successful influencers. Viewers can donate to livestreams or sponsor their gamer of choice by "gifting" them virtual items, which they can exchange for fiat or crypto currency. Extremist actors on livestreaming platforms, especially those targeting right-leaning communities such as *DLive*, bring in new users. At the same time, lucrative revenue streams make companies reluctant to wade into moderation debates. *DLive* markets itself as "the world's primary and largest blockchain streaming channel," and provides its users with crypto currency to perform transactions through its DLive Protocol and associated apps (Keierleber, 2021; DLive, 2023). While the platform made efforts to clean its public-facing website after facing scrutiny following its use by the January 6 attack on the US Capitol, the underlying protocol and content hosted on it appear to remain unchanged. The platform also does not take a share of *DLive* users' earnings, making it more lucrative for streamers looking to raise funds quickly compared with other (and more moderated) options such as *YouTube*.

Experts have advised that "as familiarity with virtual worlds rises, hopefully the FATF, FinCEN (the US Financial Crimes Enforcement Network), and other agencies throughout the world will start addressing the risks posed by in-world currencies of the virtual world" (Kelly, 2021, p. 1512). Terrorist financing expert Jessica Davis also has testified that propagandistic merchandise from violent extremist groups is being sold across streaming and gaming platforms (The Hub, 2022). Violent extremist groups, in the meanwhile, continue to experiment with new exploits: An ISIS supporter recently issued a non-fungible token (NFT), of the collectible sort that buyers pay for and collect (Tech Against Terrorism, 2022). Meanwhile, various companies are gamifying NFTs to build games with tradable avatars, increase the loyalty of customers already paying for digitalized collectibles, and building in crypto currency exchanges into simple games. While not yet exploited by VEOs, these aspects provide future concerns for financial flows that could be channeled to extremist groups. In summary: Until further research and policies are developed, extremist-related financing and money laundering remain under-evaluated risks across gaming platforms.

Radicalization Theories

Beyond the typology above, several researchers have sought to explain why radicalization can take root in gaming spaces. Before describing their efforts, it is helpful to conceptualize violent extremism (VE) and radicalization. Unfortunately, both are wide-ranging terms without unified definitions across governments, academics, and tech platforms. There are, however, some general commonalities among most thinkers: VE generally refers to a belief system (whether political, religious, or otherwise ideological in nature) that justifies the use of violence, especially against civilians, to achieve its aims and elevate its followers above others. Bak *et al.*, (2019) made an admirable attempt at a unified definition, which covers most bases:

> Violent extremism is a violent type of mobilization that aims to elevate the status of one group, while excluding or dominating its "others" based on markers, such as gender, religion, culture and ethnicity [as well as race, sexual orientation, and other markers]. In doing so, violent extremist organizations destroy existing political and cultural institutions, and supplant them with alternative governance structures that work according to the principles of a totalitarian and intolerant ideology. (p. 8)

In keeping with the above definition, they also provide three main criteria to define violent extremism:

1 *Totalitarianism and intolerance:* Violent extremist ideology legitimizes subjugation and domination over other groups, thereby depriving them of their fundamental rights
2 *An anti-status quo political project:* Violent extremism as a political project attempts to build new institutions and structures of governance, and either destroy those that exist or reform them in a fundamental manner
3 *Use of violence:* Violent extremism goes beyond cognitive radicalization, which only includes thoughts and beliefs. VE involves violent mobilization and behavior (ibid)

In the gaming context, a great deal of content from across the six proceeding typologies of harm might fall short of the VE definition but which many observers might see as extremism. For example, propaganda from violent extremist organizations often does not initially call for the use of violence and instead seeks to ideologically indoctrinate individuals to the views of the group. Savvy extremist propagandists don't lead with the most extreme content: they often start with accessible calls to defend one's brethren against an ideological struggle, build a better world or a utopia, and so on.

Hence, it is also useful to consider the definition of extremism (rather than *violent* extremism). Here too a unified definition is lacking. One of the many definitions is a conceptualization proposed by Peter Neumann (2013) that defines extremist or radicalized views without reference to violent acts: Extremism "may describe political ideas that are diametrically opposed to a society's core values, which – in the context of a liberal democracy – can be various forms of racial or religious supremacy, or ideologies that deny basic human rights or democratic principles. Or it can mean the methods by which actors seek to realize any political aim, namely by showing disregard for the life, liberty, and human rights of others" (p. 874).

Lastly, when it comes to radicalization, the United Nations High Commissioner for Human Rights provides a general definition that: "The notion of 'radicalization' is generally used [by some States] to convey the idea of a process through which an individual adopts an increasingly extremist set of beliefs and aspirations. This may include, but is not defined by, the willingness to condone, support, facilitate or use violence to further political, ideological, religious or other goals" (General Assembly, Human Rights Council report A/HRC/33/29, para. 19). (See Figure 2.1.)

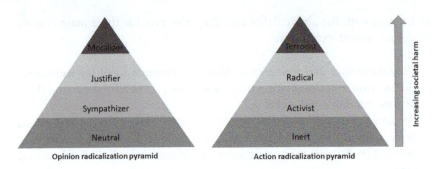

FIGURE 2.1 Two Pyramid Model Example, author's own image based on McCauley and Moskalenko (2017).

Moving beyond definitions, there is a wide range of models for radicalization developed over the last 20 years, ranging from the classic Sageman (2004), to the more recent popular theories developed by Kruglanski *et al.* (2019), Hafez and Mullins (2015), and overviews such as those from Borum (2011). As a complex, widely debated phenomenon, no single model offers a perfect empirical picture. However, the two pyramid model developed by McCauley and Moskalenko (2017) and the Attitudes-Behaviors-Corrective (ABC) model by Khalil *et al.* (2019) provide flexible approaches that are helpful when thinking about radicalization in virtual or tech-based spaces. McCauley and Moskalenko suggest that violent extremist opinions and actions are separate pathways – delineated between cognitive and behavioral radicalization – that are not inherently connected or dependent on one another. For them, the opinion pyramid shows shifts in an individual's beliefs, ideologies, and ideas. In contrast, the action pyramid indicates radicalization steps toward a willingness to commit political, social, or violent action. Critically, one can move up and down either pyramid independently of the other. Here, radicalization is a fluid, potentially nonlinear process that is not systematically predictable. Violent or radical action can occur without full opinion radicalization, while a fully cognitively radicalized individual (in terms of their opinion) will not inherently take action.

In the context of gaming communities and gaming-adjacent platforms, we can make a rough overlay in which individuals use different aspects of the gaming ecosystem to extremist ends based on where they may sit in the two pyramids (see Figure 2.2).

In this graphic, the six main extremist uses of games and gaming-adjacent platforms are situated based on an admittedly arbitrary set of levels of harm along the radicalization pyramids. For example, a deeply convicted moralizer may enjoy playing racist or violent extremist games. A

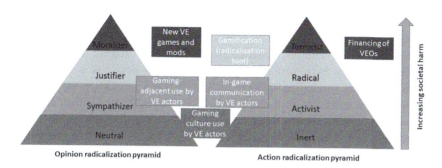

FIGURE 2.2 Two Pyramid Model with Gaming Cases, adapted from McCauley and Moskalenko (2017).

sympathizer or activist may turn to gaming-adjacent platforms such as *Twitch* or *Discord* to find like-minded communities. Gamification, especially when strategically applied, may constitute a higher risk use case: Weaponizing gamification for extremist purposes indicates both significant action and opinion-oriented radicalization. While the efficacy of the approach is still unproved, the use case merits inclusion here. Developing custom games and mods, meanwhile, shows a substantial level of opinion radicalization and the willingness to invest time and effort in their development – action. Downloading and playing these games, of course, less so. Lastly, financing through gaming platforms confers material support to extremist organizations and demonstrates action radicalization, although the type of support rendered may situate it between the terrorist and radical levels. This is still a very crude sketch, with plenty of overlaps and edge cases: communication capacities can be used to organize attacks (a high-risk terrorist action), while custom games may be played by sympathizers or justifiers and further their radicalization journey. Still, this framework allows us to join a well-known radicalization model with the typology of gaming use cases outlined previously.

Beyond the above sketch, several theorists and researchers have sought to explain terrorist and extremist uses of games via different theories. However, as with any complex phenomenon, especially given the nascent state of research into the subject, no single approach provides comprehensive logic.

From Theory to Practice

Schlegel (2021b) has written extensively on the subject and provided a useful distinction between organic and strategic uses of games and platforms by extremist actors. Drawing from their top-level grouping, we can organize an array of other theories that generally fit into organic or strategic framing, although the two are not mutually exclusive. While there seems to be limited evidence that gaming is used as a concerted strategy by many extremist organizations, gaming acts "as a means of bringing already radicalized people together" (Davey, 2021, p. 9) and as multidirectional social networking (Koehler *et al.*, 2022). Historical and role-playing games, such as *Hearts of Iron* (Paradox), *Europa Universalis* (Paradox), and *Crusader Kings* (Paradox), also offer a long history of racist mods and communities. While extremist actors may co-opt games, most of their use appears to be more organic than strategic in nature. However, strategic use cases are of more concern, and we lack a comprehensive evidence base, especially outside the USA and EU, to accurately understand the depth of strategic use. Both cases merit deep inquiry from interested researchers, practitioners, and policymakers.

Organic Use

Social Spaces

Organic use suggests that, put simply, extremists may also enjoy playing games. Across billions of gamers, there are inevitably individuals with extremist views. Additionally, they may find acceptance in – and not be kicked out of – toxic gaming spaces that are filled with misogyny (from GamerGate to the recent findings of rampant sexism in game studios), racism, and homophobia. They may also find a sense of imagined community through gaming, especially within more toxic communities. As Koehler *et al.* (2022) and Davey (2021) found in their assessments of far-right radicalization cases on gaming platforms and in far-right communities, respectively, "there is a notable extremist subset within broader gaming communities" (Davey, 2021, p. 5). The prominence of persistent, extremist content on gaming platforms seems clear: the Anti-Defamation League (ADL) found that some 20% of adult gamers in the USA were exposed to white-supremacist ideologies in 2022, along with 15% of younger users between ages ten and 17 (ADL, 2022). Those figures are increasing year on year. Similarly, global non-representative polling by UNOCT found that nearly 80% of gamer respondents had seen hateful or violent content, with 27% exposed to anti-Semitic content, and 32% encountering concerning levels of extremist content (Schlegel and Amarasingam, 2022). Both polls also found that gamers are exposed across a variety of surfaces, from in-game chats, to *Discord* servers and in audio conversations, and across games, from *Call of Duty* to *Valorant*, *DOTA 2* (Valve), and *Counter-Strike: Global Offensive* (ADL, 2022; Schlegel and Amarasingam, 2022).

Identity Fusion

The pervasiveness of extremist and harmful content across the gaming ecosystem makes a persuasive argument for the organic use case explanation, as do several recent research studies that provide reasons for why extremist ideologies may find particularly fertile soil in video-gaming cultures. Identity fusion is a construct that refers to how close one feels to a group. Typically, each of us has many layers of social identities. When one identity overwhelms the others – in this case, becoming a gamer as the primary identity – the individual is typically more willing to do substantially more to support the group. Evaluating pathways to joining violent groups has shown that this "internalization" of the group identity can directly provide a reason to enlist (Gómez *et al.*, 2011; Gómez, *et al.*, 2020). This can be a double-edged sword: providing "a sense of connection and purpose for individuals who suffer from loneliness and insecurity" while potentially luring them "into embracing extremist beliefs that lead them down the path to radicalization" (Kowert *et al.*, 2022, n.p.).

Kowert and Newhouse (2022) have illustrated how exclusionary identities (us versus them mentalities) help to create conducive environments for extremist ideologies. At the same time, the tight-knit groups present in gamer guilds, raids, and servers can help to form intense small group affinity bonds of the type shown to strengthen group identity: these can also increase risks of radicalization should one member of the group start down a pathway of radicalization (Atran & Stern, 2005; Atran, 2010; Molyneux *et al.*, 2015). Recent psychological testing by Kowert, Martel, and Swann (2022) has also shown that identity fusion among gamers is associated with numerous negative behavioral traits, including increased support for extremist ideologies. Ultimately, Kowert and colleagues find that a "fused" gamer identity in their study was associated with:

- Willingness to fight/die (for other gamers)
- Recent aggressive behaviors
- Machiavellianism (a personality trait characterized by interpersonal manipulation, being deceitful, cynical, and lacking morality)
- Narcissism, psychopathy (lack of empathy), sexism, racism
- Endorsement of beliefs and policies centered on ideas of white nationalism

Strategic Use

In contrast to organic use cases, Schlegel's (2021b) conceptualization of strategic use provides the framing for the deliberate exploitation of gaming surfaces by extremist actors. There are many logical reasons why using videogames and gaming platforms appeals to terrorist and extremist actors.

First, the *demographic appeal* is clear: Although all ages increasingly game, gamers remain a younger audience. The greatest share of gamers, at least in the USA, are between 18–34 years of age (36%), followed by those under 18 (24%) (ESA, 2022). Those are prime recruitment demographics for militaries, armed groups, and violent extremist organizations worldwide (Østby et al., 2022). As such, like any successful marketer, extremist actors may simply be seeking to reach their target audience where they are. The sheer reach of gaming platforms is also tremendous: with over 2.8 billion gamers globally, opportunities to drive home propaganda abound (Newzoo, 2022a).

Second, the innate and timely *pop culture appeal of gaming* provides an effective avenue to interact with audiences and perpetrators alike. The Christchurch attacker, for example, littered his online commentary with gaming cultural references, quotes, and indie game characters (Lakhani & Wiedlitzka, 2022). Similarly, "bottom-up" approaches to providing humorous gaming cultural references, often laced with dark humor, can effectively facilitate cognitive openings to ideological radicalization (Fielitz &Ahmed, 2021; Schlegel, 2021). The use of videogame screen-grabs in extremist memes, from *Far Cry V* to Viking-type memes, can also be leveraged to help "users create a sense of urgency that 'race war in the real world' is necessary" (Thorleifsson, 2021, p.299; Kingdon, 2023). Using memetic warfare calling on cultural tropes from gaming subcultures not only creates effective propaganda, but helps to dodge conventional online moderation efforts (Liang & Cross, 2020; Thorleifsson & Duker, 2021).

Third, those *culturally nuanced communication and outreach approaches often occur in gaming spaces without significant moderation.* As such, the strategic benefit of targeting gaming platforms looks clear. Research by the Institute for Strategic Dialogue and the Anti-Defamation League has shown that community standards, moderation, and trust and safety enforcement on many gaming and gaming-adjacent platforms are severely lacking (Davey, 2021; ADL, 2022). To illustrate this point, a questionnaire from US Congresswoman Lori Trahan in early 2023 found that nine of 14 major gaming studios had made no efforts to specifically identify or address extremist content in their online games (Trahan, 2023). While some platforms, such as *Roblox* and *Discord*, have taken robust and fairly public efforts to address extremist exploitation of their services, many others have not taken any meaningful steps.

Fourth, *the use of gamification*, or applying game-like elements outside of games, fits well into the strategic use typology. As Schlegel explains, "gamification most often means introducing points, badges, leader boards and other gaming elements into other settings" (2021c, p. 5). Gamifying experience effectively engages users and increases retention, from e-learning and educational arenas to extremist milieus. Both more competitive users (or those motivated to improve their ranking inside the group) and collaborative users keen to find interaction and belonging find gamified tactics enticing (Schlegel, 2021c).

Schlegel (2021c) also distinguishes top-down gamification, used by organizations or recruiters, and bottom-up formats deployed by individuals and small groups without direction from extremist organizations. One common tactic is the livestreaming of terror attacks, starting with the 2019 Christchurch attacks and continuing with subsequent attacks in Poway (USA), Bærum (Norway), Halle (Germany), and Buffalo (USA) (see Table 2.1 for an overview).

TABLE 2.1 Far-right attacks with gamified elements. Adapted and extended from Thorleifsson, 2021, p.7

Location	Date	Manifesto posted on	Livestream	Outlinking
Christchurch, New Zealand	15 March 2019	8chan, /pol/	Facebook	Filesharing sites by the attacker
Poway, USA	27 April 2019	8chan, /pol/	Facebook (attempt)	
El Paso, USA	3 August 2019	8chan, /pol/		
Bærum, Norway	10 August 2019	Endchan	Facebook (attempt)	
Halle, Germany	9 October 2019	Meguca	Twitch	
Hanau, Germany	19 Feb 2020	YouTube, Personal Website		Filesharing sites by supporters, Kiwifarms
Buffalo, USA	14 May 2022	Discord, Gdoc	Twitch	Filesharing sites by supporters
Bratislava, Slovakia	12 October 2022	Twitter (outlinked)		Filesharing sites by the attacker

By mixing helmet-mounted footage, often from GoPro mobile cameras, with tactical weapons and armor, attackers seek to mirror the gameplay of first-person shooter series such as *Call of Duty* or *Counter-Strike*. For their audiences, the gamified propaganda gives them a means to respond in real time, reacting and supporting the attack with emojis and rallying cries: a game with deadly outcomes (Amarasingam *et al.*, 2022; Lakhani & Wiedlitzka, 2022). At the same time, manifestos developed by a similar set of attackers draw on gaming references often ripped from imageboard "chan culture" and memetic irony designed to "mask offensive and racist material" (Thorleifsson, 2021, p. 9). Using dehumanizing humor, dark irony, and gamified hate online allows extremist users to enter into "play frames" where many treat the "activities that are occurring as both true and not true, serious and non-serious at the same time" (ibid). In this telling, both viewers watching the livestream of an attack and the experience of the perpetrator himself can feel both real and unreal, simultaneously like a game and not a game. The recent Bratislava attacker wrote in his 2022 manifesto that watching the video of the Christchurch massacre was: "truly unique – maybe it was the fact that it was livestreamed, or the video-game-like view of the whole event … The video felt 'different' to most other content that I had seen before."

Apart from livestreaming, the Halle attacker also listed his achievements in his manifesto, similar to what might come up at the end of a video game playthru. Both he and the Buffalo shooter obsessed and recorded their arsenals just as a game might give options for the kit used by a player (Thorleifsson, 2021; Amarasingam *et al.*, 2022). In any case, such strategic uses of gamification are also not unique to far-right attackers: videogame-based propaganda developed by ISIS continues to hold salience, from memes and videogames developed in 2013–2014 to new *Roblox* minigames built by ISIS sympathizers a decade later (Mahmoud, 2022; Singapore Ministry of Home Affairs, 2023).

Fifth, extremist organizations may seek to recruit and radicalize gamers based on *strategic appeals to their individual motivations for engaging with gaming content*. Researchers have outlined preliminary frameworks drawing linkages between radicalization user typologies and gamer typologies. Mahmoud (2022), for example, looks to draw comparisons between gamer types and psychological-motivational groupings that inspire individuals to join VEOs. Additionally, though she does not directly argue that VEOs seek to target individual gaming motivations, Schlegel's (2021a) application of Marczewski's HEXAD gamification typology (2015) reveals five user types: "Socializers motivated by connection to others, Competitors seeking to compare themselves to their peers, Achievers driven by the desire to understand the world, Meaning Seekers wishing to engage in meaningful action that can provide them with a sense of purpose, and Disruptors who enjoy upsetting others" (2021a, p. 60). Both researchers see clear overlaps between why individuals play videogames and why they may be drawn to VEOs, though their understandings of the strategic use of those motivations by VEOs vary. It does, however, seem likely that this nexus is understood and exploited by different VEOs, including by white supremacists who are sanguine about the role of games in their recruitment ecosystem (Young, 2022).

Conclusion

As we have seen, while updated research into radicalization, extremism, and gaming is nascent, several researchers have developed valuable theories potentially explaining the exploitation of gaming spaces. Those recent theoretical developments include:

- Typologies of gaming exploitation (Lamphere-Englund and Bunmathong, 2021; Schlegel, 2021b)
- Uses of gamification (Schlegel, 2021a; Lakhani, White, & Wallner, 2022)
- Conceptualizations of "play frames" (Thorleifsson, 2021)
- The reconfiguration of classic radicalization theories such as identity fusion and small group recruitment dynamics (Kowert, 2022), recruiter-to-gamer profile types (Schlegel, 2021; Mahmoud, 2022), and socialization or social-networking explanations (Koehler *et al.*, 2022)

In addition, the chapter reviewed how to conceptualize the popular twopyramid model radicalization model developed by McCauley and Moskalenko (2017) to assess digital radicalization processes (for example, Cohen, 2012). By retooling validated models like these, we can assemble frameworks for understanding the social functions of gaming in radicalization.

In spite of these concerns, I see games fundamentally as a source of resilience, joy, and community for billions. Stronger research, platform policy, regulatory, intervention, and awareness raising efforts are needed to build more resilient and inclusive gamer communities. The massive audience of gamers – one in four people globally – deserves greater recognition, protection, and resources to keep games as they should be: Fun, inclusive, community-building opportunities to make the world a bit better online and offline. As a gamer myself, I know we can keep games exciting, fun, and amazingly creative expeditions while preventing violent extremist exploitation of these spaces. I hope you, dear reader, will join us on that journey. If you would like to contribute to closing those research, policy, and practice gaps, I hope you consider joining the efforts of the groups including the Extremism and Gaming Research Network (EGRN), the Global Internet Forum on Counter Terrorism (GIFCT), Tech Against Terrorism (TaT), or the EU Radicalization Awareness Network (RAN).

References

Al-Rawi, A. (2016). Video Games, Terrorism, and ISIS's Jihad 3.0. *Terrorism and Political Violence*, 30(4), 740–760. 10.1080/09546553.2016.1207633.

Amarasingam, A., Argentino, M.-A., & Macklin, G. (2022). The Buffalo Attack: The Cumulative Momentum of Far-Right Terror. *CTC Sentinel*, *15*(7).

Anti-Defamation League (ADL) (2020). This is Not a Game: How Steam Harbors Extremists. https://www.adl.org/resources/report/not-game-how-steam-harbors-extremists.

Anti-Defamation League (ADL) (2022). Hate Is No Game: Hate and Harassment in Online Games 2022. https://www.adl.org/resources/report/hate-no-game-hate-and-harassment-online-games-2022.

Anti-Defamation League (ADL) (2023). Caught in a Vicious Cycle: Obstacles and Opportunities for Trust and Safety Teams in the Games Industry | ADL. www.adl.org. https://www.adl.org/resources/report/caught-vicious-cycle-obstacles-and-opportunities-trust-and-safety-teams-games.

APA Task Force on Violent Media (2015). Technical Report on the Review of Violent Video Game Literature. https://www.apa.org/pi/families/review-video-games.pdf.

Atran, S. (2010). *Talking to the Enemy*. HarperCollins.

Atran, S. & Stern, J. (2005). Small Groups Find Fatal Purpose through the Web. *Nature*, *437*(7059), 620– 620. 10.1038/437620a

Baele, S. J., Brace, L., & Coan, T. G. (2020). Uncovering the Far-Right Online Ecosystem: An Analytical Framework and Research Agenda. *Studies in Conflict & Terrorism*, 1–21. 10.1080/1057610x.2020.1862895.

Bak, M., Kristoffer, N., Tarp, D., Christina, S., & Liang, C. (2019). *Defining the Concept of "Violent Extremism": Delineating the attributes and phenomenon of violent extremism*. Geneva Centre for Security Policy. https://dam.gcsp.ch/files/2y10xuCSaBlvYTDbinjPokvyDO2XLpn5jG4va93JVUzppqj08EDHwnC.

Bateson, P. & Martin, P. (2013). *Play, playfulness, creativity, and innovation*. Cambridge University Press.

Borum, R. (2011). Radicalization into Violent Extremism I: A Review of Social Science Theories. *Journal of Strategic Security*, *4*(4), 7–36. 10.5038/1944-0472.4.4.1.

Business Research Company (2023). Online Microtransaction Global Market Report 2023 –Product Image New Online Microtransaction Global Market Report 2023. https://www.researchandmarkets.com/reports/5735105/online-microtransaction-global-market-report.

Chalmers, D. (2022). *Reality+: Virtual worlds and the problems of philosophy*. W.W. Norton.

Cohen, K. (2012). Who Will Be a Lone Wolf Terrorist? Mechanisms of Self-Radicalisation and the Possibility of Detecting Lone Offender Threats on the Internet. https://www.foi.se/rest-api/report/FOI-R--3531--SE.

Conneller, P. (2019, November 6). CS:GO Money Laundering Shut Down by Game Publisher Valve Corp. *Casino.org*. https://www.casino.org/news/csgo-money-laundering-shut-down-by-game-publisher-valve-corp.

Ćwil, M. & Howe, W.T. (2020). Cross-Cultural Analysis of Gamer Identity: A Comparison of the United States and Poland. *Simulation & Gaming*, *51*(6), 785–801. 10.1177/1046878120945735.

D'Anastasio, C. (2021, June 10). How "Roblox" Became a Playground for Virtual Fascists. *Wired*. https://www.wired.com/story/roblox-online-games-irl-fascism-roman-empire/.

Dauber, C.E., Robinson, M.D., Baslious, J.J., & Blair, A.G. (2019). Call of Duty: Jihad – How the Video Game Motif Has Migrated Downstream from Islamic State Propaganda Videos. *Perspectives on Terrorism, 13*(3), 17–31. https://www.jstor.org/stable/26681906.

Davey, J. (2021). *Gamers Who Hate: An introduction to ISD's gaming and extremism series.* Institute for Strategic Dialogue (ISD). https://www.isdglobal.org/isd-publications/gamers-who-hate-an-introduction-to-isds-gaming-and-extremism-series/.

Davey, J., Comerford, M., Guhl, J., Baldet, W., & Colliver, C. (2021). *A Taxonomy for the Classification of Post-Organisational Violent Extremist & Terrorist Content.* Institute for Strategic Dialogue (ISD). https://www.isdglobal.org/isd-publications/a-taxonomy-for-the-classification-of-post-organisational-violent-terrorist-content/.

Delcker, J. (2022, November 16). Twitter's Sacking of Content Moderators Raises Concerns – DW – 11/16/2022. https://www.dw.com/en/twitters-sacking-of-content-moderators-will-backfire-experts-warn/a-63778330.

Deterding, S., Dixon, D., Khaled, R., & Nacke, L. (2011). From Game Design Elements to Gamefulness. *Proceedings of the 15th International Academic MindTrek Conference on Envisioning Future Media Environments – MindTrek, 11*, 9–15.

Discord (2021). How Trust & Safety Addresses Violent Extremism on Discord. *Discord.com.* https://discord.com/blog/how-trust-safety-addresses-violent-extremism-on-discord.

DLive (2023). *DLive Protocol: Installation Guide.* https://docs.dlive.com/docs.

Entertainment Software Association (ESA) (2022). Essential Facts About the Video Game Industry 2022. https://www.theesa.com/wp-content/uploads/2022/06/2022-Essential-Facts-About-the-Video-Game-Industry.pdf.

Fielitz, M. & Ahmed, R. (2021). *It's Not Funny Anymore: Far-right extremists' use of humour.* Radicalisation Awareness Network (RAN). https://home-affairs.ec.europa.eu/networks/radicalisation-awareness-network-ran/publications/far-right-extremists-use-humour-2021_en.

Garcia, I. (2022). The "Call of Duty" Effect: the Role of Videogames in Extremist Radicalisation. [MSc thesis].

Global Internet Forum to Counter Terrorism (GIFCT) (July 2021). *Broadening the GIFCT Hash-Sharing Database Taxonomy: An assessment and recommended next steps.* GIFCT. https://gifct.org/wp-content/uploads/2021/07/GIFCT-TaxonomyReport-2021.pdf.

Gómez, Á., Brooks, M.L., Buhrmester, M.D., Vázquez, A., Jetten, J., & Swann, W.B. (2011). On the Nature of Identity Fusion: Insights Into the Construct and a New Measure. *Journal of Personality and Social Psychology, 100*(5), 918–933.

Gómez, Á., Chinchilla, J., Vázquez, A., López-Rodríguez, L., Paredes, B., & Martínez, M. (2020). Recent Advances, Misconceptions, Untested Assumptions, and Future Research Agenda for Identity Fusion Theory. *Social and Personality Psychology Compass, 14*(6). 10.1111/spc3.12531.

Gómez, Á., Vázquez, A., López-Rodríguez, L., Talaifar, S., Martínez, M., Buhrmester, M.D., & Swann, W.B. (2019). Why People Abandon Groups: Degrading Relational vs Collective Ties Uniquely Impacts Identity Fusion and Identification. *Journal of Experimental Social Psychology, 85*, 103853.

Hafez, M. & Mullins, C. (2015). The Radicalization Puzzle: A Theoretical Synthesis of Empirical Approaches to Homegrown Extremism. *Studies in Conflict & Terrorism*, 38(11), 958–975.

Howe, W.T., Livingston, D.J., & Lee, S.K. (2019). Concerning Gamer Identity: An Examination of Individual Factors Associated with Accepting the Label of Gamer. *First Monday*, 24(3). 10.5210/fm.v24i3.9443.

Hub, The (2022, January 10). *National Security Expert Jessica Davis on Terrorist Financing in the 21st Century*. The Hub. https://thehub.ca/2022-01-10/terrorist-financing-in-the-21st-century/.

Hunicke, R., Leblanc, M., & Zubek, R. (2004). MDA: A Formal Approach to Game Design and Game Research. https://users.cs.northwestern.edu/~hunicke/MDA.pdf.

Iqbal, M. (2023, January 9). *Fortnite Usage and Revenue Statistics (2023)*. Business of Apps. https://www.businessofapps.com/data/fortnite-statistics/.

Kaye, L.K., Kowert, R., & Quinn, S. (2017). The Role of Social Identity and Online Social Capital on Psychosocial Outcomes in MMO Players. *Computers in Human Behavior*, 74, 215–223. 10.1016/j.chb.2017.04.030.

Keierleber, M. (2021). *How White Supremacists Recruit Teen Culture Warriors in Gaming Communities*. Fast Company. https://www.fastcompany.com/90599113/white-supremacists-gaming-sites-dlive.

Kelly, S. (2021). Money Laundering Through Virtual Worlds of Video Games: Recommendations for a New Approach to AML Regulation. *Syracruse Law Review*, 71(1487). https://lawreview.syr.edu/wp-content/uploads/2022/01/1487-1512-Kelly.pdf.

Khalil, J., Horgan, J., & Zeuthen, M. (2019). The Attitudes-Behaviors Corrective (ABC) Model of Violent Extremism. *Terrorism and Political Violence*, 1–26.

Kingdon, A. (2023). *God of Race War: The utilisation of Viking-themed video games in far-right propaganda*. Global Network on Extremism and Technology (GNET). https://gnet-research.org/2023/02/06/god-of-race-war-the-utilisation-of-viking-themed-video-games-in-far-right-propaganda/.

Koehler, D. (2019). The Halle, Germany, Synagogue Attack and the Evolution of the Far-Right Terror Threat. *CTC Sentinel*, 12(11).

Koehler, D., Fiebig, V., & Jugl, I. (2022). From Gaming to Hating: Extreme-Right Ideological Indoctrination and Mobilization for Violence of Children on Online Gaming Platforms. *Political Psychology*.

Kowert, R., Botelho, A., & Newhouse, A. (2022). *Breaking the Building Blocks of Hate*. Anti-Defamation League (ADL). https://www.adl.org/sites/default/files/pdfs/2022-07/ADL_CTS_Minecraft%20Content%20Moderation%20Report_072622_v2.pdf.

Kowert, R., Domahidi E., & Quandt, T. (2014). The Relationship Between Online Video Game Involvement and Gaming-Related Friendships Among Emotionally Sensitive Individuals. *Cyberpsychology, Behavior, and Social Networking*: 447–453.

Kowert, R., Martel, A., & Swann, W.B. (2022). Not Just a Game: Identity Fusion and Extremism in Gaming Cultures. *Frontiers in Communication*, 7.

Kruglanski, A.W., Bélanger J.J., & Gunaratna, R. (2019). *The Three Pillars of Radicalization: Needs, narratives, and networks*. Oxford University Press.

Lakhani, S. (2022). *Video Gaming and (Violent) Extremism: An exploration of the current landscape, trends, and threats.* Radicalisation Awareness Network (RAN). https://home-affairs.ec.europa.eu/system/files/2022-02/EUIF%20Technical%20Meeting%20on%20Video%20Gaming%20October%202021%20RAN%20Policy%20Support%20paper_en.pdf.

Lakhani, S., White, J., & Wallner, C. (2022). *The Gamification of (Violent) Extremism: An exploration of emerging trends, future threat scenarios, and potential P/CVE solutions.* Radicalisation Awareness Network (RAN). https://home-affairs.ec.europa.eu/system/files/2022-09/RAN%20Policy%20Support-%20gamification%20of%20violent%20 extremism_en.pdf.

Lakhani, S. & Wiedlitzka, S. (2022). "Press F to Pay Respects": An Empirical Exploration of the Mechanics of Gamification in Relation to the Christchurch Attack. *Terrorism and Political Violence*, 1–18. 10.1080/09546553.2022.2064746.

Lamphere-Englund, G. & Bunmathong, L. (2021). *State of Play: Reviewing the literature on gaming & extremism.* Extremism and Gaming Research Network (EGRN). https://lovefrankie.link/extremismandgamingreview.

Lamphere-Englund, G. & White, J. (2022). *The Buffalo Attack and the Gamification of Violence.* www.rusi.org; Royal United Services Institute (RUSI). https://rusi.org/explore-our-research/publications/commentary/buffalo-attack-and-gamification-violence.

Lamphere-Englund, G. & White, J. (2023). *The Online Gaming Ecosystem: Assessing digital socialisation, extremism risks and harms mitigation efforts.* Extremism and Gaming Research Network (EGRN) and the Global Network on Extremism and Technology (GNET). https://gnet-research.org/wp-content/uploads/2023/05/GNET-37-Extremism-and-Gaming_web.pdf.

Levin, J.-C. (2023, February 17). *Welcome to the Oldest Part of the Metaverse.* MIT Technology Review. https://www.technologyreview.com/2023/02/17/1068027/ultima-online-oldest-metaverse/.

Liang, C. & Cross, M. (2020). *White Crusade: How to prevent right-wing extremists from exploiting the internet.* https://dam.gcsp.ch/files/doc/white-crusade-how-to-prevent-right-wing-extremists-from-exploiting-the-internet.

Macklin, G. (2022). Praise the Saints: The Cumulative Momentum of Transnational Extreme-Right Terrorism. In J. Dafinger & M. Florin (Eds.), *A Transnational History of Right-Wing Terrorism: Political violence and the far right in eastern and western Europe since 1900.* Routledge.

Mahmoud, F. (2022). *Playing with Religion: The gamification of jihad.* Danish Institute of International Studies (DIIS). https://pure.diis.dk/ws/files/9007170/The_gamification_of_jihad_DIIS_Report_2022_06.pdf.

Marczewski, A. (2015). User Types. In *Even Ninja Monkeys Like to Play: Gamification, Game Thinking and Motivational Design* (1st ed., pp. 65–80). CreateSpace Independent Publishing Platform.

McCauley, C. & Moskalenko, S. (2008). Mechanisms of Political Radicalization: Pathways Toward Terrorism. *Terrorism and Political Violence*, 20(3), 415–433.

McCauley, C. & Moskalenko, S. (2017). Understanding Political Radicalization: The Two Pyramids Model. *American Psychologist*, 72(3), 205–216. 10.1037/amp0000062.

Mistry, K. (2018). P(l)aying to Win: Loot Boxes, Microtransaction Monetization, and a Proposal for Self-Regulation in the Video Game Industry. *Rutgers Law Review*, *71*(537). https://www.rutgerslawreview.com/wp-content/uploads/2019/08/08_Mistry.pdf.

Molyneux, L., Vasudevan, K., & Gil de Zúñiga, H. (2015). Gaming Social Capital: Exploring Civic Value in Multiplayer Video Games. *Journal of Computer-Mediated Communication*, *20*(4), 381–399. 10.1111/jcc4.12123.

Neumann, P.R. (2013). The Trouble with Radicalization. *International Affairs*, *89*(4), 873–893.

Newzoo (2022a). *The Games Market in 2022: The Year in Numbers*. Newzoo. https://newzoo.com/resources/blog/the-games-market-in-2022-the-year-in-numbers.

Newzoo (2022b, July 26). *Newzoo Global Games Market Report 2022*. Newzoo. https://newzoo.com/resources/trend-reports/newzoo-global-games-market-report-2022-free-version?utm_campaign=GGMR2022&utm_source=press.

Østby, G., Rustad, S.A., Haer, R., & Arasmith, A. (2022). Children at Risk of Being Recruited for Armed Conflict, 1990–2020. *Children & Society*. 10.1111/chso.12609.

Pisoiu, D. (2022). *Can Serious Games Make a Difference in P/CVE?* GNET. https://gnet-research.org/2022/09/05/can-serious-games-make-a-difference-in-p-cve/.

Radicalisation Awareness Network (RAN). (2020). *Extremists' Use of Video Gaming - and Narratives*. Radicalisation Awareness Network (RAN). https://home-affairs.ec.europa.eu/system/files/2020-11/ran_cn_conclusion_paper_videogames_15-17092020_en.pdf.

Radicalisation Awareness Network (RAN). (2021). Digital Grooming Tactics on Video Gaming & Video Gaming Adjacent Platforms: Threats and Opportunities. https://home-affairs.ec.europa.eu/system/files/2021-05/ran_c-n_conclusion_paper_grooming_through_gaming_15-16032021_en.pdf.

Reddit r/GrandTheftAuto. (2016). *ISIS Use GTA V and My Mod for Propaganda*. Reddit. https://www.reddit.com/r/GrandTheftAutoV_PC/comments/4rk35o/comment/d527bix/?utm_source=reddit&utm_medium=web2x&context=3.

Robinson, N. & Whittaker, J. (2021). Playing for Hate? Extremism, Terrorism, and Videogames. *Studies in Conflict & Terrorism*, 1–36. 10.1080/1057610x.2020.1866740.

Roblox (2023a). *Developer Economics | Roblox Creator Documentation*. Create.roblox.com. https://create.roblox.com/docs/production/monetization/economics.

Roblox (2023b). Roblox Reports Fourth Quarter and Full Year 2022 Financial Results. https://ir.roblox.com/news/news-details/2023/Roblox-Reports-Fourth-Quarter-and-Full-Year-2022-Financial-Results/default.aspx.

Sageman, M. (2004). *Understanding Terror Networks*. University of Pennsylvania Press.

Schlegel, L. (2020). Jumanji Extremism? How Games and Gamification Could Facilitate Radicalization Processes. *Journal for Deradicalization*, *23*, 1–44. https://journals.sfu.ca/jd/index.php/jd/article/view/359/223.

Schlegel, L. (2021a). Connecting, Competing, and Trolling: "User Types" in Digital Gamified Radicalization Processes. *Perspectives on Terrorism, 15*(4). https://www.universiteitleiden.nl/binaries/content/assets/customsites/perspectives-on-terrorism/2021/issue-4/schlegel.pdf.

Schlegel, L. (2021b). *Extremists' Use of Gaming (-Adjacent) Platforms: Insights regarding primary and secondary prevention measures.* Radicalization Awareness Network (RAN). https://home-affairs.ec.europa.eu/system/files/2021-08/ran_extremists_use_gaming_platforms_082021_en.pdf.

Schlegel, L. (2021c). *The Gamification of Violent Extremism & Lessons for P/CVE.* Radicalisation Awareness Network (RAN). https://home-affairs.ec.europa.eu/system/files/2021-03/ran_ad-hoc_pap_gamification_20210215_en.pdf.

Schlegel, L. (2022). *Playing Against Radicalization: Why extremists are gaming and how P/CVE can leverage the positive effects of video games to prevent radicalization.* GameD. https://www.scenor.at/_files/ugd/ff9c7a_9f5f3687937b4f3384e2b0a7eac8c33f.pdf.

Schlegel, L. & Amarasingam, A. (2022). *Examining the Intersection Between Gaming and Violent Extremism.* United Nations Office of Counter-Terrorism (UNOCT). https://www.un.org/counterterrorism/sites/www.un.org.counterterrorism/files/221005_research_launch_on_gaming_ve.pdf.

Seng, M. (2023, February 19). *"Roblox" und Rechtsextremismus: Das Kinderspiel mit Nazicontent.* www.zeit.de; Zeit Online. https://www.zeit.de/digital/games/2023-02/roblox-rechtsextremismus-gaming-kinder-inhalte/seite-2.

Singapore Ministry of Home Affairs (MHA) (2023, February 21). *Issuance of Orders Under the Internal Security Act Against Two Self-Radicalised Singaporean Youths.* Ministry of Home Affairs. https://www.mha.gov.sg/mediaroom/press-releases/issuance-of-orders-under-the-internal-security-act-against-two-self-radicalised-singaporean-youths/.

Southern Poverty Law Center (SPLC) (2021). *Meet DLive: The livestreaming platform used by Trump's Capitol insurrectionists.* https://www.splcenter.org/hatewatch/2021/01/07/meet-dlive-livestreaming-platform-used-trumps-capitol-insurrectionists.

Tech Against Terrorism (TaT) (2022). *State of Play: Trends in terrorist and violent extremist use of the internet.* https://www.techagainstterrorism.org/wp-content/uploads/2023/01/FINAL-State-of-Play-2022-TAT.pdf.

Thorleifsson, C. (2021). From Cyberfascism to Terrorism: On 4Chan/Pol/Culture and the Transnational Production of Memetic Violence. *Nations and Nationalism, 28*(1). 10.1111/nana.12780.

Thorleifsson, C. & Düker, J. (2021). *Lone Actors in Digital Environments.* Radicalisation Awareness Network (RAN). https://home-affairs.ec.europa.eu/system/files/2021-10/ran_paper_lone_actors_in_digital_environments_en.pdf.

Trahan, L. (2023). *Summary of Responses from Gaming Companies.* U.S. House of Representatives. https://trahan.house.gov/uploadedfiles/summary_responses_to_letter_game_companies_online_harassment_extremism.pdf.

Trip, S., Bora, C.H., Marian, M., Halmajan, A., & Drugas, M.I. (2019). Psychological Mechanisms Involved in Radicalization and Extremism. A Rational Emotive Behavioral Conceptualization. *Frontiers in Psychology, 10*(437). 10.3389/ fpsyg.2019.00437.

Twitch Tracker (2023). Twitch Top Streamers. https://twitchtracker.com/channels/ranking.

United Nations High Commissioner for Human Rights (2016). Report on Best Practices and Lessons Learned on How Protecting and Promoting Human Rights Contribute to Preventing and Countering Violent Extremism: Report of the United Nations High Commissioner for Human Rights. https://digitallibrary.un.org/record/845276?ln=en.

White, J. & Lamphere-Englund, G. (2023). A View from the CT Foxhole: Jessica White and Galen Lamphere-Englund, Co-Conveners, Extremism and Gaming Research Network. *CTC Sentinel, 16*(3). https://ctc.westpoint.edu/a-view-from-the-ct-foxhole-jessica-white-and-galen-lamphere-englund-co-conveners-extremism-and-gaming-research-network/.

3

EXTREMIST GAMES AND MODIFICATIONS

The "Metapolitics" of Anti-Democratic Forces

Mick Prinz

Videogames are a supremely political medium as players regularly find themselves in the middle of profoundly political scenarios. For instance, the action shooter *Far Cry 6* (Ubisoft) puts the protagonist inside a totalitarian regime on a fictional Caribbean island inspired by Cuba, while *Red Dead Redemption 2* (Rockstar Games) has the player take part in the women's rights movement during the era of the "Wild West". But the politics of a game tends to enter the frame even before the story starts. Decisions about whether to have a male or female protagonist, the developers' inclusion (or not) of non-binary gender models, and the possible involvement of groups affected by discrimination when designing the game can all roughly indicate a videogame studio's stance towards the world. When it comes to gaming, political values and narratives are a matter of negotiation. A diverse array of worldviews is displayed across the spectrum of popular videogames. Extreme right-wing actors in particular have realized that videogames and the platforms they provide constitute a fertile ground for approaching or hectoring certain groups of people, connecting like-minded individuals, and spreading hateful and oppressive ideologies.

This chapter examines how the far-right is working hard to weaponize and exploit gaming culture for its own means. It is important to make clear from the outset that the gaming world does not have a "neo-Nazi problem." However, gaming has become a central pillar of our modern society, which fundamentally struggles with racist, misogynist and anti-Semitic attitudes – and videogame circles and gaming communities are far from immune to this. Far-right stances presented in gaming chats and across gaming (-adjacent) platforms often remain unchallenged Some gaming platforms,

DOI: 10.4324/9781003388371-4

such as *Steam* (https://steamcommunity.com), even host games developed within the far-right scene and user-created variations on existing games – known as modifications or "mods" – relaying far-right content and narratives. In other words, far-right gamers often find it all too easy to spread their dehumanizing views in videogame-related contexts.

Most of the research on the use of bespoke videogames and mods by extremist actors has focused on how far-right extremist actors in particular are seeking to exploit gaming for their ends. However, this does not mean that gaming is irrelevant in the context of other types of extremism. Therefore, this chapter will begin with a brief review of the current state of knowledge on the use of videogames and mods by jihadists before taking a deep dive into the production of bespoke games and mods by right-wing extremist actors. Readers should note that the chapter is based largely on the author's own research and focuses on German far-right actors specifically.

Jihadist Videogames and Mods

While substantially less popular as a research topic than the nexus between right-wing extremism and gaming, there is ample evidence of a "gaming jihad" across various geographical locations and groups (Lakomy, 2019). For more than two decades, several jihadist actors have sought to employ gaming in their propaganda efforts (Dauber *et al.*, 2019). Already in the early 2000s, numerous jihadist activities were connected to video gaming. For instance, the 9/11 attackers, who were part of Al Qaeda, allegedly trained for their attack with flight simulator games. Al Qaeda also produced modifications of commercial videogames and turned, for instance, the video game *Quest for Saddam* (Petrilla Entertainment) on its head by producing a mod called *Quest for Bush* and made adaptations that places the player in the shoes of a suicide bomber, who is trying to kill the president of the United States (Al-Rawi, 2018; Schlegel, 2020). The Lebanese Hezbollah did not modify existing games, but published its first bespoke videogame, the first-person shooter *Quds Kid*, in 2000 (Rose, 2018). Subsequently, Hezbollah has developed and published several sequences to *Quds Kids*, including *Special Forces I*, *Special Forces II*, and most recently *Holy Defense*. In an interview with Middle Eastern Eye, the game developer of *Holy Defense* and other individuals affiliated to Hezbollah explained that the main appeal of all of Hezbollah's games is that they are based on real events rather than fantasy and that Hezbollah believes it "must use technology to influence the minds of young people and teenagers" (Rose, 2018).

In spite of the early use of videogames by jihadist actors, the issue only gained prominence among researchers and policymakers with the rise of the so-called Islamic State (ISIS). ISIS published sophisticated and professionally produced propaganda, which utilized and made reference to popular entertainment products such as Hollywood movies, music videos, and videogames. For instance, the group employed original footage from the popular first-person shooter game *Call of Duty* (Activision) in its propaganda videos (Lakomy, 2019; see also Dauber *et al.*, 2019). The group also produced a bespoke videogame for children. The "educational" game *Huroof* prompts children to match letters of the alphabet with images of tanks or other military equipment, e.g. B for bomb, K for *kufr* [infidel] (Schlegel, 2020; Mahmoud, 2022). The app was designed to be a "fun" introduction to the group's propaganda, familiarize the youngest group members with ideological content, and normalize violence and weapons from a young age to prepare the children for their future in the "caliphate." Allegedly, ISIS supporters have also produced a mod of the popular video game *Grand Theft Auto* (Rockstar Games; Al-Rawi, 2018). The mod is called *Salil al-Sawarem* [The clanging of the swords], which is also the name of a popular religious chant used by ISIS. However, researchers were unable to locate the game itself – the only available information is a trailer for the mod. Hence, it is unclear whether the mod was actually produced or not (Al-Rawi, 2018; Mahmoud, 2022).

More information on the use of bespoke games and mods by jihadist actors can be found in Lakomy's (2019) work, which provides a comprehensive overview of the use of videogames by various jihadist groups in different locations, and in Mahmoud's (2022) recent report on the "gamification of religion." This chapter now turns to the use of videogames and mods by right-wing extremists and far-right actors.

Far-Right Games – Propaganda with a Limited Reach

Right-wing actors have been exerting their influence via computer games for more than three decades. One of the first examples of bespoke far-right games was programmed in the 1980s. Its name? *Concentration Camp Manager.* Instead of finding oneself in an island paradise or a medieval village, the player's task was to systematically murder the alleged enemies of the far right. The game glorified the Shoah[1] by prompting players to systematically murder Jews as efficiently as possible. Depending on the version, the game also included other racist and ableist depictions. While this propaganda game existed in various versions for the Commodore Amiga,[2] its reach was largely limited to far-right circles. This was due not only to its dehumanizing setting, but to the off-putting design and because it was placed on the "Index" in Germany – a list of entertainment media that may not be advertised, because they are deemed "dangerous to young people" by the German authorities. In addition to banning the distribution, it is also no longer permitted to promote the game in Germany (Bundesanzeiger, 2014). Little is known about the development team but it is certain that the game failed to reach a broader audience.

Many other far-right propaganda games use a pseudo-humorous pretext to spread their dehumanizing ideologies. One example is an amateurishly programmed first-person shooter that has popped up on the gaming platform *Steam*. If the player enters a far-right dog whistle (i.e. coded language typically only understood by a particular group of people "in the know") as a cheat code, they are able to unlock the perpetrator of the Christchurch shootings as a game protagonist. This serves to glorify the attack that took place on March 15, 2019 in Christchurch, New Zealand, during which a right-wing terrorist killed 51 people. Another game combines pornographic visual novel elements with aspects of a top-down shooter.[3] In this game, players shoot their way through various battlegrounds from the Second World War while playing as "Adolf Hitler." This is augmented by dialogue and scenes inspired by *hentai* porn.[4] The game is not available in all national *Steam* stores, although this is due to the sexual content rather than the elements glorifying National Socialism. Another game serves as a good example of how titles containing far-right content are tolerated on the platform. This racist videogame falls within the subgenre of rogue-like games and assigns players the task of killing as many police officers as possible by taking on the role of a black protagonist with glowing red demonic eyes. The action takes place in a US suburb, and entertains various xenophobic narratives, such as the criminalization of nonwhite people, while trivializing police violence. *Steam* is home to plenty of other problematic content, including some generated by far-right profiles, groups and users – very little of which is ever blocked by the platform. Later, this chapter examines various toxic mods developed by the far right, which are free to download on *Steam*.

Right-wing populists and some far-right parties are also seeking to harness the potential of videogames to spread their content. One example is a browser game that caused a furor in Austria in 2010. During an election, the Freedom Party of Austria (FPÖ) published a point-and-click game on its homepage that challenged players to put a halt to noisy muezzin calls, minarets, and mosques as they rise from the bottom of the screen. Titled *Moschee baba*, the short propaganda game is reminiscent of an Islamophobic version of the videogame classic *Moorhuhn* (known as "Crazy Chicken" in English; Ravensburger Interactive Media; Augsburger Allgemeine, 2010). Political parties using video games for election purposes is not a new phenomenon: Joe Biden's election campaign used video games such as *Among Us* (Inner Sloth) and *Animal Crossing* (Eguchi & Nogami, 2001) to engage gamers with political content. The symbiosis of video games and politics is a predictable development, but it becomes problematic when titles are used as a vehicle to deliver fake news and toxic narratives. The FPÖ game, for example, ends with right-wing populist election phrases that hint at the alleged "Islamization" of Austria and create a sense of urgency to act.

The New Right's Dystopian Jump'n' Run Title

The number of far-right videogame productions remains small for now and most bespoke games are characterized by their clumsy presentation and sloppy programming. Craving attention and attempting to provoke political enemies are a key reason why these racist and anti-Semitic pieces of software are developed in the first place. Appealing to individuals who are not yet part of far-right circles and propagating right-wing views are the main goals of these extremist developers, although success remains limited. Even though far-right developers try to reach and appeal to new gamers, games often reach mostly those who already support far-right ideologies and achieving to reach gamers at large beyond far-right circles remains a goal that is reached only sporadically.

Kvlt Games, a right-wing development studio, has also explicitly expressed the desire to get young people interested in the ideas of the New Right via videogames.[5] Financed by the German far-right think tank Ein Prozent [One Percent], the studio – which is largely confined to the efforts of a single person – designed the game *Heimatdefender: Rebellion* [Defender of the Homeland]. Released in 2020, the 2D jump'n' run title gives players control of key figures of the New Right, such as Martin Sellner (head of the Identitarian Movement in Europe)[6] or Götz Kubitschek (co-founder of the right-wing Institute for State Policy (Institut für Staatspolitik; IfS)), as they fight against the alleged enemies of the far-right across a fictitious, dystopian Europe (Huberts, 2021). As part of a patriotic resistance movement in the year 2084, the players make their way through various European capitals, battling against "spineless" populations that are kitted out in rainbow flags and leftist symbols. The game incorporates many far-right references and narratives, including books by the European right-wing publisher Antaios that are intended to further encourage players to engage with far-right material. This is in addition to in-game dialogue with leading radical right-wing figures who explicitly call on the player to take an active role against the allegedly leftist mainstream. The level bosses and final boss in the game represent actual "enemies" of the far-right and the player has to defeat politicians such as the former German chancellor Angela Merkel, employees of democratic NGOs such as Anetta Kahane (founder of the German Amadeu Antonio Foundation), George Soros (investor and regular punchbag for many anti-Semitic groups), and individuals such as the German left-wing satirist Jan Böhmermann.

In other words, *Heimatdefender* is the summation of many different racist, anti-Semitic and anti-feminist narratives in a single videogame. However, the developers' goal – to drum up enthusiasm for an alternative right-wing worldview – did not work. After protests from parts of the gaming community, *Steam* removed the game from its store and the game has been indexed in Germany, meaning it may no longer be advertised. As of spring 2023, the studio is working on a follow-up title, *The Great Rebellion*, a reference to the well-established conspiracy narrative known as the Great Reset.[7] Numerous far-right perpetrators have made reference to this narrative in their manifestos in the past.

Patriotic Gaming Jams

Kvlt Games, the studio behind this and upcoming propaganda games, is closely involved in the far-right Identitarian Movement and has received occasional financial support from a politician belonging to the far-right party Alternative for Germany (AfD; Franz & Prinz, 2021). This suggests that even right-wing politicians believe video games can serve as a catalyst for shaping political views. Alongside *Heimatdefender*, Kvlt Games has managed to keep its foot in the gaming door with other projects. For example, it has organized a series of "homeland jams" – co-working sessions attended by several games developers who pool their resources to develop a basic videogame concept and pitch initial demos that could pave the way for follow-up projects to *Heimatdefender*. Unsurprisingly Kvlt Games' video-game jams have prompted a slew of racist, misogynist, and anti-Semitic gaming content. One such jam led to a game prototype prompting the player to assume the role of a supermarket clerk who has to shoot invading looters, all of whom bear the face of George Floyd. In another prototype, the player drives a bulldozer to destroy the US Federal Reserve. The jam also resulted in a pitch outlining a game in which "space Nazis" from the moon liberate the earth from "woke" forces. By and large, these pseudo-humorous game concepts remain both in the initial prototype stage and the far-right bubble in which they are conceived. Here, too, the main goal is to create digital spaces in which entertainment software turns far-right ideologies into an interactive experience. As already stated, the production of full bespoke games remains a niche field for the far right. It is more often the case that developers make modifications to existing games in order to push their beliefs on players. Before taking a closer look at far-right mods, it is important to first consider three central reasons as to why the far right seeks to weaponize the gaming world at all.

Why Is the Far Right Turning to Gaming? Three Key Reasons

Right-wing populist and far-right actors have long used videogames and their platforms as tools to spread propaganda. These misanthropic parties and groups focus primarily on gaming (-adjacent) platforms – and the discussions taking place there – where moderation is the exception rather than the norm. These groups set up, for instance, *Discord* (a popular third-party chat application; https://discord.com) servers and generate *Steam* groups where racist, misogynist, and anti-Semitic narratives, and popular conspiracy ideologies can be freely exchanged. Sometimes, these discussions piggyback on existing debates in the gaming world, such as attempting to normalize the anti-transgender narratives surrounding the game *Hogwarts Legacy* (Avalanche Software) or to reproduce xenophobic stereotypes on *Steam* about the Black Lives Matter movement. Political discourses in digital gaming spaces are thus often instrumentalized by right-wing extremists. By contrast, the production of bespoke games to spread far-right narratives is a rare practice. However, even if videogames produced within far-right circles do not yet appear to have much traction in the wider world and remain limited in their reach, they are nevertheless indicative of the various strategies employed as part of the alleged "culture war by the right."

Extremist actors use "metapolitics"[8] to spread their narratives in digital gaming spaces and gradually normalize them. Part of this "metapolitics" strategy involves pushing propaganda games into mainstream society to generate attention (Strick, 2021). These actors believe that by constantly repeating the titles and narratives of the games, the ideologies they serve will be promoted – whether deliberately or unwittingly. Some of these so-called propaganda games are discussed in more detail below to demonstrate the strategies and narratives at play. However, on the whole, it is important to paraphrase rather than repeat such names, especially when discussing far-right games in an educational context. Ultimately, one of the goals of the far right is to use the pop-cultural appeal of video games to sell their ideology. It is therefore advisable not to reproduce the names of these games so as not to give them even more attention outside right-wing circles. Nevertheless, as stated earlier, while developers of far-right videogames may strive to reach new audiences and use the games to generate attention in society at large, they have had little success so far (see also Robinson & Whittaker, 2021).

Gaming as a Networking Tool

By the time social media took off as part of Web 2.0, it was clear that extremists were exploring strategic ways to use the internet for their own purposes. For years, Twitter threads and Facebook groups were flooded with racist and anti-refugee discourses. While the degree of visibility such discourses receive depends on the (actions of the) platform in question, the problem continues to exist today. If the far right continues to be given free access to digital channels, they will use them to spread their propaganda. Gaming is no exception in this regard, exemplified by right-wing content on gaming (-adjacent) platforms such as *Twitch* (https://www.twitch.tv), *Steam*, and *Discord*. These platforms are used by virtually every gamer to play videogames together, talk to one another, and upload their own content. And although far-right users on these channels constitute a loud minority and the vast majority of players expressing no misanthropic views whatsoever, this vocal minority nevertheless poses a risk. Even as loud minorities, far-right actors seek to launch hate campaigns, bombard people with hostility, and employ strategies such as silencing are used to censor democratic actors and marginalized groups to shape and even dominate digital discourses. Extremists feel at home on these platforms for two key reasons: first, moderation by the platform operators is often light, although this depends on the platform in question. Second, "normal" players put up little resistance to far-right views. Many gamers continue to choose to look the other way when these actors express extremist views and ignore hateful content (see also Schlegel & Amarasingam, 2022). All too often, players seemingly believe that "it's just a game – it doesn't matter."

As a consequence of this lack of resistance, far-right agitators use gaming (-adjacent) platforms to meet and communicate with one another. This is especially the case on *Steam*. Numerous far-right groups have founded groups on the platform, including Wehrmacht fan groups and New Right groups – both of which have long been banned from other social media channels. *Steam* also hosts fans of the Atomwaffen Division[9] as well as various right-wing brotherhoods and "Germanic gaming clans." The shooting in the Olympia shopping mall in Munich in the summer of 2016 exemplifies the potential detrimental effects of such groups. During the shooting, a right-wing terrorist driven by a racist ideology killed nine people. In the period leading up to the killings, he contacted other far-right actors in an anti-refugee *Steam* group. One user who was in touch with the Munich perpetrator went on to kill two people in New Mexico, USA, just 18 months later (Ayyadi, 2018). Despite the fact that this group is now blocked, there are many other groups in which right-wing views are freely shared. Platforms such as *Discord*, *Twitch* and *YouTube Gaming* (https://www.youtube.com/GAMING) also host far-right agitators whose aim is to bring extremists together. For example, a video published by a right-wing Twitch streamer shows him in discussion with the chairman of the far-right National Democratic Party of Germany (NPD) about how to unite the right in Germany after it had splintered into various factions. Far-right actors are therefore using digital gaming spaces – both within and outside their own groups – to link up and mobilize.

This networking is also facilitated through the development of modifications. In the comments sections related to these modifications, far-right supporters exchange information, arrange to play together or link to other groups. For example, it is not uncommon for *Steam* users to log inordinate amounts of time on extremist-created bespoke games (e.g., *Hatred*) as a signal of their ideology to identify themselves to other potential radicalized users within the broader *Steam* community. Groups adhering to conspiracy theories are also building up in gaming-related digital spaces. For example, there are *Grand Theft Auto*-related online servers that host and connect QAnon supporters.[10] In addition, right-wing extremist video games often link to further networking opportunities of anti-democratic groups – for instance, by referencing and linking to propaganda output or writings from right-wing extremist groups.

Gaming as a Tool for Mobilization

Although it may be one of the often stated goals of the far right, these groups have thus far largely failed to entice outsiders into their extremist world by using videogames as a gateway. In many instances, however, gaming is a form of escapism and a potential opportunity to appeal to those "comrades" who may be less inclined to take direct action. This is the reason why gaming-related events are frequently held within far-right circles. In addition to the "homeland jams" discussed above, these circles put on patriotic gaming evenings and nationalist esports tournaments (see Thomas, 2021 on far-right gaming tournaments in the UK). While playing the strategy game *Starcraft II* (Blizzard Entertainment), for example, these gamers discuss "good" and "bad" foreigners. Because gaming is an extremely popular leisure time activity, it stands to reason that the far right will continue to use it to attract attention to their cause. For example, the leader of the Identitarian Movement in Europe, Martin Sellner, streamed a video in May 2022 in which he sought to explain the Russian invasion of Ukraine using video games and cutscenes to illustrate his arguments. Ultimately, all the video shows is that the far-right activist's knowledge of video game culture is lacking. Even so, this is a clear attempt to use the medium to sell a New Right narrative in a socially acceptable way. The aim of the videogame footage is to appeal to viewers who would usually not watch Sellner's videos or engage with far-right ideas. Mobilizing people for right-wing extremist groups through their own games and modifications, by the same token, is a rare occurrence Occasionally, people are approached via gaming chats or, for example, in *Roblox* (Roblox Corporation), but this is the exception. In contrast, it is more common to reach people via the entire cultural asset of games, i.e., via gaming (-adjacent) platforms, streams or tours of existing videogames.

Gaming as Part of Far-Right Metapolitics

The third key reason for the far-right's foray into the world of video games is "metapolitics." But what is meant by this term when the New Right uses it and how does it crop up in gaming communities? Metapolitics is a strategy devised by New Right groups to influence the language and mindset of the population in various areas of society. The aim is to gradually replace the current "mainstream" political discourse with ethnically charged and nationalist thinking by continually reproducing right-wing rhetoric on social media and across other media channels such as videogames and gaming-related platforms. Metapolitics involves propagating far-right ideology as widely as possible. When, for example, various gaming communities discussed a possible boycott of the video game *Hogwarts Legacy* – with the spotlight being shone primarily on Harry Potter creator J.K. Rowling's anti-transgender stance – the far right jumped on the discourse (Rafael & Prinz, 2023). The tense atmosphere surrounding the discussions about the game on *Twitch* and *Twitter* comment threads initiated by gaming influencers with a broad audience was harnessed as a way to push conspiracy ideologies and anti-transgender narratives onto a grand stage. This strategy was also used to corrupt other relevant debates, such as #metoo and #blacklivesmatter – in these cases, through racist or misogynist narratives.

Gaming platforms are also awash with extremist content – some more obvious than others – that, for example, encourages users to read the terrorist manifesto published by the Atomwaffen Division or broadcasts the myth (widely held in right-wing circles) of a "pure Wehrmacht." Another example of metapolitical action can be found on *Reddit* (https://www.reddit.com/), which has a subreddit (a forum on the platform) of 136,000 followers, where anti-feminist memes and comments are posted that refer to an allegedly "woke"/leftist gaming landscape. *Discord* and *Twitch*, two platforms popular among gamers, are also home to far-right accounts that seek to cloak their content in a socially acceptable guise, although they are increasingly being subject to pushback from the platforms' operators. *Discord* is used by gamers primarily for its voice chat function during play or to speak to one another in various chatrooms and on different servers when not playing. Since 2022 in particular, *Discord* has increasingly been deleting servers (group chats) bearing far-right names or symbols from its server lists (Allyn, 2021). Even so, many servers with less conspicuous names continue to exist.

Metapolitics can also be found in the games discussed above, whether by featuring the slogan of the Identitarian Movement, giving antagonists a rainbow flag, or including writings that set out New Right theories. However, racist, anti-Semitic and misogynist ideologies are spread through existing gaming ecosystems much more frequently than via the far-right's own productions. The next section discusses the nature of these mods and the strategy behind them.

Far-Right Mods Designed for the General Public

It is hardly surprising that far-right supporters also play videogames that are enjoyed by the public at large and that have no obvious, explicit ties to dehumanizing ideologies. For many of these popular games, developers provide various tools allowing users to create their own content and publish it in community areas on relevant platforms, i.e., to develop "mods." Extremist gamers, too, are inclined to make use of these options. The idea is to tailor popular games more closely to their own ideologies. Mods are designed to be accessible to a wider audience and mods with problematic content are available for many popular games in the *Steam Workshop*.[11] There are, for example, too many far-right mods to count for videogames that take place in the First or Second World Wars, with right-wing fans creating additional content for war strategy games such as *Hearts of Iron IV* (Paradox Development Studio) or *Company of Heroes* (Relic Entertainment), which allows players to assume the role of the Waffen SS as a supposedly legitimate actor. Elsewhere, a mod adds Adolf Hitler as a character who leads his own troops into battle (Kampf & Prinz, 2022). These mods can often be downloaded effortlessly and often for free. Far-right modifications are found on other sites, too, such as *Nexus Mod Manager*, giving gamers the chance to guide avatars in Wehrmacht uniforms through the world of *Fallout 3* (Bethesda Softworks) or swing the "axe of racism" in *Skyrim* (Bethesda Game Studios). The latter is a role-playing game based on battles between different races, meaning the topic of racism is an integral part of its world. The creator of the "axe of racism" mod further adds, on the page description for this modification: "Don't you wish *Skyrim* was a little more racist?" Alongside mods that glorify National Socialism, there are creations that hypersexualize female characters in role-playing games (more so than they already are) and even render them naked. In that sense, anti-feminism is another avenue through which right-wing mod developers infiltrate various games.

Then there are videogames that rely on their players' own creative input to exist. These, too, are stages for right-wing metapolitics. Sandbox videogames such as *Minecraft* (Mojang Studios) and *Roblox* in particular are hotbeds of far-right content. *Roblox* is a platform through which user-generated content can be created and uploaded (Prinz, 2023). The platform has been online since 2006 and has become increasingly popular in the years since. There are more than 200 million active users on *Roblox* each month, the majority of whom are between nine and 12 years of age and based in Canada and the USA. Sandbox platforms such as *Roblox*, which are based on co-creation by its community and allow such content to be uploaded to the system, are a playground for toxic and far-right actors. Present among the more than 24 million playable "experiences," as maps and mods on *Roblox* are called, are misogynist, racist, and radical right-wing creations. One of these recreates the mass shooting in Buffalo. In May 2022, a right-wing extremist killed ten people for racist reasons at a Tops Friendly Markets supermarket and livestreamed the act on *Twitch* for a few minutes. Plenty of content that venerates the right-wing terrorist and allows people to play through the shooting can be found on *Roblox*. The shooter himself, the Black Sun (a Nazi symbol), and the site of the attack are all displayed as realistically as possible on one of the platform's maps. Meanwhile, the computer-controlled NPCs are based on racist stereotypes. These "experiences" may be very much in the minority, but they are theoretically able to be found and played by all *Roblox*'s young player base. *Minecraft* is another platform containing maps that allow players to commit terrorist acts and maps that relativize or deny the Shoah. Although teams of moderators remove explicitly far-right content from the platform's library, the response tends to be a passive one and happens only when content is reported by players themselves. The active removal and explicit prohibition of such content in the platform guidelines would be desirable.

More Digital Civic Courage Is Needed in Gaming

The far-right gamers, games, and mods described in this chapter represent a minority and a niche phenomenon in the world of gaming. They should not be understood to be representative of the heterogeneous, multifaceted gaming culture and gaming communities. However, there are undeniably digital gaming spaces that are subject to little to no moderation and only timid pushback to far-right content is displayed by gamers, developers, and influencers. These spaces are used as staging grounds by far-right accounts. Many individuals continue to stay silent when racist or anti-Semitic comments are issued, when female players are exposed to hostility in comment threads, or when supposedly harmless mods with far-right content pop up in the *Steam Workshop*. More courage is required in all these cases. A study published by the Anti-Defamation League shows that 86% of all gamers have experienced hate speech in gaming. However, only 33% of gamers report that they speak up for themselves when attacked (ADL, 2022).

There is a simple solution: virtually every game and every major gaming platform has a reporting feature. Extremist content can also be reported via external hotlines.[12] However, responsibility should not be placed on the players alone. Platform operators and law enforcement authorities also need to take a stronger stand against far-right efforts to infiltrate gaming and to understand how these digital spaces are used. Gaming influencers and streamers can also make a contribution: they play videogames in front of thousands of other players, making it important for them to speak out against such content and serve as role models in one way or another. There is huge potential in having these people – with their exceptional reach – take an unequivocal stance against various forms of misanthropy. Those with little to no experience in the world of gaming can be called on, too. This target group cannot afford to simply dismiss videogame culture; instead, it is essential that parents, teachers, and social workers use the positive effects and opportunities offered by videogames without exaggerating or ignoring the downsides described in this chapter.

Notes

1 Term for the persecution and extermination of European Jews during National Socialist rule in Germany and Europe.
2 The Commodore Amiga is a series of computers that were widely used in the 1980s and 1990s.
3 A top-down game is a game that offers an elevated viewpoint above the action. The overhead perspective is called top-down.
4 A specific form of pornography in comic style.
5 The term "New Right" is a self-designation of right-wing extremist intellectuals who strive for an ideological and strategic modernization of right-wing ideologies and at the same time want to distance themselves from the "Old Right," which is strongly associated with Nazism..
6 The "Identitarian Movement" is a right-wing extremist youth movement that is close to the "New Right" and wants to "liberate" right-wing extremism from the veneration of National Socialism in order to make it more acceptable.
7 The Great Reset is a right-wing conspiracy narrative arguing that society is being secretly reorganized by elites, including by replacing native populations with foreigners.
8 "Metapolitics" is a concept of the extreme right and refers to actions that further their political agenda even in spaces not associated with politics, including the gaming sphere.

9 The Atomwaffen Division (AWD) is a right-wing terrorist organization founded in the USA in 2015, composed mostly of neo-Nazis and white supremacists.
10 QAnon is a conspiracy movement that originated in the USA and claims, among other things, that COVID-19 is a "globalist bioweapon," that 5G makes us all sick, and that anyone wearing a mask is subordinate to the "New World Order."
11 A platform area on which user-generated content can be uploaded.
12 e.g., https://www.ma-hsh.de/service/beschwerde.html [in German].

References

Activision (2003). *Call of Duty.* [Videogame]

ADL (2022). Hate Is No Game: Hate and Harassment in Online Games 2022. https://www.adl.org/resources/report/hate-no-game-hate-and-harassment-online-games-2022.

Allyn, B. (2021). Group-Chat App Discord Says It Banned More Than 2,000 Extremist Communities. https://www.npr.org/2021/04/05/983855753/group-chat-app-discord-says-it-banned-more-than-2-000-extremist-communities.

Al-Rawi, A. (2018) Video Games, Terrorism, and ISIS's Jihad 3.0. *Terrorism and Political Violence, 30*(4), 740–760.

Augsburger Allgemeine (2010). "Moschee Baba": Österreich: Online-Spiel der FPÖ sorgt für Empörung. https://www.augsburger-allgemeine.de/panorama/Moschee-Baba-Oesterreich-Online-Spiel-der-FPOe-sorgt-fuer-Empoerung-id8414181.html.

Avalanche Software (2023). *Hogwarts Legacy.* [Videogame]

Ayyadi, K. (2018). Das OEZ-Attentat und der international vernetzte virtuelle Rechtsextremismus. https://www.belltower.news/das-oez-attentat-und-der-international-vernetzte-virtuelle-rechtsextremismus-48668/.

Bethesda Game Studios (2011). *Skyrim.* [Videogame]

Bethesda Softworks (2008). *Fallout 3.* [Videogame]

Blizzard Entertainment (2010). *Starcraft II.* [Videogame]

Bundesanzeiger (2014). Bundesprüfstelle für jugendgefährdende Medien: Bekanntmachung Nr. 6/2014 über jugendgefährdende Trägermedien. https://www.bundesanzeiger.de/pub/publication/YkQsSxY1gMez55KKCBa?0.

Dauber, C., Robinson, M., Baslious, J., & Blair, A. (2019). Call of Duty: Jihad – How the Video Game Motif Has Migrated Downstream from Islamic State Propaganda Videos. *Perspectives on Terrorism, 13* (3), 17–31.

Eguchi, K. & Nogami, H. (2001). *Animal Crossing.* [Videogame]

Franz, P. & Prinz, M. (2021). "Toxische Spielestudios" in Amadeu Antonio Foundation (Eds), *Unverpixelter Hass: Toxische und rechtsextreme Gaming-Communitys* (pp.34–38). https://www.amadeu-antonio-stiftung.de/wp-content/uploads/2022/02/unverpixelter-hass-netz-final.pdf.

Huberts, C. (2021). "Rechte Falschspieler:innen in Gaming-Communitys" in Amadeu Antonio Foundation (Eds), *Unverpixelter Hass: Toxische und rechtsextreme Gaming-Communitys* (pp.54–57) https://www.amadeu-antonio-stiftung.de/wp-content/uploads/2022/02/unverpixelter-hass-netz-final.pdf.

Inner Sloth (2018). *Among Us.* [Videogame]

Kampf, R. & Prinz, M. (2022). Die Gaming-Plattform Steam und ihr verhaltener Umgang mit Rechtsextremismus. https://www.belltower.news/zur-gamescom-die-gaming-plattform-steam-und-ihr-verhaltener-umgang-mit-rechtsextremismus-137639/.

Lakomy, M. (2019). Let's Play a Video Game: Jihadi Propaganda in the World of Electronic Entertainment. *Studies in Conflict & Terrorism*, 42(4), 383–406.

Mahmoud, F. (2022). Playing with Religion: The Gamification of Jihad. Danish Institute for International Studies. https://pure.diis.dk/ws/files/9007170/The_gamification_of_jihad_DIIS_Report_2022_06.pdf.

Mojang Studios (2011). *Minecraft*. [Videogame]

Paradox Development Studio (2016). *Hearts of Iron IV*. [Videogame]

Petrilla Entertainment (2003). *Quest for Saddam*. [Videogame]

Prinz, M. (2023). Rechte Erlebnisse. *TAZ (28.01.2023)*. Print edition.

Rafael, S. & Prinz, M. (2023). Hogwart's Legacy: Zwischen Transfeindlichkeit, Antisemitismus, und rechten Entwicklern. https://www.belltower.news/hogwarts-legacy-zwischen-transfeindlichkeit-antisemitismus-und-rechten-entwicklern-146533/.

Ravensburger Interactive Media (1999). *Moorhuhn*. [Videogame]

Relic Entertainment (2006). *Company of Heroes*. [Videogame]

Robinson, N. & Whittaker, J. (2021). Playing for Hate? Extremism, Terrorism, and Videogames. *Studies in Conflict & Terrorism*. Online First. 10.1080/1057610X.2020.1866740.

Rockstar Games (1997). *Grand Theft Auto*. [Videogame]

Rockstar Games (2018). *Red Dead Redemption 2*. [Videogame]

Roblox Corporation (2006). *Roblox*. [Videogame]

Rose, S. (2018). "Holy Defence": Hezbollah Issues Call of Duty to Video Gamers. *Middle East Eye*. https://www.middleeastye.net/news/holy-defence-hezbollah-issues-call-duty-video-gamers.

Schlegel, L. (2020). Jumanji Extremism? How Games and Gamification Could Facilitate Radicalization Processes. *Journal for Deradicalization*, 23, 1–44.

Schlegel, L. & Amarasingam, A. (2022). Examining the Intersection Between Gaming and Violent Extremism. United Nations Office of Counter-Terrorism. https://www.un.org/counterterrorism/sites/www.un.org.counterterrorism/files/221005_research_launch_on_gaming_ve.pdf.

Strick, S. (2021). *Rechte Gefühle – Affekte und Strategien des digitalen Faschismus*. Transcript.

Thomas, E. (2021). The Extreme Right on DLive. Institute for Strategic Dialogue. https://www.isdglobal.org/wp-content/uploads/2021/08/03-gaming-report-dlive-1.pdf.

Ubisoft (2021). *Far Cry 6*. [Videogame]

4

DIGITAL GAMES AS VEHICLES FOR EXTREMIST RECRUITMENT AND MOBILIZATION

Alex Newhouse and Rachel Kowert

Extremist activity and movements have been increasingly migrating online. Today, digital spaces are being leveraged by extremists of all ideologies for recruitment, group formation, propaganda creation and dissemination, organization, and mobilization. This is due to the many affordances provided within these digital environments, such as their accessibility (for more on this, see Kowert & Newhouse, 2023), as well as the ineffectiveness of current moderation strategies to identify and moderate these kinds of digital behavior. The movement towards digital engagement among extremist groups has also affected the way extremism exhibits itself within society: Moving away from discrete groups that rely on in-person connections to grow, and towards geographically diffuse, organizationally fluid, and decentralized networks. While this can be found across spaces on the internet, such as online forums and social media, there is a particular concern about how this is manifesting in digital gaming spaces.

In this chapter, we will explore the nature of this shift to digital gaming spaces by presenting evidence of how gaming spaces are currently being exploited by known extremist movements and their support networks. This will begin with an overview of extremism in games, including a survey of key terms, the unique susceptibility of gaming spaces for extremist exploitation, and the presentation of several case studies where extremist radicalization, recruitment, and mobilization have been documented. The chapter will end with suggestions for immediate steps that can be taken by game developers and trust and safety teams to better address the threats that games-based extremism poses.

DOI: 10.4324/9781003388371-5

Background

There are many ways to define extremism. For the purposes of this chapter, we use the definition of extremism introduced in Berger (2018): "[T]he belief that an in-group's success or survival can never be separated from the need for hostile action against an out-group" (p. 38). From this definition, extremism relies on the establishment of a strict boundary between an in-group (or "tribe", family, etc.) and an out-group. Importantly, for an entity to meet the threshold of extremism, a person does not actually have to engage in hostile action but rather just promote it as necessary. For example, inciting violence within a group would be considered extremist action even though the individual is not engaging in the violent acts themselves. Hostile actions encompass a host of common tactics employed by extremists, including hate speech, vandalism, harassment, propagandization, and disinformation. Terrorism, the use or threatened use of violence, is the most well known of these tactics (Bale *et al.*, 2019, p. 8).

While extremist networks have historically relied on geographical proximity to organize and mobilize, the internet has provided a lower threshold for connection, allowing like-minded individuals to connect in more easily accessible ways. Evidence for this can be found in even the earliest days of the internet. Some of the first users of nascent social media were white supremacists: For example, Louis Beam, leader of various divisions of the Ku Klux Klan and pioneer of the concept of "leaderless resistance," established Aryan Nations Liberty Net in 1984 (Smith, 2021). In the 1990s, elements of terroristic jihadist movements such as Al Qaeda moved some of its propaganda and recruitment onto the internet as well (Weimann, 2008). While extremist groups can, and do, leverage a variety of digital environments (see Littler & Lee, 2021), digital games have become an area of particular concern (Kowert & Newhouse, 2021). This is because digital games are thought to have the potential to be used as a tool for radicalization for many reasons, including their accessibility, content, lack of effective moderation, and various cultural factors such as identity fusion (for more on this, see Kowert & Newhouse, 2023). As such, extremist movements have seemingly embraced games as the new frontier for identity creation and mobilization.

History of Extremist Recruitment and Mobilization in Gaming Spaces

Extremist activity has occurred in digital games for decades, but the signs have become clear only in retrospect. One of the earliest and most notable incidents of extremist use of digital gaming spaces took place in the game *Habbo Hotel* (Sulake) in 2006. Ostensibly in response to perceived racial discrimination by the game developers, a network of individuals co-ordinated to raid the game's world to disrupt the game for other players. In particular, these campaigns assumed in-game avatars with "Afro" hair and black skin and blocked access to sections of *Habbo Hotel*'s world. At certain points, they even arranged their players into a swastika shape – an act (and image) that has become a meme in its own right since then. Participants frequently employed racist, sexist, and generally crude and offensive language, both in in-game chat and in discussions of the campaigns online. These actions had the impact of bringing the game to a halt – an overt display of coordination and hostility toward the developer (and other players) of an unprecedented scale (Vichot, 2009).

The *Habbo Hotel* incident was one of the first documented early incarnations of extremist-related action in digital gaming spaces. This incident was novel not only in the scope of its coordination but also in the scale of involvement by decentralized networks including *4chan*'s /b/ imageboard and the *Something Awful* forums.[1] Although it is impossible to state confidently how many individuals harbored extremist views, the communities that participated in the *Habbo Hotel* raids – *4chan* (Tuters & Hagen, 2020; Baele *et al.*, 2021; Zelenkauskaite *et al.*, 2020) and elements of *Something Awful* (Herrman, 2014; Wofford, 2017; Beran, 2019) in particular – transformed over time into some of the most important focal points of far-right agitation, white supremacist beliefs, and even the incitement of real-world violence.

It is important to note that those who took part in these events insisted that toxic language and symbols were satirical and part of the process of "griefing" (i.e., a common practice among game players to irritate and annoy other players; Dibbell, 2008) and were not intended to cause serious harm. This is important, as it allowed the perpetrators to evade individual responsibility behind the shield of what has come to be known as "edgelord humor": Expressing a hateful or heinous sentiment and, in the light of pushback or criticism from others, suggesting that the things they were saying are in jest. While true intent among griefers and "edgelords" is hard to assess, evidence suggests that these behaviors have contributed to widespread normalization of hateful language in gaming spaces as part of the "culture" of games (Kowert, 2021; Kowert & Crevoshay, 2022).

Indeed, following the *Habbo Hotel* campaigns, many of these same participants dubbed themselves "Patriotic Nigras" and spent several years coordinating disruptions of *Second Life* (Linden Lab) and harassment of its users, which included increasingly shocking, hostile, and offensive actions against its targets. Researchers have noted that participants in "Patriotic Nigras" raids disseminated racist propaganda and conducted sexist and racist vandalism in the game (Giles, 2007). When asked to comment, members relied largely on the argument that everything was done satirically and to get a rise from people who took the game too seriously (Giles, 2007), thus demonstrating how the normalization of hate and harassment in gaming spaces has provided an opening for this kind of activity within these environments.

It is also worth noting that research following the *Habbo Hotel* raids revealed that they were carried out by a complex, decentralized, and multiplatform network of individuals with a wide range of beliefs and motives. This supports the contention that the organization and mobilization of extremist activity in digital spaces has correspondingly changed the way extremist groups organize and mobilize in non-digital spaces. While this is only one example of extremist ideologies and behaviors within digital gaming spaces, a lot of questions about how these environments are being used for the recruitment and mobilization of extremist groups, remain.

Games for Recruitment: Unique Attributes and the Radicalization Process

It has been suggested that digital games spaces may be particularly vulnerable to recruitment to extremist causes. This includes recruiting new members into extremist organizations with no previous experience or exposure as well as further radicalizing existing members or believers and recruiting them into more active extremist movements.

As previously described, recruitment into extremist movements has traditionally required extensive time and resources and often a shared geographical location. Recruitment in online spaces has reduced the need for geographical closeness. While it still necessitates significant time and effort, finding groups of potential like-minded individuals is easier.

Recruitment in online games is functionally different from traditional forms of off- and online recruitment. As social, playful spaces, gaming environments can "emotionally jumpstart" relationships between players, accelerating the formation of close, tight-knit interpersonal connections. In essence, a player may learn to trust someone much more quickly than they would in traditional, non-digital relationships, because of the presence of a shared, stressful activity (Yee, 2002). Although empirical measurement of the impact of this phenomenon on extremism is ongoing, it closely fits theoretical models of the radicalization process. Studies have shown that close personal relationships can drive radicalization and mobilization to violence, specifically because of the influence of trust on a person's cognitive openness to extremist beliefs (for example, Hafez (2016) shows that kinship and friendship bonds can cause particularly rapid mobilization to violence in new recruits to jihadist groups). Therefore, if someone was using digital games to recruit new members to their cause, they have essentially a series of built-in trust building exercises to "jumpstart" a sense of trust and emotional closeness with any potential target (Kowert, 2015; Radicalisation Awareness Network, 2021). Thus, we hypothesize that games provide a particularly pernicious combination of the decentralization and scale of social media combined with the trust-building power of in-person interaction.

In addition, the visual and narrative elements of games can be leveraged to further reinforce extreme worldviews that are common across extremist ideologies, such as racism, misogyny, and hate for specific ethnic groups (Phelan *et al.*, 2023). Game content can be thought of as the "mood music" for radicalization. While game content in and of itself is unlikely to be a radicalizing force on its own, the narratives, images, and other related content can be used as a tool to leverage radicalization efforts. For example, the game *Hearts of Iron IV* (Paradox Interactive), a military strategy game, is centered on the events of the Second World War and has been found to play a prominent role in the rhetoric and community-building of contemporary neo-Nazi and neofascist communities. This is a consequence of a number of factors (many of which are explained later), but it in particular the game's approach to the Second World War's history provides a "blank slate" for living out alternative history fantasies (Aschim, 2020). This game has been used specifically as a touchpoint for players who endorse radical beliefs to forge bonds in games and game-adjacent spaces, such as *Reddit* forums dedicated to the game (Andrews & Skoczylis, 2022).

The use of *bespoke* games[2] by extremist groups is largely seen as a tool to solidify beliefs that have already been established through other radicalization processes. A recent example of extremist use of bespoke games can be found in the proliferation of mass-shooter simulators across digital gaming marketplaces. Shooter simulators, which can best be described as game modes that put players in the role of the perpetrators of mass shootings, were first documented following the Columbine shooting with the 2005 release *Super Columbine Massacre RPG* (Orland, 2015). This game shocked audiences by giving players the ability to play as the perpetrators of the school shooting. Although the creator's motivations remain debated and the game sparked significant controversy in the 2000s, it was merely the first of a trend of games and creations aiming to put players in the role of mass shooters. In 2018, for instance, Russian developer Revived Games released *Active Shooter*, a game that lets users choose to play as either a mass shooter or a law enforcement agent trying to stop the shooting (Kan, 2018). Users of gaming platforms such as

Roblox (Roblox Corporation), *Garry's Mod* (Facepunch Studios), and *Minecraft* (Mojang) have also generated numerous game modes and maps aimed at simulating school shootings. In addition, a number of creators have created explicitly *ideological* shooter simulators, including recreations of the white supremacist shootings in Christchurch, New Zealand (Brandom, 2021).

It is important to note that the use of bespoke gaming spaces is not limited to shooter simulators. For example, Holocaust simulators are also well documented in gaming spaces (Miller & Silva, 2021). Typically built in sandbox creation environments such as *Minecraft* or *Roblox*, users craft environments to resemble the concentration camps of Nazi Germany, including simulated gas chambers and swastika iconography. *Roblox* users have created detailed concentration and death camps complete with mechanics that allow the administrators of these games to explicitly assume the role of Nazi camp guards (Howes & Bennett, 2022). *Minecraft* users have also recreated Nazi-run death camps such as Auschwitz (Miller & Silva, 2021), while we have confirmed that *Garry's Mod* users have built detailed death camp role-playing game modes and shared videos of them online.

Cultural considerations must also be considered in the context of gaming spaces. There is a normalization of hateful ideologies within gamer cultures and can provide a welcoming environment for extreme worldviews than many other places on the internet (for more on this, see Kowert & Newhouse, 2021, 2023). This cultural normalization of hate and harassment has created a vulnerability for the propagation of more extreme ideologies, making them more conducive spaces for recruitment. For example, if racial slurs are commonplace within gaming spaces, taking those slurs from racist language to overt hate speech is a less noticeable change within the social landscape.

Taking all these factors into consideration – the emotional jumpstarting of relationships, game content, and cultural norms of games – has led games to be described as "cultural assets of influence" in the context of radicalization (Kowert & Newhouse, 2021). That is, digital games are being specifically targeted for radicalization efforts due to the combination of their unique structural and cultural aspects. Consequently, evidence suggests that games can have a significant impact on the process by which recruits are radicalized.

Radicalization Process

The exact details and cadence of a person's radicalization to extremism is unique to them alone. Although almost universally dependent on social networks and community-building, radicalization processes emerge based on the particular characteristics of each individual, to the extent that scaling up counter-radicalization programming poses daunting challenges (see the wide body of literature attempting to evaluate the effectiveness of countering violent extremism (CVE) programming, such as Romaniuk, 2015; Vidino & Hughes, 2015; Holmer, Bauman, & Aryaeinejad, 2018).

What starts a person's radicalization process, whether they eventually carry out violence, which ideological currents they immerse in, and even how long it takes the new recruit to be mobilized to violence all depend on an array of psychological, social, political, and emotional factors. Some new recruits may carry out attacks only a relatively short time after starting on their radicalization pathway, as occurred with the far-right perpetrator of the mass shooting in Buffalo, NY, in 2022 (Bindner & Gluck, 2022). Others may spend decades in radicalized communities without ever picking up a weapon. This trend is especially notable among ideologues and propagandists, who rarely hold the guns themselves (Scrivens *et al.*, 2022). In other cases, individuals may only temporarily join online chatrooms about certain extreme viewpoints, falling away from active participation from apathy, regret, disruption of the chat room by content moderators, or other factors (Koehler, Fiebig, & Jugl, 2022).

In spite of the array of possible manifestations, radicalization generally occurs as a steady build-up of increasingly extreme beliefs. This has led researchers to discuss radicalization in terms such as "pathway," "funnel," or "ladder" (Kowert & Newhouse, 2021; Rosenblat & Barrett, 2023). Although none of these terms is perfectly accurate, they are all useful for illustrating radicalization systems; the authors have observed extremists themselves discussing recruitment in these terms, as well.

Although empirical work is still in its nascent stages, researchers have proposed different mechanisms by which games and the radicalization process interact. As in other contexts, individuals can be attracted to radicalizing material and communities for different reasons and based on different stimuli. Schlegel (2021), for instance, proposes applying five user types within games to gamified radicalization. The author suggests that games may be able to facilitate radicalization on different axes, such as through competitive mechanics for "competitor" user types, puzzle-solving and collaborative augmented reality mechanics for "achiever" types, and community status markers for "socializer" types.

Anecdotal and observational evidence suggests that extremists conceptualize these interactions at least to some degree and attempt to take advantage of them to find new recruits. Some CVE practitioners have observed hardened extremists using particular, highly charged words and phrases to identify potential recruits in large public lobbies in multiplayer video games. Individuals who react positively to these actions (e.g., laughing at racial slurs) are then invited into private lobbies, where they are further vetted and enticed with increasingly exclusive access to highly connected communities (Harbinger, 2020).

These types of process in games also frequently integrate other dynamics that have been associated with radicalization. Videogame communities can be avid users of edgy, dark humor that incorporates hateful and harassing elements; this type of "edgelord" humor is frequently weaponized by extremists to increase the appeal of radical messages (Huey, 2015; Nagle, 2017; Hodge & Hallgrimsdottir, 2019; Crawford, Keen, & Suarez-Tangil, 2020).

Although more research is needed to establish generalizable evidence for these interactions, they have already appeared in several real-world cases involving violent extremists. In 2022, for instance, two teenage boys spoke with law enforcement about their successful radicalization into an extremist group through online games (Koehler, Fiebig, & Jugl, 2022). Their process mirrors the dynamics that have been observed by Picciolini and others (Bayoumy & Gilsinan, 2019). Their introduction to their respective radicalization pathways came via a recruiter with whom they had frequently enjoyed playing games. Over a short period of time, they built trust in the recruiter, and they were invited to join an external *Discord* community that was already populated with more radicalized individuals. Once here, they were asked to do increasingly more dangerous and insidious tasks, such as performing the Hitler salute at school. Eventually, the tasks turned more violent, and, at this point, the boys were cognizant enough to understand the repercussions of these actions and they sought out law enforcement for support. It is notable that the boys note in their police report that they did not want to perform any of the actions asked of them, but they continued to do so because they wanted to remain a part of the *Discord* and gaming community associated with it. The feelings of belonging and community support they felt had proved to be the most salient factors keeping them immersed in a radicalizing environment.

Games for Mobilization

In addition to recruitment, it is hypothesized that extremist groups are using games to mobilize established networks. That is, using these spaces to not only recruit new members, but also organize, communicate, and mobilize established networks to online and offline action. This is most commonly thought of as creating linked, established networks of extremist groups within gaming platforms. While traditional mobilization would require geographical centrality in the group structure, games allow people to connect across geographical spaces. Another important consideration is that traditional mobilization typically requires extensive efforts to hide or disguise communications. In digital gaming spaces, this is not the case. As noted above, a lot of extremist content hides behind the guise of "edgelord humor," making it difficult to moderate with traditional practices. Images and memes are also difficult to detect and determine their relationship to extremist propaganda without the use of subject matter experts as well as extensive, individual moderation efforts, which is both expensive and, as it stands today, not considered feasible at scale.

However, even the most basic prohibitions are missing within gaming spaces. As discussed in the 2023 report from the NYU Center for Business and Human Rights: "[M]any large and profitable gaming and gaming-adjacent companies have delayed in taking adequate steps to prevent bad actors from misusing their sites and causing harm" (p. 21). For example, as it stands today, only one gaming platform (*Roblox*) specifically prohibits extremist action through their terms of service or a violation of their code of conduct. This has made the mobilization of extremist groups in gaming spaces relatively frictionless. In the aforementioned report of the two teenagers were attempted to be radicalized through online games, the players noted to the police in their report that even when the individuals who were actively radicalizing them were deplatformed due to their behavior they quickly regained access with new accounts (Koehler, Fiebig, & Jugl, 2022). Thus, there is not only an ineffectiveness for moderating content, but also restricting access by known bad actors even after they are identified.

Radicalization and Mobilization within Digital Games: A Series of Case Studies

The above examples were provided to illustrate some of the ways in which the tools and opportunities within digital gaming spaces are being utilized by extremists to recruit and mobilize. While these case studies are important for understanding how digital games have been exploited in the past, they provide little insight into the contemporary patterns and scope of extremist exploitation across gaming networks. To better understand the contemporary use of digital gaming spaces by extremist actors, we undertook a series of case studies across two popular gaming platforms, *Roblox* and *Steam*, and one popular online digital game, *Hearts of Iron IV* (Paradox Development Studio). We chose these three cases because of their known use by extremists and their ease of access to data that demonstrates their role in extremist activity. Each of these gaming environments is described in more detail below.

Roblox

Roblox is a game platform that revolves around the creation, sharing, and engagement with content created by the users themselves. The game developer provides a suite of creation tools and social network functionality, and players create experiences, in-game items, and groups. This combination has proved extraordinarily popular: since its launch in 2006, *Roblox* has accumulated over 65 million daily active users (Statista, 2023). Its developer is worth over $20 billion, making it one of the most valuable game studios in the world (Levy, 2021). *Roblox* stands out because of its emphasis on providing a low-friction sign-up experience coupled with extensive social networking capabilities. Roblox's core feature is its game creation engine, but its networking affordances make it a prominent social media platform in its own right. For example, within Roblox, users are able to:

- Form friendships
- Follow players and have other players follow them
- Organize into groups, and create role hierarchies in those groups
- Create alliances and declare adversaries between one's group and other groups
- Create and sell cosmetic items for *Roblox* avatars
- Create and share experiences[3]
- Communicate with other users through in-game chat, a group's shared "Wall," and comments on content

This is not a comprehensive list: *Roblox*'s social networking and content-sharing features are extensive and constantly evolving. Each of these features, however, can directly or indirectly indicate a relationship, which means that *Roblox* is also a uniquely rich platform for conducting social network analysis (SNA) to map player networks with possible affiliation to extremist movements.

Steam

Steam is a popular videogame marketplace for PC games. Owned by the large gaming corporation Valve, *Steam* is generally considered the de facto place for developers to sell their games and players to buy and play them. It occupies a similar role to the *PlayStation Network* on *Playstation* consoles and *Xbox Live* on *Xbox* consoles, providing the infrastructure for engagement within and around games. Over time, Valve has built *Steam* into a games-centric social network in addition to a marketplace. Its affordances include:

- *Steam* Workshop, where players can share and discuss game modifications (or "mods," which are player created changes to the game, such as changing the leader of Germany in the game *Civilization IV* [Activision] from Otto von Bismarck to Aldof Hitler)
- *Steam* Community, which allows developers to host forums about their games where players can discuss and leave feedback, and for players to create groups
- *Steam* store pages that host player reviews for games
- The ability to make friends with other users

Since its creation, *Steam* has become a giant in the videogame industry, and it is estimated to facilitate a majority of all PC game sales worldwide. This has allowed *Steam* to emerge as a focal point for videogame activity broadly, becoming more than just a marketplace. Its friends list, messaging, community forums, game modifications, and profile features have built *Steam* into a de facto social network for PC gamers. This includes far-right extremists, who have exploited *Steam*'s lax content moderation to develop networks of organization and communication.

Hearts of Iron IV

In 2016, strategy game developer Paradox Interactive released *Hearts of Iron IV*, the fourth installment in the grand strategy wargame series. Focusing on the theaters of the Second World War, players are tasked with navigating through the complex strategic and tactical decisions facing wartime commanders, including diplomacy, espionage, resource allocation, and combat. *Hearts of Iron IV* was released to critical and commercial acclaim for its ambition and fully fledged commander simulation systems.

Hearts of Iron IV is also a particularly beloved game among far-right extremists (Andrews & Skoczylis, 2022). In order to show its prominent role in far-right extremism, we survey far-right online communities for mentions of the game and investigate far-right discourse around it. We also show how player-created modifications have allowed far-right extremists to customize and live out alternative, fascistic histories in the game.

The intricate detail with which *Hearts of Iron IV* simulates the Second World War and the complete flexibility in which country and leader players can control made the game popular among strategy game fans. It also brought a host of far-right extremists to the game, especially following the creation of alternative history modifications such as Kaiserreich that allows players to interact with a world where the Axis Powers achieved victory.

Results

Roblox

To assess the prevalence and nature of extremist activity in *Roblox*, we employed SNA in addition to qualitative investigation to examine a network of individual users exhibiting indicators of far-right extremist beliefs on *Roblox*. All the data collected is open source, and we use *Roblox*'s API via the PyRoblox Python library to collect social network and user data. We surface a seed group through manual investigation, and then map that group's two-step ego network (i.e., its allies, and all of its allies' allies). We also collect every group's members and any content attached to these groups at the time of collection.

In addition to its core game mechanics and creator modes, *Roblox* has become a robust social networking platform in its own right. It also allows for a wide array of customizations, from user-created avatar items including t-shirts and hats to game modes, thumbnails, and groups. Subsequently, these features provide significant opportunities for signaling to other players, such as in the case of a member of an in-group signaling their identity to other members of that group.

Using manually identified seed accounts and scaled social network analysis, we find several examples of hardened, neo-fascist extremist networks that have exploited *Roblox*'s affordances to communicate with one another, signal their adherence to their ideology, and evade content moderation. We explore two case studies here, one of which was active until disrupted by *Roblox* in April 2022, and the other that has reshuffled in response to content moderation but continued activity through the time of this writing (March 2023).

We identified the first network via keyword search for users with the term "Floyd" in their usernames, as we previously observed neo-fascists using ironic or satirical references to George Floyd in usernames across social media platforms. After reviewing several *Roblox* accounts, we selected one that demonstrated significant engagement with other groups, users, and in-game content. The first indication that this user was involved in an extremist network appeared in their account's "About" section, where Roblox players will often list their interests, characteristics about themselves, and other information. This particular user declared that their account was "Home of *Patriotic Front Aesthetics // R E C L A I M*." These are both indicators of adherence to neo-fascism and white supremacy, and they are also both examples of tactics to evade content moderation. "Patriotic Front Aesthetics" is an adversarial spelling of "Patriot Front," a white supremacist and neo-fascist network that has been active in vandalism, flyering, and street marches throughout the United States (CTEC, 2022). "R E C L A I M," meanwhile, is a reference to one of Patriot Front's key slogans, "Reclaim America." Interspersing letters with spaces is a common meme in far-right circles, designed to draw particular attention to certain words by evoking monospace fonts from early computer systems.

This user also promoted Patriot Front in their deliberate choice of content to display in their "Favorites" section on their profile. *Roblox* allows users to select up to six pieces of content to highlight as favorites, which displays those pieces of content's thumbnails in a prominent position on the user's profile page. In the investigated user's case, they employed a creative strategy to evade moderation while still promoting a cohesive message: each of their favorited items was a "shell," containing essentially nothing but the thumbnail. The thumbnails were carefully designed to look mostly innocent individually, but to form an image when arrayed in order side-by-side. In this case, the favorites created a cohesive Patriot Front propaganda poster. This is displayed in Figure 4.1.

Utilizing the significant social network capabilities of *Roblox*, this user also participated in an extensive and seemingly decentralized in-game neo-fascist network. In the real world, Patriot Front is deeply connected to other neo-fascist groups and networks, including National Socialist Club 131 (NSC-131), the Proud Boys, the Base, and, most notably, Active Clubs, Will2Rise, and Robert Rundo (Newhouse, 2021; CTEC, 2022). Members generally treat Patriot Front as a brand more than a group, leveraging its aesthetics and uniforms as convenient for certain marches while still collaborating and crossing over with many other neo-fascist entities. This is in line with the evolution of neo-fascism and militant accelerationism over the past ten years, in which activists have increasingly stressed loose connections and temporary alliances over strict membership and hierarchies (Newhouse, 2021; Upchurch, 2021). This *Roblox* user and other users in their orbit operate similarly in the game, establishing affiliations with large numbers of different *Roblox* groups that often promote quite disparate real-world entities.

FIGURE 4.1   "Favorites" section from user Justice4Floyd's profile page on Roblox.

The investigated user was a high-ranking member of the group "Justice 4 Floyd," which is another sarcastic reference to George Floyd. The group's thumbnail displays a black shield with a white outline, which is likely a reference to Wehrmacht SS Division shields. These logos have been adopted and modified by terrorist networks such as Atomwaffen Division and far-right troll networks such as Bowl Patrol (Upchurch, 2021). Justice 4 Floyd had 50 members, and it also listed nine other groups as allies. Each of these nine groups also had allies. In order to collect these relationships, we logged all of the allies of Justice 4 Floyd (i.e., all groups that identified a formal friendly connection with this group) and the allies of those allies, creating what is often referred to as a "two-step ego network." From this, we were able to document extensive collaborative behaviors across dozens of groups and users. This can be seen in Figure 4.2.

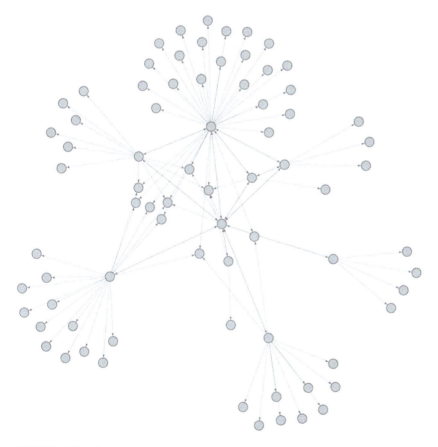

FIGURE 4.2 Two-step network from the "Justice 4 Floyd" seed group. Arrow marks node for "Justice 4 Floyd".

We found three main categories of extremist signaling in these groups: Indirect or evasive promotion of extant contemporary fascist movements, direct references to historical groups and individuals, and fictional or fabricated terms that are stylistically similar to fascist rhetoric.

Of the first category, we identified groups named "Pzatriot Front" (an adversarial spelling of Patriot Front), "New Republic of Kekistan" (a reference to 4chan's extreme-right /pol/ imageboard), and "New Hampshire 2nd Infantry Platoon" (which used a profile picture that included the logo of Nationalist Social Club 131). Groups in the second category included references to Golden Dawn, Elohim City, the Covenant, Sword, and Arm of the Lord, and The Order. Finally, groups in the third category included "Condor Division," "British Nationalist Vanguard Party," and "Followers of Christ Nationalist Workers Party."

Based on long-term monitoring of *Roblox*, we believe that this network represented just one small portion of the total ecosystem of far-right extremism on the platform. We also observed significant and often fairly nuanced adversarial evolution in response to content moderation actions. We have detected *Roblox* groups being rapidly recreated after bans, often with slight variants on their group name. We have also seen entire alliance networks become reformulated and restructured in the aftermath of enforcement sweeps, during which time users exploit gaps in the enforcement and the ease of account creation on *Roblox* to fluidly and swiftly adapt.

Steam

In order to investigate the presence of far-right extremism on *Steam*, we collect data using *Steam*'s public API and conduct SNA on the relationships between players within groups. In early 2022, we identified a *Steam* account using the pseudonym "AstroZelea." Using hashtags related to George Floyd and having logged dozens of hours in *Hearts of Iron IV*, we hypothesized that this account was active in far-right communities, as sarcastic or degrading references to Floyd are common in right-wing online spaces. We investigated this account and discovered that it had interacted with another banned account called "CommanderFKD." Together, these two accounts provided strong evidence that we had detected the online activity of the Feuerkrieg Division, one of the most notorious far-right accelerationist entities of the past ten years (Newhouse, 2021; Upchurch, 2021). "CommanderFKD" (or just "Commander") is the alias used by the founder and former leader of Feuerkrieg Division, a teenage boy based in Estonia (Newhouse, 2021). After founding the organization in 2018, Commander forged a transnational network of accelerationists dedicated to extreme violence and neo-fascist and neo-Nazi ideologies. Several members of

Feuerkrieg were arrested for various crimes, including firearms charges and plotting terrorist attacks throughout Europe.

Following a brief hiatus, Feuerkrieg Division re-emerged in 2021 alongside another entity, Injekt Division, the leader of which nearly committed a mass shooting at a Wal-Mart in Texas (Newhouse, 2021). According to social media accounts linked to Feuerkrieg and reports by journalists, Commander had begun collaborating with another youth, using many aliases including "Hergle Zelea," based in the United States. Feuerkrieg, primarily via Commander and Hergle Zelea, became particularly active in far-right internet communities, forging many ephemeral Telegram coalitions and forming accounts on various other platforms (Shadnia *et al.*, 2022). Because of its plots of violence and harassment campaigns, Feuerkrieg Division has been proscribed in the United Kingdom, Australia, and Canada.

Based on the similarities between the names "Astro Zelea" and "Hergle Zelea," and taking into consideration the account called "CommanderFKD," we believe that there is a strong probability that these two accounts were directly associated with the Feuerkrieg Division. Further, these members of this designated terrorist organization were promoting extreme-right beliefs and building networks openly on *Steam*. Their profile walls and *Steam* groups had many comments expressing hate and extremist views, including a meme post of a swastika that is frequently used across all of *Steam*. This particular Feuerkrieg network was disrupted in mid-2022, and we have not detected re-emergence since then. However, their use of friend lists, profile walls, and groups to promote their ideologies is common among far-right extremists, and many other extremist networks are exploiting *Steam* at the time of this writing.

One particularly sophisticated and extensive network is associated with "Trollwaffen," a loose association of hardened extremists and online trolls that uses the aesthetics of accelerationist movements like Atomwaffen Division and Feuerkrieg Division to raid, harass, and spread hate in online communities. Trollwaffen is defined by rapid expansion, evolution, and restructuring in response to content moderation, with affiliated users creating dozens of accounts in quick succession to overwhelm enforcement efforts. While Trollwaffen accounts generally espouse nonviolence, they frequently promote antisemitism and racism, and they participate in doxxing activities.

Trollwaffen accounts are particularly attention hungry and often explicitly attempt to gain media coverage for their adversarial and antisocial behavior, so we will not name any specific accounts in this chapter as they are still active on *Steam*. The particular network's structure on *Steam* is similar to that of right-wing extremists on *Roblox*: Organized under an informal, decentralized banner, a set of groups create alliances to "fight" against another faction of affiliated groups. One particular group we investigated, which promotes a combination of Chinese Communism and Islamism, lists over a dozen allies and over a dozen enemies. Another features a comments wall from members that is saturated with racial and ethnic slurs, anti-LGBTQ hate, and other extremist rhetoric.

In spite of aesthetics adopted from a wide-ranging assortment of ideologies and movements from Maoism to eco-fascism, the membership of this Trollwaffen network shows clearly that far-right accelerationism has a dominant influence. Many members' profiles exhibit explicit references to far-right extremism, including the Sonnenrad, pictures of neo-fascist terrorists, logos from groups such as Atomwaffen Division, and the use of characters including the German Iron Cross in conjunction with terms such as "ethno-state." One particular user adopted for their profile picture a photograph Devon Arthurs, co-founder of Atomwaffen Division and alleged murderer of two Atomwaffen members.

Hearts of Iron IV

In our investigation, we identified thousands of discussions of *Hearts of Iron IV* (HOI4) in far-right communities. In the leaked *Discord* logs from far-right networks compiled by the activist collective Unicorn Riot, for instance, there are well over 1,000 mentions of the game, the vast majority of which are positive. *4chan* users also discuss the game hundreds of times per week, according to data collected by the Open Collective's Social Media Analysis Tool. We reviewed hundreds of these messages to understand the motivations behind far-right extremists' fascination with *Hearts of Iron IV*. We identified several different roles that *Hearts of Iron IV* plays, including tactical exploration, in-group signaling, and radicalization.

Radicalization can take the form of introducing newcomers to consolidated extremist movements and hardening the identities of existing extremists. According to comments by extremists in internal discussion channels that later leaked, the game can contribute to both phases of radicalization. Spending significant time attempting to establish fascist domination in the game is seen as a baseline threshold of radicalization, as seen when a user describes well-known neo-fascist Matthew Heimbach as "not even HOI4 pilled" following Heimbach's supposed disengagement with the neo-fascist movement. In a now defunct *Discord* server linked to The Right Stuff podcast community, a user even states specifically: "HOI4 radicalized me."

Due to its opaque systems and steep learning curve, *Hearts of Iron IV* is often used more as an in-group symbol on gaming platforms than it is actually played. On *Steam* in particular, users exhibiting far-right sympathies (identified via membership in explicitly white supremacist groups or via the use of slurs, extremist language, or other indicators in their profile) often artificially inflate their playtime in *Hearts of Iron IV* and select it as their "favorite" game, to be highlighted at the top of their profile. One *Steam* user, for instance, whose profile has design elements evocative of the fashwave aesthetic (Kelley, 2017), stopped playing *Hearts of Iron IV* when they hit 666 hours played – a "meme" number in far-right communities because of its mainstream association with satanism. Others cover their *Steam* profiles in badges, images, and art from the game.

The alternative future imagined by *Hearts of Iron IV* and its universe of mods has given rise to a thriving culture of fanart, fan fiction, and other types of fan-produced content, which may provide for an "on-ramp" to radicalized communities for newcomers. *Hearts of Iron IV* content has become popular across social media platforms, especially video-sharing sites including YouTube. In our investigation, we identified dozens of videos sharing content from the game that have attracted highly engaged audiences that often promote fascistic and white supremacist ideals. This trend is apparent on songs from The New Order mod, which envisions a world in which Nazi Germany won the Second World War, but the resulting world order drives society to total collapse. Fanart and music created for the mod's playable nations attract hundreds of comments praising the style and rhetoric of these nations. For the most ideologically extreme nations – such as Henrich Himmler's SS State of Burgundy – comments from outright fascist users are often intermixed with other, more innocent comments about the mod, which can provide an air of plausible deniability to endorsements of real-world extremism. "This is fire bro," wrote one user with a profile picture of Himmler. "The Black Sun will rise and we will try again," stated another user with "88" in their username.[4] These videos garner hundreds of thousands – if not millions – of views, and fascist comments can often be immediately found in the most visible set of comments right below these videos. While we do not assert that the creators of these videos or the mods are extremist, the evidence suggests that the game and its mods can provide readily available onboarding for newcomers into extremist communities.

Moving Forward

Game developers have increasingly focused on providing players more customizability and more opportunities to connect with others. This has resulted in games becoming more social, expansive, and popular than ever before, which has helped millions of people to forge strong, healthy digital relationships. However, these same features can become vulnerabilities if content moderation and community management lags behind.

Our three case studies also demonstrate how the exploitation of games can take different forms. *Hearts of Iron IV* and its mods, for instance, can provide a framework to explore fantasies of fascist domination, genocide, and revenge, which has resulted in many extremists declaring that the game played an instrumental role in radicalizing them and thus should be considered an important tool for recruitment. *Roblox*, meanwhile, gives players significant capacity to create alliances and build networks while also providing extensive customization to create profiles, avatars, maps, and modes that explicitly endorse and promote extremist ideologies. Finally, *Steam* has established a community-building toolbox on the back of its marketplace, which has allowed extremist networks such as Trollwaffen to mount online "wars" that result in the proliferation of aesthetics and rhetoric associated with movements like eco-fascism, Nazism, Italian fascism, anti-LGBTQ hate, and more.

Much of this exploitation results from conventional wisdom in content moderation not keeping up with the evolution of extremist tactics. While player reports and content queues work for some types of toxic behavior, extremist radicalization and organization requires a more flexible, long-term, and comprehensive disruption and mitigation approach. In both *Roblox* and *Steam*, we detected significant adversarial and evasive behavior in direct response to content moderation: Groups were reformulated with slightly different names; users shuffled around to different groups; users evaded bans with new names and alternative accounts. This indicates that content moderation paradigms must shift to meet the new characteristics of the extremist threat in games, through the use of network mapping and disruption, actor-based analysis, and positive interventions to incentivize prosocial behaviors.

The games industry as a whole should also take the threat of exploitation by extremist networks more seriously. Game developers have lagged behind social media companies in joining and supporting organizations such as the Global Internet Forum on Counter-Terrorism (GIFCT) and Tech Against Terrorism, in spite of the availability of existing resources to build extremism mitigation capacity. As the "social networkification" of games continues to accelerate, however, it is imperative that the games industry rise to the occasion and ensure that adapting to and countering these threats is made an essential part of the game development process.

Conclusion

As we have shown in this chapter, extremist groups have the capacity to build large, sophisticated, consistently evolving networks on gaming platforms. They can also exploit the mechanics of games themselves to build propaganda and strengthen extremist identity. Often in plain sight, far-right extremists are using games to spread hate, find like-minded individuals, plan harassment campaigns, and radicalize others. As unique online spaces, greater attention must be placed on understanding how extremist groups are utilizing these spaces and how to best address this digital vulnerability.

Notes

1 The Habbo Hotel raids were early examples of leaderless, large-scale, co-ordinated disruption campaigns launched entirely virtually. They arose "organically," in that there was little to no oversight or command exerted over the campaign. However, participants coordinated with one another extensively, organizing raids in the threads on 4chan and *Something Awful*.
2 In this chapter, we refer to "bespoke games" as games purpose built by extremists for their purposes.
3 Roblox "experiences" are user-created games built on the Roblox platform. They can be single player or multiplayer, and they involve custom mechanics, goals, and roles on a purpose-built map.
4 The Black Sun is a reference to the Sonnenrad, an esoteric fascist symbol most associated with Himmler's SS. 88 is a common far-right meme standing for "Heil Hitler" as H is the eighth letter of the alphabet.

References

Andrews, S. & Skoczylis, J. (2022, February 17). Understanding Attitudes to Extremism in Gaming Communities. GNET. https://gnet-research.org/2022/02/17/understanding-attitudes-to-extremism-in-gaming-communities/.

Aschim, J. (2020). Playing Hitler: The Representation of Nazism in *Hearts of Iron IV* [Master's thesis], Inland Norway University. https://brage.inn.no/inn-xmlui/bitstream/handle/11250/2740422/Aschim.pdf.

Baele, S.J., Brace, L., & Coan, T.G. (2021). Variations on a Theme? Comparing 4chan, 8kun, and Other chans' Far-Right "/pol" Boards. *Perspectives on Terrorism*, *15*(1), 65–80. https://www.jstor.org/stable/26984798.

Bakioglu, B. (2009). Spectacular Interventions of Second Life: Goon Culture, Griefing, and Disruption in Virtual Spaces. *Journal of Virtual Worlds*, *1*(3), 4–21.

Bale, J., Hynes, N., & Reidy, T. (2019). Assessing the Risk of Islamist Terrorists Using Human Vectors to Deploy Pathogens. https://www.middlebury.edu/institute/sites/www.middlebury.edu.institute/files/2020-07/CTEC_Bale_Bioterrirsm_Report_0.pdf?fv=B5Ma5CoX.

Bayoumy, Y. & Gilsinan, K. (2019, August 6) A Reformed White Nationalist Says the Worst Is Yet to Come. The Atlantic. https://www.theatlantic.com/politics/archive/2019/08/conversation-christian-picciolini/595543//

Beran, D. (2019). *It Came From Something Awful*. Macmillan.

Berger, J.M. (2018). *Extremism*. MIT Press.

Bindner, L. & Gluck, R. (2022, July 1). The Buffalo Attack – Insights From the Suspected Terrorist's Diary. GNET. https://gnet-research.org/2022/07/01/the-buffalo-attack-insights-from-the-suspected-terrorists-diary/.

Brandom, R. (2021, August 17). Roblox is struggling to moderate re-creations of mass shootings. The Verge. https://www.theverge.com/2021/8/17/22628624/roblox-moderation-trust-and-safety-terrorist-content-christchurch.

Center on Terrorism, Extremism, and Counterterrorism (CTEC) (2022, May 31). Dangerous Organizations and Bad Actors: The Patriot Front. https://www.middlebury.edu/institute/academics/centers-initiatives/ctec/ctec-publications/dangerous-organizations-and-bad-actors-patriot.

Crawford, B., Keen, F., & Suarez-Tangil, G. (2020). Memetic Irony and the Promotion of Violence within Chan Cultures. Centre for Research and Evidence on Security Threats. https://crestresearch.ac.uk/resources/memetic-irony-and-the-promotion-of-violence-within-chan-cultures/.

Dangerous Organizations and Bad Actors: The Patriot Front (2022, May 31). Center on Terrorism, Extremism, and Counterterrorism. https://www.middlebury.edu/institute/academics/centers-initiatives/ctec/ctec-publications/dangerous-organizations-and-bad-actors-patriot.

Dibbell, J. (2008, January 18). Mutilated Furries, Flying Phalluses: Put the Blame on Griefers, the Sociopaths of the Virtual World. Wired. https://www.wired.com/2008/01/mfgoons/?currentPage=1.

Facepunch (2006). *Gary's Mod*. [Videogame]

Giles, J. (2007). Serious Grief. *New Scientist, 195*(2619), 52–53.

Hafez, M. (2016). The Ties that Bind: How Terrorists Exploit Family Bonds. *CTC Sentinel*, (9), 2.

Harbinger, J. (2020, February 27). Christian Picciolini | Breaking Hate Part Two (No. 318) [Audio podcast episode]. https://www.jordanharbinger.com/christian-picciolini-breaking-hate-part-two/.

Hearts of Iron IV (2016). [Videogame]

Herrman, J. (2014). Internet Terror Cell Neutralized. The Awl. https://www.theawl.com/2014/04/internet-terror-cell-neutralized/.

Hodge, E. & Hallgrimsdottir, H. (2019). Networks of Hate: The Alt Right, "Troll Culture," and the Cultural Geography of Social Movement Spaces Online. *Journal of Borderlands Studies, 4*, 563–580.

Holmer, G., Bauman, P., & Aryaeinejad, K. (2018). Measuring Up: Evaluating the Impact of P/CVE Programs. United States Institute of Peace. https://www.usip.org/sites/default/files/2018-09/preventing-countering-violent-extremism-measuringup.pdf.

Howes, S. & Bennett, S. (2022, February 19). Revealed: The "Nazi Gas Chambers" in a Metaverse Game Played by Children as Young as Seven Around the World. Daily Mail. https://www.dailymail.co.uk/news/article-10531139/The-Nazi-gas-chambers-metaverse-game-played-children-young-seven-world.html.

Huey, L. (2015). This is Not Your Mother's Terrorism: Social Media, Online Radicalization and the Practice of Political Jamming. *Journal of Terrorism Research, 6*(2).

Kan, M. (2018, May 30). Creator of "Active Shooter" Speaks Out: I'm No Psychopath. PCMag. https://www.pcmag.com/news/creator-of-active-shooter-speaks-out-im-no-psychopath.

Kelley, B. (2017). Fashwave, the Electronic Music of the Alt-Right, Is Just More Hateful Subterfuge. Southern Poverty Law Center. https://www.splcenter.org/

hatewatch/2017/10/17/fashwave-electronic-music-alt-right-just-more-hateful-subterfuge.

Koehler, D., Fiebig, V., & Jugl, I. (2022). From Gaming to Hating: Extreme-Right Ideological Indoctrination and Mobilization for Violence of Children on Online Gaming Platforms. *Political Psychology*, 44(2). 10.1111/pops.12855.

Kowert, R. (2015). *Video Games and Social Competence*. Routledge.

Kowert, R. (2020). Dark Participation in Games. *Frontiers in Psychology*, 11(598947). https://www.frontiersin.org/articles/10.3389/fpsyg.2020.598947/full.

Kowert, R. (2021). Toxic, Schmoxic: Normalization of Hate in Gaming Spaces. Meaningful Play Conference 2021, East Lansing, Michigan.

Kowert, R. & Crevoshay, E. (2022). Harassment of Game Makers: Prevalence and Impact. https://f1000research.com/articles/11-1518/v1.

Kowert, R. & Newhouse, A. (2021). Landscape of Extremist Behaviour in Games. Game Developers Conference 2021, San Francisco, California

Kowert, R. & Newhouse, A. (2023). Digital Games as Cultural Assets of Influence. In *The Sociology of Violent Extremism*. Oxford University Press.

Levy, A. (2021, March 9). How Indie Game Makers Turned Roblox into a $30 Billion Company. CNBC. https://www.cnbc.com/2021/03/09/roblox-ipo-how-game-developers-built-a-30-billion-platform.html.

Littler, M. & Lee, B. (Eds.) (2021). *Digital Extremisms: Readings in violence, radicalisation and extremism in the online space*. Palgrave Macmillan.

Miller, C. & Silva, S. (2021, September 23). Extremists Using Video-Game Chats to Spread Hate. BBC. https://www.bbc.com/news/technology-58600181.

Minecraft (2011). [Videogame]

Nagle, A. (2017). *Kill All Normies: Online culture wars from 4chan and tumblr to Trump and the AltRight*. Zero Books.

Newhouse, A. (2021). The Threat Is the Network: The Multi-Node Structure of Neo-Fascist Accelerationism. *CTC Sentinel*, 14(5), 17–25.

Orland, K. (2015, November 8). Columbine Massacre RPG Creator Banned from College Campus, Film Festival [Updated]. Ars Technica. https://arstechnica.com/gaming/2015/11/columbine-massacre-rpg-creator-banned-from-college-campus-film-festival/.

Phelan, A., White, J., Wallner, C., & Paterson, J. (2023). Introductory Guide to Understanding Misogyny and the Far-Right. Centre for Research and Evidence on Security Threats. https://crestresearch.ac.uk/resources/introductory-guide-to-understanding-misogyny-and-the-far-right/.

Radicalisation Awareness Network (2021). Digital Grooming Tactics on Video Gaming and Video Gaming Adjacent Platforms: Threats and Opportunities. chrome-extension://efaidnbmnnnibpcajpcglclefindmkaj/ https://home-affairs.ec.europa.eu/system/files/2021-05/ran_c-n_conclusion_paper_grooming_through_gaming_15-16032021_en.pdf.

Romaniuk, P. (2015). EVALUATING CVE MEASURES: PROGRESS AND PRAGMATISM. In *Does CVE Work?: Lessons learned from the global effort to counter violent extremism* (pp.35–38). Global Center on Cooperative Security. http://www.jstor.org/stable/resrep20265.9.

Roblox (2006). [Videogame]

Rosenblat, M.O. & Barrett, P.M. (2023). Gaming the System: How Extremists Exploit Gaming Sites and What Can Be Done to Counter Them. NYU Stern Center for Business and Human Rights. https://bhr.stern.nyu.edu/tech-gaming-report.

Schlegel, L. (2021). Connecting, Competing, and Trolling: "User Types" in Digital Gamified Radicalization Processes. *Perspectives on Terrorism*, 15(4), 54–64.

Second Life (2003). [Videogame]

Schrock, A. & boyd, d. (n.d.). Online Threats to Youth: Solicitation, Harassment, and Problematic Content. Berkman Center for Internet & Society. https://cyber.harvard.edu/sites/cyber.law.harvard.edu/files/RAB_Lit_Review_121808_0.pdf.

Scrivens, R., Davies, G., Gaudette, T., & Frank, R. (2022). Comparing Online Posting Typologies among Violent and Nonviolent Right-Wing Extremists. *Studies in Conflict & Terrorism*, 1–23. 10.1080/1057610x.2022.2099269.

Shadnia, D., Newhouse, A., Kriner, M., & Bradley, A. (2022). Militant Accelerationism Coalitions: A Case Study in Neo-Fascist Accelerationist Coalition Building Online. Tech Against Terrorism. https://www.techagainstterrorism.org/wp-content/uploads/2022/06/CTEC__TAT-Accelerationism-Report-.pdf.

Smith, L. (2021, January 26). Lone Wolves Connected Online: A History of Modern White Supremacy. New York Times. https://www.nytimes.com/2021/01/26/us/louis-beam-white-supremacy-internet.html.

Statista (2023). Daily Active Users (DAU) of Roblox Games Worldwide from 4th Quarter 2018 to 2nd "uarter 2023. https://www.statista.com/statistics/1192573/daily-active-users-global-roblox/.

Tuters, M. & Hagen, S. (2020). (((They))) rule: Memetic antagonism and nebulous othering on 4chan. *New Media & Society*, 22(12), 2218–2237.

Upchurch, H.E. (2021). The Iron March Forum and the Evolution of the "Skull Mask" Neo-Fascist *Network*. *CTC Sentinel*, 14(10), 27–37.

Vichot, R. (2009). "Doing it for the Lulz?": Online Communities of Practice and Offline Tactical Media [Master's thesis]. Georgia Institute of Technology. https://smartech.gatech.edu/bitstream/handle/1853/28098/vichot_ray_200905_mast.pdf?sequence=1&isAllowed=y.

Vidino, L. & Hughes, S. (2015). Countering Violent Extremism in America. Program on Extremism. https://extremism.gwu.edu/sites/g/files/zaxdzs5746/files/CVE%20in%20America.pdf.

Weimann, G. (2008). WWW.Al-Qaeda: The Reliance of al-Qaeda on the Internet. In *Responses to Cyber Terrorism* (pp. 61–69). IOS Press.

Wofford, T. (2017). Fuck You and Die: An Oral History of Something Awful. Vice News. https://www.vice.com/en/article/nzg4yw/fuck-you-and-die-an-oral-history-of-something-awful.

Yee, N. (2002). Befriending Ogres and Wood-Elves – Understanding Relationship Formation in MMORPGs. nickyee.com. http://www.nickyee.com/hub/relationships/home.html.

Zelenkauskaite, A., Toivanen, P., Huhtamäki, J., & Valaskivi, K. (2020). Shades of Hatred Online: 4chan Duplicate Circulation Surge During Hybrid Media Events. *First Monday*, 26(1). 10.5210/fm.v26i1.11075.

5

EXTREMISM ON GAMING (-ADJACENT) PLATFORMS

Jacob Davey

The study of the intersection between gaming and extremism has focussed largely on a few key areas: the presence of gamers and gaming culture in extremist communities, with a particular focus on the #GamerGate scandal of 2014, which saw significant mobilization of gamers in a large-scale harassment campaign (Peckford, 2020); the gamification of extremism (Schlegel, 2020); the co-option of gaming aesthetics and culture by extremists (Munn, 2019); the creation of (bespoke) games by extremists (Robinson & Whittaker, 2021); and potential vulnerabilities that might make gamers susceptible to radicalization (Condis, 2020).

However, although there is a growing corpus of literature around the topic, one area that requires more thorough investigation are gaming (-adjacent) platforms. These are digital platforms that were originally created to support the broader gaming community online, either by facilitating community building and conversation between gamers, or to allow gamers to livestream their activity. Accordingly, they can be seen as the digital infrastructure that surrounds gaming, a cornerstone of global gaming communities, and essential to the transmission of gaming culture.

One example of a gaming (-adjacent) platform is *Steam* (https://store.steampowered.com/). *Steam* is, at its core, a videogame distribution service. Launched in September 2003 as a software client for Valve's games, it expanded in 2005 to distribute third-party titles. However, since its launch it has introduced a range of other functionality, including social networking and community building. Accordingly, *Steam* can be seen to be both a gaming platform and a gaming-adjacent platform.

DOI: 10.4324/9781003388371-6

Twitch (https://www.Twitch.tv/) is another major platform that can be considered gaming adjacent. *Twitch* is a wildly popular livestreaming site – it had 31 million daily active users as of March 2023 (Ruby, 2023), and is primarily used to broadcast gaming to a global audience. Although the streaming of games makes up the majority of its activity, it is also used for broader communication with popular streamers through its "just chatting" feature (Hutchinson, 2020). In addition to *Twitch*, there are a range of other less popular alternative livestreaming platforms including *DLive* (https://DLive.tv/) and *Bigo* (https://www.bigo.tv/).

Perhaps the most well-known gaming (-adjacent) platform is *Discord* (https://Discord.com/). *Discord* is a chat platform that allows users to communicate with instant messaging and video and chat calls and was originally created to facilitate communication between gamers. One key function of *Discord* is the ability for users to create "'servers" – spaces in which groups of individuals can communicate and build communities. The platform has a sizable user base which is expected to grow to 196.2 million monthly active users and 514 million registered users in 2023 (Turner, 2023).

These platforms share similar functions to other social media platforms, and, in the case of *Discord* and *Twitch*, have made active efforts to expand their user base beyond the core constituent of gamers. It has long been noted that extremists are early adopters of technology (Bartlett, 2014), and, accordingly, it should be recognized that by providing opportunities for people to build networks, broadcast to other users, and share content, these gaming-adjacent platforms provide opportunities for extremists to connect and advance their worldview.

This is starkly illustrated by several high-profile cases of extremist use of gaming (-adjacent) platforms. In recent years, there have been a number of incidents of extremist activity on *Discord*. Perhaps most notoriously, the white supremacist attacker who killed ten in Buffalo, New York (USA) in May 2022, used a private *Discord* server as he planned his attack, sharing his diary and manifesto with friends on the platform (Thompson *et al.*, 2022). The platform was similarly used by the planners of the 2017 Unite the Right rally, which saw hundreds of right-wing extremists gather in Charlottesville, Virginia (USA), and culminating in a vehicular attack on counter-protestors that left one individual, Heather Heyer, dead, and 35 others injured (Davey & Ebner, 2017). Additionally, German far-right extremists utilized the platform to coordinate efforts to disrupt the 2017 German federal election through targeted harassment and the use of 'meme warfare' - the targeted spamming of ideological content in the form of memes with the intention of injecting extremist talking points into wider discussion around the election (Davey & Ebner, 2017). Furthermore, livestreaming platforms have been utilized by extremists. *Twitch* was used to broadcast a 2019 attack on a synagogue in Halle (Germany), which left two people dead (Wong, 2019), and also the 2022 attack in Buffalo (Hern & Milmo, 2022). *DLive* was similarly used by several users to livestream the 2021 insurrection at the US Capitol (Hayden, 2021).

The above examples illustrate the concerning use of gaming (-adjacent) platforms by extremists, and, in and of themselves, demonstrate the importance of analyzing these platforms to those who wish to understand and counter extremists' digital strategies. The urgency of this need is compounded by the growth in popularity of these platforms. Both *Discord* and *Twitch* are seeing steady increases in their user bases, driven, in part, by strategies designed to broaden the user base of these platforms beyond gamers. This expansion provides an opportunity for established extremist communities to radicalize and reach new audiences. This is of particular concern when the central role of online communications in radicalization is considered – between 2010 and 2020, the Profiles of Individual Radicalization in the US (PIRUS) dataset, the largest database of open-source information on radicalized individuals in the USA, showed a 413% rise in the internet playing the primary role in the radicalization process for those under the age of 30 compared to the previous decade. Accordingly, analyzing gaming-adjacent platforms provides the opportunity to better understand the ways in which extremists engage in gaming and gaming culture, but also, a potential window to understand how extremist gamers interact with broader communities online.

There is a small but growing corpus of literature on gaming (-adjacent) platforms. This includes work led by the Institute for Strategic Dialogue (ISD) tracking extremist use of *DLive, Twitch, Steam,* and *Discord* (Davey, 2021), work from the Anti-Defamation League (ADL) exploring extremist use of *Steam* (ADL, 2020), and helpful summaries that provide broader overviews of the most salient overviews of extremist activity on these platforms, from the Radicalization Awareness Network (Lakhani, 2021), and the United Nations Office of Counter Terrorism (Schlegel & Amarasingam, 2022). However, analysis on this topic is far from comprehensive and there is the need for further research on this important set of platforms.

This chapter provides insights gleaned from scoping analysis conducted at ISD of two gaming (-adjacent) platforms: the chat and community building service *Discord* (Gallagher *et al.*, 2021), and the video game distribution and community service *Steam* (Vaux *et al.*, 2021). These two platforms are selected due to their shared role as community incubators, and, accordingly, they provide useful comparison points by which to understand the dynamics underpinning circles of extremists. To ensure depth of analysis this comes with a tradeoff, and other types of gaming (-adjacent) platform – particularly streaming services such as *Twitch* and *DLive* are left out here. This chapter seeks to provide insight into the way extremists use these platforms, why they are used, as well as insights into the role gaming appears to play among extremist communities.

Research Approach and Limitations

This chapter focusses specifically on right-wing extremist use of gaming (-adjacent) platforms – although this should not suggest that no jihadists or other extremist movements are using gaming (-adjacent) platforms for their ends. Right-wing extremists are here understood to be groups and individuals that exhibit at least three of the characteristics of nationalism, racism, xenophobia, anti-democracy, and strong-state advocacy, as laid out by Cas Mudde in *The Ideology of the Extreme Right* (Mudde, 2000). These insights are informed by previous analysis conducted at the Institute for Strategic Dialogue (ISD), an independent non-profit working to counter extremism.

The reason this particular set of extremists is focussed on here, as opposed to Islamist, anarchist, far-left, or the emerging cohort of "mixed or unclear" extremists, is shaped both by pressing need and by pragmatism. The contemporary extreme right, more so than any other extremist community, has been noted for its deep connection with online gaming culture – indeed, Gamergate has been seen by many as a pivotal moment in the formation of the so-called "alternative right" (Condis, 2020). However, it is possible that there has been a greater focus of right-wing extremism with gaming spaces because this cohort of actors is louder and easier to find and accordingly easier to analyze as well. To better evidence the wide range of extremist users of gaming (-adjacent) platforms would come at the expense of depth of analysis on one cohort. Therefore, to maintain focus this chapter hones in on this key cohort of extremists. Accordingly, this analysis shouldn't be taken to suggest that other types of extremist actor are not using gaming (-adjacent) platforms.

The findings presented here on extreme right-wing activity on gaming (-adjacent) platforms are derived from a digital ethnographic methodology, and primarily present a qualitative analysis of communities and their shared content drawn from the analysis of 45 public groups on *Steam* and 24 servers on *Discord* – all of which primarily served to host right-wing extremist communities. This ethnographic analysis was conducted within a strict ethical framework and relied on observations of publicly accessible material – accordingly, it does not provide deep analysis into interpersonal activity such as voice chats, in-game discussion, or activity in private channels. Accordingly, the lack of insight into these areas of the platforms and the understanding of social dynamics that could have been gleaned here should be recognized as a limitation in this research.

These channels were primarily identified through an "extremist first" approach, whereby the native search functionality on each platform was used to identify channels or communities that appeared to be affiliated with extremist movements or groups, or that used terminology and imagery associated with the extreme right wing. On *Steam*, this was accompanied by network mapping and expansion. This methodological approach also provides a limitation to this piece, as it provides analysis on trends within identified extremist communities, rather than revealing insight on the ways in which extremists interact with broader, non-radicalized users on these platforms. Accordingly, it is recognized that this chapter is limited in providing insight into potential radicalization dynamics.

Discord: An Insight into Youth Radicalization and Splintering Ideology

Discord is a platform that has seen significant growth in recent years – growing from 25 million registered users in 2016 to 196.2 million monthly active users and 514 million registered users in 2023 (Turner, 2023). These users are diverse – running from gamers, to communities for co-working, to other interest groups. However, the platform is also frequently associated with fringe internet culture, including extremism (Heslep & Berge, 2021). At the time of writing, the platform has been at the center of a major leak of US intelligence reports – apparently driven by a 21-year-old airman who shared the material with a community of young people brought together by their appreciation for racist memes (Browning & Thompson, 2023).

Beyond its association with major extremist events, the platform has also been frequently identified for its widespread use by far-right extremists for community building, coordinated trolling, and the ease with which hateful communities can be identified (Heslep & Berge, 2021). One key concern with regards to the extreme right currently is the radicalization of youth, as there is a wealth of evidence pointing towards an increase of young people becoming involved in extremist movements and perpetrating attacks (Pandith & Ware, 2021; CTP, 2023). The role of *Discord* in youth radicalization was starkly revealed by the Buffalo shooter who was 18 at the time he committed the attack and for whom the platform – among other fringe sites – played a crucial role in his broader radicalization (Amarasingam *et al.*, 2022).

During analysis conducted at ISD of 25 *Discord* servers, we found a number of instances where channels surveyed users for their age and gender. Although not necessarily representative of the entire extremist ecosystem on the platform, this analysis suggested that users skewed young. Of 62 instances where users provided their age, 45 users self-reported their age as between 13–17 years old, with only 17 users reporting to be above 18. The average age for users in the sample was 15. This finding raises an important consideration around the broader role of gaming (-adjacent) platforms: as a potential vector in youth radicalization. Although the average gamer is 35 years old, there are 51.1 million children gaming in the US (Jovanovic, 2023). On *Discord*, just under 40% of users are aged 18–24 (Susic, 2023), while on *Twitch* – another important gaming (-adjacent) platform – 22.3% of users are aged 16–24 (Clement, 2022). Given the valuable role these platforms play in nurturing internet culture, and the well documented overlaps between internet culture and contemporary extremism (Fielitz & Ahmed, 2021), this should be of particular concern for policymakers, analysts, and practitioners seeking to counter radicalization.

Over the course of ISD's analysis on *Discord*, we also identified ways in which youth radicalization can play out. Through qualitatively analyzing conversations, we found that these servers seem to initially operate as spaces for young people to explore and ask questions about the extreme right. On the surface, these seem relatively naïve – in one example, a young person inquired where they can find Nazi content online. However, in several instances we found that these inquisitive young people were directed to extremist channels on other platforms, including *Telegram* – which hosts a wide range of largely unmoderated white supremacist communities, including those that promote terrorism (Guhl & Davey, 2020). This "off-ramping" can happen for a number of reasons, including individuals moving to other platforms for more privacy, less moderation, or the opportunity to integrate into more radicalized communities.

Beyond off-ramping to other platforms there is evidence that community dynamics on *Discord* can reward radicalization with deeper access to more privileged and secretive communities. Analysis of 2017 efforts to disrupt the German Federal elections identified a channel called Reconquista Germanica, which was dedicated to coordinated trolling with the aim of rewarding the far-right AfD party in the polls (Davey & Ebner, 2017). In this instance, the deeper commitment to the cause individuals showed – by creating memes or harassing opponents – the greater access they were given to more and more exclusive chats. In this fashion, engaging in extremist activity on *Discord* becomes gamified – turning radicalization into a real life role-playing game (RPG).

The loose structure afforded by a multitude of *Discord* servers also potentially lends itself to another key trend that is associated with contemporary youth radicalization – the splintering of movements and ideologies. In recent years, the extreme right has undergone a "post-organizational" dynamic (Davey *et al.*, 2022), whereby the role of organized groups has diminished as looser online communities shape the extremist ecosystem, and radicalization is increasingly characterized by online inter-actions with myriad ideologies and communities. Of the 25 extreme right *Discord* servers analyzed, none was affiliated with specific extremist orga-nizations. Although they shared content from specific groups – including the terrorist organization Atomwaffen Division[1] – they instead functioned as looser discussion communities, mirroring the broader use of the platform. Accordingly, this highlights how gaming adjacent platforms, among other fringe digital services, are likely playing a role in broader transformations in the entire dynamic of right-wing extremism.

Steam: The Role of Gaming in Extremist Communities

Steam is the largest single distribution site for PC games, catering to more than 120 million active users monthly, and providing access to over 50,000 games (Dean, 2023). However, beyond this, it also has community features that enable users to connect with friends, participate in discussion forums, and join groups. While many groups serve as hubs for gamers with shared interests, some have been created to enable networking among individuals supporting right wing extremism.

To identify the 45 channels analyzed here, keyword searches were conducted using a curated list of terms associated with extreme right-wing ideology and organizations, resulting in an initial list of 36 *Steam* groups. *Steam*'s architecture means that the members of any group are publicly visible, and, if a user has made their profile public, all the groups that they are a member of are also visible. Therefore, an automated web crawler was used to collect the URLs of the profile pages of those users belonging to the original 36 groups identifying groups that had members in common. A crawler was then deployed to collect all of the groups each of those users was a member of, providing a wider picture of these extreme right-right group members' activity on *Steam* groups, their interconnectedness, and relative significance within such communities, identifying 35,151 groups.

These groups were then ranked by the number of users common with the original seed list of groups. These ranked groups were then assessed and coded for relevance to extreme right mobilization, based on the content available in the group. The top 200 of these ranked groups were assessed for content relevant to right-wing extremism. Through this pro-cess we were left with a cohort of 45 groups that hosted far-right extremist communities. The largest of these groups had 4,403 members, the smallest had seven members, and the average number of members across these groups was 329. The network of 45 channels, which often have members in common, span the extreme right-wing ideological spectrum. This network connects supporters of far-right political parties, such as the British National Party,[2] with groups promoting neo-Nazi organizations, such as Misanthropic Division.[3] Based on a qualitative assessment of visible content channels were categorized based on the types of movement they identified with (see Table 5.1).

A qualitative analysis of publicly accessible comments and chats in these communities suggests that *Steam*'s primary function within the broader extremist online ecosystem is to provide a hub for individual extremists to connect and socialize. In comparison to *Discord*, *Steam* is notable for the presence of more communities affiliated with specific right-wing extremist groups and organizations. Through our analysis, we found channels linked to various organized extremist groups, such as Generation Identity,[4] the Nationalist Front,[5] and the Nordic Resistance movement.[6] This is potentially linked to a few key dynamics.

TABLE 5.1 Overview of different types of extremist channel identified

Coding	Description	No. of groups
UK groups	These groups are specifically related to the UK and cover a range of right wing extremist talking points	8
US-focussed groups	Groups associated with US forums, figures and movements	8
Neo-Nazi	Groups affiliated with known neo-Nazi organizations, or explicitly aligning themselves with Nazi ideological positions or symbols	6
Terrorist or paramilitary groups	Groups that are known to have engaged in acts of terrorism or been involved in paramilitary activities	2
Fascist	Groups openly praising historical fascist movements or associated with neo-fascist groups	8
White nationalist	Groups purporting to promote the interests of people of European ancestry while claiming not to be supremacist	4
Far-right political parties	Groups affiliated with far-right political parties that have taken part in elections	4
Generic far-right extremists	Groups not directly affiliated with a particular group, movement or ideology, which nevertheless host extreme right-wing content	6

Our analysis found that *Discord* groups were primarily relatively short lived, potentially suggesting a high attrition rate as channels are removed through platform moderation. However, on *Steam*, some channels were still active after ten years on the platform – suggesting that it can act as a space for building lasting communities that are better suited to organized movements. The demographic distribution of users on these platforms also presents another possible answer to these differences – while *Discord* users skew young, a majority of *Steam* users are aged over 30 (Wise, 2023), and, accordingly, extremists on the platform potentially became engaged with the extreme right before the acceleration of post-organizational dynamics.

Perhaps unsurprisingly for a platform designed to facilitate multiplayer gaming online, gaming plays a central and multifaceted role in many of the *Steam* communities analyzed here. In a number of instances, gaming appears to act as an ideological signifier, with groups associating with games such as *Lock Her Up: The Trump Supremacy* (Three Guys Game Studio). Additionally, a number of communities where users are supportive of far-right extremism are specifically set up around historical strategy games. While these games do not have any extremist content, they do appeal to extreme right-wing ideology, by allowing users to play out fantasies of destroying Muslim factions during the Crusades, or winning the Second World War for the Nazis. These included the popular *Total War* (Sega) series, and many of the strategy games released by Paradox Interactive, such as *Hearts of Iron IV*, *Europa Universalis*, and *Crusader Kings*. Some of these games also allowed for alternate history scenarios, catered to by mods, some of them designed by white supremacists (Winkie, 2018). The largest of all the *Steam* groups examined was called "Deus vult!." The phrase originates with Pope Urban II's call for Christians to join the first Crusade in 1095, but has become a popular refrain among players of the *Crusader Kings* series, and additionally for the extreme right to whom Muslims are seen as an enemy. There is also an extremist mod for *Crusader Kings* of this name, which allows players to merge their Crusader kingdom with that of Nazi Germany, and gas or enslave Muslims. This large group was frequently active at the time of analysis.

In the Deus Vult group, a discussion thread, titled "Political feelings. Speak your mind," asked other users whether they were in the group because of their feelings towards Muslims, or whether it was just an interest in the Crusades. At least 22% of the replies from users suggested racism against Muslims as a reason for joining the group. This demonstrates how for some extremist users of *Steam*, online strategy games allow them to play out extremist fantasies with like-minded individuals, allowing communities to collectively reinforce their ideologies.

More broadly, however, our analysis suggests that gaming seems to be largely used as a means of community building rather than as a deliberate strategy for radicalization or recruitment, with individuals who are already engaged with far-right extremism using *Steam* as a platform to connect with like-minded individuals over a shared hobby. Due to the ethical framework governing this analysis, researchers did not attempt to engage in any online games with these communities, and thus it remains a possibility that this in-game socializing provides an opportunity for broader coordination and planning.

As well as connecting individuals who support far-right extremism, a number of groups encouraged members to join conversations on outside platforms. For example, in one group, a user posted a link to the *Telegram* channel for a White Lives Matter march. Users also linked to outside platforms related to gaming and extremism, including links to GamerUprising, a far-right forum linked to the neo-Nazi site The Daily Stormer, as well as the official websites of extremist movements. We also found evidence of individuals asking communities affiliated with specific groups for advice on how to join these groups. As with *Discord* then, the analysis of *Steam* groups reveals how communities can use gaming (-adjacent) platforms to "off-ramp" interested followers into spaces where more egregious extremist activity takes place. Accordingly, in both *Discord* and *Steam*, we can chart a dynamic whereby the gaming adjacent platforms act as an intermediary before individuals engage in potentially more extreme spaces.

Raiding Activity and the Gamification of Harassment

In both *Discord* and *Steam*, communities were observed engaging in raiding – the coordinated trolling and harassment against communities and users who are deemed to be political, social, and racial enemies. This mirrors the use of the term in massively multiplayer online role playing games (RPGs), where clans of gamers aim to defeat their rivals.

On *Discord*, the users analyzed seemed to primarily engage in raids against pro-LGBTQ servers, with two of the servers analyzed primarily set up to function as hubs for extreme right-wing raiding activity. Raids largely occurred through a dynamic by which an individual user would identify communities to target. Following this, groups of users would join these channels in a coordinated fashion to post harassing, hateful, and shocking content with the aim of distressing users, driving them off channels, or having the target channel banned by *Discord* as a result of the bulk of unpleasant material dropped into chats. On servers devoted to this activity, specific channels were used to host links to servers that were the targets of raids. Raiders encouraged each other to be as offensive as possible with the aim of upsetting or angering users on the raided server, and channels often had content banks of offensive memes and content to be shared on raided servers.

Similar dynamics occurred across the *Steam* groups analyzed. In one example, a member of a group named after Ian Stuart, the frontman of the British white power band Skrewdriver, shared a link to a channel set up for Israeli gamers, encouraging other members to "help me raid this juden group" (*Juden* being German for Jews). The comments section of the Israeli group shows that neo-Nazi and anti-Semitic comments were consistently posted in the group just two minutes after the instructions for the raid had been posted in the Ian Stuart group. In another example, members of a group asked users to post negative reviews on games in the *Steam* store which they feel "silence criticism, manipulate scores, maltreat employees and push SJW [social justice warrior] agendas."

In the same way that engagement with extremist *Discord* servers gamifies radicalization, the use of raids demonstrates the gamified nature of harassment on gaming adjacent platforms – with the cyberbullying of opponents becoming a game in and of itself. Users clearly relish taking part in this subversive activity, and the combative activity of raiding serves to strengthen in-group activity, suggesting that this "fun" extremist activity could itself help facilitate radicalization.

Conclusion

This chapter provided an overview of dynamics on two gaming (-adjacent) platforms that facilitate the growth of close, deep communities. Just as gaming acts as a way of bringing people together and forging friendships, so do to these extremist channels. Across both *Discord* and *Steam*, we can see how engagement in these extremist communities itself becomes gamified, with group participation in extremist activity strengthening interpersonal bonds and loyalty to specific ideologies or movements. Accordingly, gaming (-adjacent) community platforms can be seen to act as a bridge – bringing game-like activity into extremist activism.

We can also see how extremists use gaming (-adjacent) platforms designed to build communities of gamers to strengthen their extremist movements. In the case of *Discord*, we can see how the rapidly expanding platform has become a vector for youth radicalization, providing a safe space for young people to tentatively explore "edgy" ideologies. On *Steam*, we can see how communities of already radicalized individuals use their channels to maintain close bonds. A comparison of these platforms also reveals how digital spaces can act as mirrors to extremism at different moments in time, but also drive shifts in the broader dynamics under-pinning extremist mobilization globally. On *Steam*, we see an older demographic operating on closely networked communities that match older extremist movements. This is likely a reflection of a lack of mod-eration on the platform given the longevity of these channels, but also highlights how the shared hobby of gaming can help strengthen a long-lasting and closely knit extremist community. On *Discord*, we instead see a very young demographic interacting with a range of channels that are not expressly affiliated with a particular extremist group or organization, but instead with a loosely shared ideology. This is potentially a reflection of the broader dynamic underpinning the platforms use – with individuals engaging with a diverse range of communities – but also strongly mirrors the disparate and loosely defined post-organizational nature of contem-porary right-wing extremism and radicalization.

When extrapolated, these trends also potentially provide insights into the broader relationship between gaming and extremism. Although it is easy to characterize the gaming extremism nexus as one that is reflective of an overwhelmingly toxic gaming culture, or one whereby extremists lurk in games with the intention of luring in vulnerable young people, the dynamic revealed by this analysis is one which is perhaps more complex and reflective of the broader ways in which people make friends online – building close bonds over a shared hobby.

Finally, we can also see how gaming adjacent platforms can act as a bridge between more popular platforms, and more explicit and egregious closed spaces. On *Discord*, interested young people were directed to white supremacist channels on *Telegram*, where they could find deeper ideo-logical content. Although differing slightly in the broader culture under-pinning channels, there is similar evidence on *Steam* of communities using their channels as spaces to direct potentially interested individuals to deeper extremist communities and content.

This analysis highlights the multifaceted ways in which extremists use gaming adjacent platforms to build communities, however, it is by no means exhaustive, and the gaps present in this analysis highlight several promising directions that future research could take. In particular, while this work focusses solely on right-wing extremists, conducting similar analysis of other extremist communities would be particularly valuable. Additionally, analysts did not seek to join the extremist communities they identified in game, in part due to ethical concerns around such research. However, if ethical methodologies for in-game analysis can be developed, then future research of gaming (-adjacent) platforms could be used to identify particular gaming spaces that are relevant to the analysis of extremism, facilitating a more holistic analysis of this important research area.

Notes

1 Atomwaffen Division is an international neo-Nazi terrorist network founded in the United States, but with a presence across North America and Europe.
2 The British National Party (BNP) is a fascist political party based in the United Kingdom.
3 Misanthropic Division is an international neo-Nazi group based in Ukraine, which has been described as a paramilitary organization.
4 Generation Identity is a racist movement originating in France, with a presence across Europe. Its followers advocate for the buildout of society separated across ethnic lines, and are strongly focussed on the supposed replacement of ethnic Europeans by non-Europeans through migration and demographic shifts.
5 The Nationalist Front is a loose coalition of right-wing extremists and white supremacists based in the United States created to unite various extremist groups under a shared umbrella.
6 The Nordic Resistance Movement is a neo-Nazi movement present across the Nordic States.

References

ADL (April 29 2020). This Is Not a Game: How Steam Harbors Extremists. ADL. https://www.adl.org/resources/report/not-game-how-steam-harbors-extremists.

Amarasingam, A., Argentino, M.A., & Macklin, G. (July 2022). The Buffalo Attack: The Cumulative Momentum of Far-Right Terror. *CTC Sentinel*, 15(7). https://ctc.westpoint.edu/the-buffalo-attack-the-cumulative-momentum-of-far-right-terror/.

Bartlett, J. (2014, November 4). Why Terrorists and Far Right Extremists Will Always Be Early Adopters. Daily Telegraph. https://www.telegraph.co.uk/technology/11204744/Why-terrorists-and-far-Right-extremists-will-always-be-early-adopters.html.

Browning, K. & Thompson, S. (2023, April 11). An Online Meme Group Is at the Center of Uproar Over Leaked Military Secrets. New York Times. https://www.nytimes.com/2023/04/11/business/discord-leaked-military-documents.html.

Clement, J. (2022, August 12). Distribution of Twitch.tv Users Worldwide as of May 20202, by Age Group. Statista. https://www.statista.com/statistics/634057/twitch-user-age-worldwide/.

Condis, M. (2020). Hateful Games – Why White Supremacist Recruiters Target Gamers. In J. Reyman & E.M. Sparby, *Digital Ethics – Rhetoric and Responsibility in Online Aggression* (pp. 143–159). Routledge.

Counter Terrorism Policing (2023, March 9). Young People Arrested on Suspicion of Terrorism Related Offences in UK Continues to Rise. Counter Terrorism Policing. https://www.counterterrorism.police.uk/young-people-arrested-on-suspicion-of-terrorism-related-offences-in-the-uk-continues-to-rise/.

Davey, J. (2021, August). Gamers Who Hate: An Introduction to ISD's Gaming and Extremism Series. Institute for Strategic Dialogue. https://www.isdglobal.org/isd-publications/gamers-who-hate-an-introduction-to-isds-gaming-and-extremism-series/.

Davey, J., Comerford, M., Guhl, J., Baldet, W., & Colliver, C. (January 2022). A Taxonomy for the Classification of Post-Organizational Violent Extremist &

Terrorist Content. Institute for Strategic Dialogue. https://www.isdglobal.org/wp-content/uploads/2022/01/A-taxonomy-for-the-classification-of-post-organisational-terrorist-content.pdf.

Davey, J. & Ebner, E. (2017, October). The Fringe Insurgency – Connectivity, Convergence and Mainstreaming of the Extreme Right. Institute for Strategic Dialogue. https://www.isdglobal.org/isd-publications/the-fringe-insurgency-connectivity-convergence-and-mainstreaming-of-the-extreme-right/.

Dean, B. (2023, March 27). Steam Usage and Catalog Stats for 2023. Backlinko. https://backlinko.com/steam-users.

Fielitz, M. & Ahmed, R. (2021, March). It's Not Funny Anymore. Far-Right Extremists' Use of Humour. Radicalisation Awareness Network. https://home-affairs.ec.europa.eu/system/files/2021-03/ran_ad-hoc_pap_fre_humor_20210215_en.pdf.

Gallagher, A., O'Connor, C., Vaux, P., & Davey, J. (2021, August). Gaming and Extremism: The Extreme Right on Discord. Institute for Strategic Dialogue. https://www.isdglobal.org/isd-publications/gaming-and-extremism-the-extreme-right-on-discord/.

Guhl, J. & Davey, J. (2022, June). A Safe Space to Hate: White Supremacist Mobilization on Telegram. Institute for Strategic Dialogue. https://www.isdglobal.org/wp-content/uploads/2020/06/A-Safe-Space-to-Hate2.pdf.

Hayden, M.E. (2021, January 7). Meet DLive: The Livestreaming Platform Used by Trump's Capitol Insurrectionists. SPLC. https://www.splcenter.org/hatewatch/2021/01/07/meet-dlive-livestreaming-platform-used-trumps-capitol-insurrectionists.

Heslep, D.G. & Berge, P. (2021). Mapping Discord's Darkside: Distributed Hate Networks on Disboard. *New Media & Society*, 0(0). 10.1177/14614448211062548.

Hern, A. & Milmo, D. (2022, May 16). Online Hate Under Scrutiny After Buffalo Shooter Streamed Massacre on Twitch. The Guardian. https://www.theguardian.com/us-news/2022/may/16/buffalo-shooter-twitch-streamed-online-hate.

Hutchinson, A. (2020, September 2). Twitch Continues Expansion Beyond Gaming with Global Roll Out of Watch Parties. Social Media Today. https://www.socialmediatoday.com/news/twitch-continues-expansion-beyond-gaming-with-global-roll-out-of-watch-part/584623/.

Jovanovic, B. (2023, May 25). Gamer Demographics: Facts and Stats About the Most Popular Hobby in the World. Dataprot. https://dataprot.net/statistics/gamer-demographics/.

Lakhani, S. (2021). Video Gaming and (Violent) Extremism: An Exploration of the Current Landscape, Trends and Threats. European Commission. https://home-affairs.ec.europa.eu/system/files/2022-02/EUIF%20Technical%20Meeting%20on%20Video%20Gaming%20October%202021%20RAN%20Policy%20Support%20paper_en.pdf.

Mudde, C. (2020). *The Ideology of the Extreme Right*. Oxford University Press.

Munn, L. (2019, June 1). Alt-Right Pipeline: Individual Journeys to Extremism Online. https://firstmonday.org/ojs/index.php/fm/article/view/10108.

Pandith, F. & Ware, J. (2021, March 22). Teen Terrorism Inspired by Social Media Is on the Rise. Here's What We Need to Do. NBC News. https://www.nbcnews.com/think/opinion/teen-terrorism-inspired-social-media-rise-here-s-what-we-ncna1261307.

Paradox Interactive (2000) *Europa Universalis*. [Videogame]

Paradox Interactive (2004) *Crusader Kings*. [Videogame]

Paradox Interactive (2016) *Hearts of Iron IV*. [Videogame]

Peckford, A. (2020). *Right Wing Extremism in a Video Game Community? A qualitative content analysis exploring the discourse of the Reddit GamerGate community r/KotakuInAction*. Simon Fraser University Press.

Robinson, N. & Whittaker, J. (2021). Playing for Hate? Extremism, Terrorism and Videogames. *Studies in Conflict & Terrorism*. 10.1080/1057610X.2020.1866740.

Ruby, D. (2023). Twitch Statistics 2023. Demandsage. https://www.demandsage.com/twitch-users/.

Schlegel, L. (2020). Jumanji Extremism? How Games and Gamification Could Facilitate Radicalization Processes. *Journal for Deradicalization*, 50–92.

Schlegel, L. & Amarasingam, A. (2022, October 5). Examining the Intersection Between Gaming and Extremism. United Nations Office of Counter-terrorism. https://www.un.org/counterterrorism/sites/www.un.org.counterterrorism/files/221005_research_launch_on_gaming_ve.pdf.

Sega (2000) *Total War*. [Videogame]

Susic, P. (2023, February 22). 39+ Discord Statistics: Users, Servers, Demographics, Revenue (2023). Headphones Addict. https://headphonesaddict.com/discord-users/.

Thompson, C., Tucker, E., & Sisak, M. (2022, May 17). Online Diary: Buffalo Gunman Plotted Attack for Months. AP News. https://apnews.com/article/buffalo-supermarket-shooting-19514b0c6524bd428f4167ad9b490a12.

Three Guys Game Studio (2018). *Lock Her Up: The Trump Supremacy*. [Videogame]

Turner, A. (2023, July). Discord Users – How Many People Use Discord? Bankmycell. https://www.bankmycell.com/blog/number-of-discord-users/.

Vaux, P., Gallagher, A., & Davey, J. (2021, August). Gaming and Extremism: The Extreme Right on Steam. Institute for Strategic Dialogue. https://www.isdglobal.org/isd-publications/gaming-and-extremism-the-extreme-right-on-steam/.

Winkie, L. (2018, June 6). The Struggle Over Gamers Who Use Mods To Create Racist Alternate Histories. Kotaku. https://kotaku.com/the-struggle-over-gamers-who-use-mods-to-create-racist-1826606138.

Wise, J. (2023, April 4). How Many People Use Steam in 2023? Earthweb. https://earthweb.com/how-many-people-use-steam/.

Wong, J.C. (2019, October 10). Germany Shooting Suspect Livestreamed Attempted Attack on Synagogue. The Guardian. https://www.theguardian.com/world/2019/oct/09/germany-shooting-synagogue-halle-livestreamed.

6

HATE AND EXTREMISM ON GAMING PLATFORMS

Insights from Surveys with the Gaming Community

Amarnath Amarasingam and Daniel Kelley

Terrorist groups across the ideological spectrum use gaming-related content and spaces for a variety of reasons, in a variety of ways, and with varying degrees of success, both strategically and organically. Discussions around games and extremism are reminiscent of the debates around the potential connection between violent videogames and violence that first erupted in public discussions in the 1990s. However, unlike the debates of the 1990s, current discussions on gaming and extremism center less on media effects and focus more on the strategic use of these interactive media for nefarious purposes (Rosenblat and Barrett, 2023; Wells *et al.*, 2023).

The allure of the vast and interconnected gaming community has drawn extremist actors to exploit gaming-related content and spaces, employing diverse strategies to achieve their goals. These tactics can encompass a wide spectrum, from carefully planned and coordinated efforts to more spontaneous and organic activities within gaming communities. By leveraging the immersive and interactive nature of gaming, these extremist groups aim to amplify their messages, radicalize vulnerable individuals, and establish a presence in virtual environments where they can freely propagate their extremist beliefs. This intersection between gaming and extremism poses significant challenges for online safety, counterterrorism efforts, and the preservation of inclusive and tolerant gaming spaces.

What is often missing from these debates are the voices of gamers themselves, and their experiences on these platforms. That is the focus of this chapter. This chapter first provides a short review of some of the relevant previous research on gaming and extremism, as well as experiences of gaming communities with respect to extremism and hate.

DOI: 10.4324/9781003388371-7

Following this, the chapter summarizes results from two surveys that the authors have conducted with gaming communities. The first survey was supported by the United Nations Office of Counter Terrorism (Schlegel & Amarasingam, 2022) and the second is the survey conducted by the Anti-Defamation League (ADL Center for Technology and Society, 2022d) which has been conducted every year since 2019. The chapter closes by looking at some recent trends by tech companies to address hate and extremism on their platforms.

Past Debates: Gaming and Violence

Since the 1990s, violent videogames, especially first-person shooters, have been repeatedly blamed by the media as the main impetus for school shootings throughout the USA. This was true of the Columbine school shooting in 1999, the Heath high school shooting in 1997, the Sandy Hook killings in 2012, and the Parkland shooting in 2018 (Campbell, 2018). As such, the impact of violent videogames has been a hot topic among psychologists, sparking much debate as to whether exposure to violent videogames increases violent, aggressive, or antisocial behavior (Kowert & Quandt, 2016). Those in support of this view argue that repeated exposure to violent videogames desensitizes youth and normalizes extreme violence, resulting in decreased sympathy for others and increased antisocial behaviors such as delinquency, aggression, and violence (Anderson & Bushman, 2001; Anderson & Murphy, 2003; Gentile *et al.*, 2004; Carnagey, Anderson & Bushman, 2007; Greitemeyer & McLatchie, 2011). The other side of the debate denies or cannot substantiate any significant causal relationship between repeated exposure to violent videogames and increased antisocial behaviors (Williams & Skoric, 2005; Unsworth *et al.*, 2007). Some studies even found violent videogames actually reduced aggression (Colwell & Kato, 2003; Barnett & Coulson, 2010). In addition to the primary debate, psychologists have considered whether violent videogames in and of themselves are the problem or whether certain predispositions, such as violent upbringings or psychiatric disorders, contribute to a youth's susceptibility to violence.

In several meta-analytic reviews of the effects of playing violent videogames on aggression, Craig A. Anderson, alongside various co-authors, found that videogames do indeed increase aggression (Anderson & Dill, 2000; Anderson & Bushman, 2001; Anderson, 2003; Anderson & Murphy, 2003). However, many of Anderson's studies have been critiqued for inherent flaws in methodologies, such as the comparative nature of his past experiments, use of unclarified outcome measures, failing to cite any peer-reviewed studies supportive of his conclusion, ignoring conflicting research findings, and weak evidence considering the gravity of their assertions (Bensley & Van Eenwyk, 2001, pp. 254–255; Freedman, 2001; Hilgard *et al.*, 2017). In 2015, the American Psychological Association (APA) concluded that aggressive videogames might be related to aggression; however, its findings were also accused of flawed methods and potential biases (Elson *et al.*, 2019; Ferguson, 2019, p. 440). In 2020, the APA updated its findings to state that "there is insufficient scientific evidence to support a causal link between violent video games and violent behavior" (American Psychological Association, 2020).

A comprehensive, two-year-long study conducted in 2019 found that "it would take 27 h/day of explicit violent gameplay to produce clinically noticeable changes in aggression" (Ferguson, 2008, p. 1447). The study had a large sample size of 3,034 youth and employed nonsensical outcomes to compare the statistical relevance of the findings; the effect sizes for aggression and prosocial outcomes were comparable to the nonsensical outcomes. As such, the evidence from this study is in line with other longitudinal studies and does not support the conclusion that aggressive videogames are a predictor of later aggression or reduced prosocial behavior in youth (Ferguson, 2008; von Salisch *et al.*, 2011; Breuer *et al.*, 2015; Lobel *et al.*, 2017). To date, roughly two dozen longitudinal studies have generally found a weak relationship between violent videogames exposure and aggression levels in youth (Ferguson & Wang, 2019, p. 1440).

The power of hindsight shows us that the panic around violent videogames was misguided in its media-in/behavior-out approach. The effects of these debates and the insistence of lawmakers to engage in scientifically uninformed arguments about the potential negative impact of violent videogames, continues to make it difficult to publicly discuss real-world harms that may be happening in and around gaming spaces. However, over the last few years, there has been some work starting to explore games and extremism specifically. This work has varied wildly in its theoretical framework and approaches. Much of this literature focuses on the variety of uses of games by extremists (i.e., for training, for desensitization, etc.) but also game and gaming (-adjacent) platforms – but rarely on the experiences of gamers themselves of hate and extremism.

Current Debates: Games and Extremism

In spite of the fact that games and extremism is a topic receiving more attention by researchers, policymakers, and members of the gaming industry, it still fuels debates in regards to its prevalence and impact. The UNOCT and ADL surveys were created to help build a foundation of knowledge to inform these debates and avoid the overgeneralizations and ill-informed scientific evidence that formed the basis of the previous discussions around videogames and violence. In the next section, we will discuss the outputs of the UNOCT and ADL gamer surveys. These surveys explored a range of aspects of games and gaming cultures including gamification, livestreaming, and game-adjacent spaces. While these different areas are discussed more extensively throughout the book, we wanted to briefly mention them below before moving into a more detailed discussion of several large-scale surveys of gamers themselves and their experiences.

Gamification refers to the "use of game attributes" such as rewards and rankings "in contexts which are traditionally considered non-gaming environments" (Schlegel, 2018, 2020). Gamification has been observed on right-wing extremist *Discord* servers, in private chat groups and on chanboards displaying virtual scoreboards of right-wing extremist perpetrators. Using the appeal of games in extremist contexts is not a new phenomenon. Since the early days of the internet, extremists and terrorist groups have developed videogames specifically designed to spread their ideologies and recruit gamers, such as Al Qaeda's "Quest for Bush" released in 2003, ISIS's version of *Assassin's Creed* "Salil al-Sawarim," its children's app "Library of Zeal," and the new app "The Dawn of Glad Tidings" (Schlegel, 2018).

Livestreaming is another area of interest. Livestreaming refers to the broadcasting of live video footage across a social media platform. Today, there are several popular livestreaming platforms (e.g., *Twitch*, *Facebook Live*, *YouTube*) that host a wide range of content, from videogame play, to cooking demonstrations, to crocheting. Extremists have also utilized these platforms. The right-wing extremist, livestreamed attack in Christchurch, New Zealand, which appropriated the first-person shooter-style of popular videogames, sparked a new trend in 2019: The "gamification of terrorism." The Christchurch attacker pioneered the trend by using a helmet camera to replicate the first-person shooter style from popular first-person shooter games such as *Call of Duty* (developed by Infinity Ward) and livestreaming the attack for others to watch. One of the first comments under the livestreamed video on the now deleted image and message board *8chan* remarked: "Get the high score" (Schlegel, 2018). Soon after the Christchurch attack, users in far-right online communities began livestreaming similar attacks in Pittsburgh, El Paso, Poway, Halle, and Buffalo on streaming services including *Facebook*, *Discord*, and *Twitch* (Amarasingam *et al.*, 2022). The Halle synagogue attacker also released a manifesto filled with gamer references such as his "objectives" and "achievements" (Mackintosh & Mezzofiore, 2019).

In addition to gamification and livestreaming, researchers have also noted the importance of in-game chats and gaming culture on these platforms and how they may normalize and perpetuate racism, misogyny, and other forms of hate (Kowert *et al.*, 2022; Rosenblat & Barrett 2023). This aspect of extremism and gaming, however, is relatively understudied. To address some of these ongoing gaps in the research, extremism researchers have ventured to survey members of the gaming community to get a sense of the kinds of content they are seeing on gaming platforms, how they are responding to the presence of hate speech and extremism when they do encounter it, and their views on what gaming platforms need to do better. The results of two large-scale surveys, which both authors of this chapter helped carry out, will be summarized and examined below. The first is the survey of 622 gamers carried out by researchers Linda Schlegel and Amarnath Amarasingam, supported by the United Nations Office of Counter Terrorism (UNOCT), and the second are the yearly surveys conducted by the team at the Anti-Defamation League (ADL).

The UNOCT Survey

In 2022, the United Nations Office of Counter Terrorism launched a survey asking generalized questions about gamers' personal experiences, the types of content they are exposed to, and how they respond to hateful and extremist speech in these spaces (Schlegel & Amarasingam, 2022). A total of 622 gamers took part in the survey, with 74% identifying as males, 15% identifying as females, and 11% identifying as other or nonbinary. Most respondents were located in North America (54%) and Europe (29%). While the survey has its limitations and its findings cannot be generalized to other geographical regions, it still provides valuable insights, especially since the voices of gamers themselves have been largely absent from the literature on gaming and extremism so far. In response to the open-ended questions, many participants offered detailed and elaborate answers, which enabled the researchers to look deeply at the challenges and benefits users experience in gaming-related spaces.

Play Patterns

One initial finding was that survey respondents spend vastly different amounts of hours a week gaming, with 39% spending ten hours or fewer and 28% spending more than 21 hours. This suggests that the survey's sample includes both casual gamers and gamers for whom it is a daily activity; 51% of the sample play videogames alone, 35% play with others, and 14% do both (Schlegel & Amarasingam, 2022, p. 13). The survey respondents also play a diverse variety of games, with the most popular options being role-playing, shooter, and strategy games. Most of the players (85%) spend less than $100 a month on games. In terms of the gaming

(-adjacent) platforms they use, the most popular were *Discord* (83%; discord.com), *Twitch* (45%; twitch.tv), *YouTube* (39%; youtube.com), and *Reddit* (24%; reddit.com). Other platforms that were also mentioned include *Twitter* (twitter.com), *Steam* (store.steampowered.com), and *Facebook* (facebook.com), while only 1% of respondents used *4Chan*, *Instagram* (instagram.com), *Slack* (app.slack.com), *Skype* (skype.com), and *Snapchat* (snapchat.com).

Player Experiences with Hate: In Game and Game Adjacent

The majority of the survey was focused on probing respondents regarding their experiences with toxic, hateful, violent, and extremist content and behavior in video games and on gaming (-adjacent) platforms. When asked to elaborate on the negative aspects of gaming and gaming (-adjacent) platforms, some participants noted problems with the games themselves, such as bugs or the increasing monetization of online gaming, or the problem of being distracted from the real world as a result of spending too much time playing videogames. More prominently however, respondents frequently complained about toxicity in gaming communities, such as individuals who specifically target people of color or LGBTQ+ gamers (Schlegel & Amarasingam 2022, p. 14). When asked whether they had witnessed any problematic or toxic behavior in gaming spaces, 85% of survey participants responded in the affirmative. Instances of this behavior were primarily verbal, with most perpetrators using in-game chats or voice-based communication. Participants cited examples of misogyny, racism, xenophobia, antisemitism, homophobia, and transphobia, as well as some examples of ableism. More generally, participants reported that they were told to kill themselves, or the casual use of slurs and comments that were meant to reinforce negative stereotypes, such as "ur gay," "you play like a girl," and frequent use of the N-word (Schlegel & Amarasingam 2022, p. 14).

When asked how often they had been exposed to content they would deem hateful or violent, 62% said "a little" or "none at all," while only 14% said "a great deal" or "a lot" (Schlegel & Amarasingam 2022, p. 14). There are a few potential reasons for this apparent imbalance. It is possible that the survey respondents did not deem the insults they reported witnessing as hateful or violent. It is also possible that the question was misunderstood by some respondents. When participants were asked how often they encountered specific forms of hate, such as misogyny, xenophobia, extremist content, anti-Semitism, Islamophobia, and homophobia, 30% to 34% had witnessed significant amounts of misogyny, racism, xenophobia, or homophobia, while only 15% to 16% noted witnessing similar levels of extremism, anti-Semitism, or Islamophobia (Schlegel & Amarasingam 2022, p. 14).

Positive Experiences

Gaming certainly does not only consist of these negative aspects, however. If it did, very few people would want to spend any time in gaming spaces. Generally speaking, survey respondents emphasized the many positive aspects of gaming and the range of benefits players experience. A primary theme in the open-ended replies was that videogames as such are not the problem and should not be blamed for hateful or extremist conduct. Extremists are merely seeking to exploit the attractiveness and popularity of videogames and gaming spaces. Respondents explained that gaming communities should thus be treated and understood as places of interaction with like-minded individuals which largely yield positive outcomes for those involved (Schlegel & Amarasingam, 2022, p. 18).

When respondents were asked what they liked about playing videogames, the most common answers were challenge/competition (35%), escapism (21%), community (16%), and relaxation (14%). When asked about the positive outcomes of gaming, the most prominent themes were again community (36%), skill development (24%), relaxation (16%), and entertainment (15%). This, of course, makes sense. Connecting with others and socializing mean that gamers become part of a community while enjoying a relaxing and entertaining hobby. These social opportunities allow gamers to interact with like-minded individuals from around the world, which has become an increasingly important way of socializing. Other notable reasons for and positive outcomes of playing noted in the survey included: high-quality storytelling and design, feelings of accomplishment, unique immersive experiences, and educational opportunities. Overall, many survey participants explained that videogames and the social connections they have made in gaming communities have "helped them through difficult times, are a source of joy, provide a feeling of belonging, and are relaxing and entertaining" (Schlegel & Amarasingam, 2022, p. 21).

Main Takeaways

There were many important takeaways from the UNOCT survey. First, participants in the focus groups and surveys consistently highlighted the positive outcomes of videogames and gaming communities. They emphasized how games fostered a sense of community, belonging, and acceptance, particularly during the COVID-19 pandemic. Many participants stressed that video games themselves were not the problem and should not be blamed for violent or hateful behavior. When asked about the positive aspects of gaming, key themes emerged, including community, entertainment, escapism, relaxation, challenge and competition, and skill development. Hence, extremism studies too should be careful to not paint gaming as intrinsically dangerous or gaming communities as hotbeds of radicalization. Rather, counter-extremism efforts should acknowledge and utilize the positive outcomes of gaming.

Second, in spite of the positive aspects, participants across all phases of the study discussed the negative impacts of gaming. Toxicity in gaming communities was a prevalent complaint, with individuals targeting and dehumanizing females, people of color, and LGBTQIA+ gamers, which deterred them from certain games or genres. This indicates that some gaming communities are spaces in which hateful conduct is normalized and often goes unchallenged. When faced with hateful, toxic, or extremist content, participants reported various reactions, including, most prominently, ignoring or blocking the individual and leaving the digital gaming space, as well as reporting or reacting in some way, although reporting and reacting were much less frequently named than ignoring and blocking. This suggests that incentivizing players to use report functions and following up on their reports is necessary.

Third, participants in the focus groups noted that while extremist content may be easily found in public gaming communities, the majority is shared in private groups and servers, making it challenging to determine where it is most prevalent without infiltrating closed groups. Instances of casually racist, homophobic, and misogynistic language were more common than specific targeting based on religious identity or explicit extremist conduct. Examples of violent and hateful language also included death threats, threats of violence, doxing, DDOS attacks (i.e., malicious attempt to disrupt a server or network to overwhelm with internet traffic to temporarily or permanently disrupt service), and threats of real-life actions. This suggests that counter-extremism efforts in gaming spaces may be most useful when they emphasize countermeasures to racism, homophobia, misogyny, or other problematic perceptions rather than explicitly extremist content and narratives.

Finally, lack of moderation in online games and gaming-related platforms was a significant concern expressed by the participants. Extremists are able to disseminate their ideas more widely due to the accessibility and lack of moderation in these spaces. Participants felt that further moderation and accountability were necessary, including warnings, in-game penalties, bans, IP-bans, deplatforming, and escalation of extreme cases to law enforcement. However, they believed that lasting change in gaming culture should be driven by the gaming community itself rather than external stakeholders. This suggests that counter-extremism efforts should include participation from the gaming community rather than being implemented top down.

The ADL Surveys

The Anti-Defamation League (ADL) Center for Technology and Society has conducted yearly assessments about extremism in online multiplayer games through its annual survey of hate and harassment in online games since 2019. Each of these surveys was done in collaboration with Newzoo, a leading videogame market analytics firm and has included a nationally representative sample of adult gamers in the USA. Starting in 2021, the survey also included a nationally representative sample of teens, aged 13–17, in the USA. In 2022, the survey also added pre-teens aged ten to 12.

ADL's survey has found that, for adults, harassment in online multiplayer games has increased every year since 2019 to a high of 86% of adults experiencing harassment in 2022. Severe harassment has also increased every year since 2019 to a high of 77% of adults experiencing severe harassment in 2022. In ADL's survey, harassment and severe harassment are made up of a number of in-game behaviors, namely:

- Trolling/griefing (deliberate attempts to upset or provoke someone)
- Another online player embarrassing them
- Offensive name calling
- Threats of physical violence
- Sustained harassment or harassment that occurs over numerous game sessions or a longer period of time
- Stalking (online monitoring/information gathering used to threaten or harass)
- Sexual harassment
- Discrimination by a stranger (due to age, gender, ethnicity, sexual orientation, etc.)
- Doxing, which is having personally identifying information made public
- Swatting, i.e. when a stranger makes a false report to emergency services to target someone

Severe harassment consists of all of the above behaviors excluding trolling, embarrassment, and offensive name calling.

The ADL survey has also examined how players are targeted by hate. ADL defines hate as forms of harassment or abuse that are based on a person's actual or perceived identity (e.g., race, religion, color, gender, gender identity, national origin, age, disability, sexual orientation, disability). Every year since 2019, women have been the identity group that are most often targeted by hate in online multiplayer games among adults in the USA. In 2022, 47% of adult women players were targeted by hate in online games. At the same time, women are the identity group that has seen the steepest decline in hate – a ten-point decrease from 57% of women being targeted by hate in online games in 2019. While this amount is still unacceptably high, this decrease over time should be further studied.

The identity group that has seen the largest increase in hate between 2019 and 2022 are Asian Americans. In 2019, 28% of Asian American adults were targeted by hate in online multiplayer games. In 2022, 40% of Asian American adults were targeted by hate in online multiplayer games. This aligns with spikes in anti-Asian American hate that occurred in the USA, following the COVID-19 pandemic and the scapegoating of Asian Americans that occurred as part of the pandemic. This trend points to how online games can mirror the hateful experiences seen elsewhere, both online and off, rather than purely existing as a subculture or discreet space separate from broader trends in American society.

The ADL survey has also looked at the games in which players most often experience harassment. Looking across the 16 games that we collected data on since 2019, the game where players reported the least harassment was *Minecraft* (Mojang Studios) in 2021; 46% of adults reported experiencing harassment in *Minecraft* in 2021. Since 2019, the game where players reported the most harassment was *Counterstrike: Global Offensive* (Valve Corporation) in 2022; 86% of adults experienced harassment in *Counterstrike: Global Offensive* in 2022. That at least roughly half of adult gamers stated that they experienced harassment in every one of 16 games across a variety of genres over four years speaks to how hate and harassment are not problems specific to one type of game or game content but rather span all games with an online multiplayer component.

Lastly, and perhaps most saliently, the ADL survey looked at the impacts that experiences of harassment have on players, both on how harassment changes how they play online and how harassment in online games changes their behavior and emotional state in their offline life. In terms of offline impacts, every year since 2019 nearly one in ten players has felt the need to reduce the risk to their physical safety as a result of an experience of harassment in online games. The number of players that have contacted the police because of an experience of harassment in online games has roughly doubled in the years since the survey began from 5% in 2019 to 11% in 2022. In terms of in-game impacts, the number of players who have quit games because of harassment has been steadily increasing from 19% of adult players in 2019 to 33% of adult players who quit a game because of harassment in 2022. At the same time, the number of players who said that in-game harassment has no impact on their experience in online games has been decreasing from 27% in 2019 to 19% in 2022.

What these trends point to is an environment in online games in which hate and harassment are rampant and increasing, where players – especially players from historically marginalized identities – are feeling more threatened and less safe. All these trends make online games a fertile ground for extremist ideologies – belief systems steeped in multifaceted manifestations of hate against multiple groups – to take root.

White Supremacy

In terms of extremism, these surveys have focused on asking about the exposure that players have had to white supremacist ideologies in online games. The reason for this is that white supremacist extremism is the most lethal form of extremism in the United States. ADL's data shows that from 2013 to 2022, right-wing extremists were responsible for 75% of all extremism-related murders in the USA, and of that, 73% of those murders were committed by extremist white supremacists (ADL Center on Extremism, 2023).

The survey focused on whether players heard phrases that contain explicit white supremacist dogma. This includes "the superiority of whites and the inferiority of non-whites" and "a home for the white race." The dominance of the "white race" over other races is a cornerstone of the extremist white supremacist ideology, as is the idea that the "white race" should live by itself in a "whites-only society" (ADL Center on Extremism, n.d.). This idea is also known as white nationalism (ADL Center on Extremism, n.d.). In the first ADL survey in 2019, a broad question was asked about these concepts and it was found that 23% – nearly a quarter – of adults responded saying they had an encounter with these kinds of concept in online multiplayer games (ADL Center for Technology and Society, 2019). This result was extremely concerning and so, in subsequent years, ADL researchers refined their methodology to ensure greater accuracy in prevalence estimates by asking participants to give an example of their experiences in an open-ended question.

In 2020 and 2021, researchers asked about the same core concepts of white supremacist ideologies but also asked respondents to fill out an open text box that described their experience (ADL Center for Technology and Society, 2020, 2022a, 2022b). If they filled it out with text indicating they'd prefer not to elaborate or if they elaborated with something relevant, they were included in the final count. If they provided an experience that didn't seem relevant to white supremacy, they were taken out of the count. The result of this is that in 2020 and 2021, the amount that adult players experiencing white supremacy was closer to one in ten (9% and

8% respectively). In 2022, while still keeping this conservative methodology in place, ADL researchers found that 20% of adults had been exposed to white supremacist ideologies in online multiplayer games (ADL Center for Technology and Society, 2022d).

In 2022, we also asked players in which games they most often experienced exposure to white supremacist ideologies. For adults, it was *Call of Duty* (Activision, 44%) and *Grand Theft Auto* (Rockstar Games, 35%). For teens 13–17, it was *Dota 2* (Valve, 29%) and *PUBG* (Krafton, 27%). For ten to 12-year-olds, it was *PUBG* (32%) and *Counterstrike: Global Offensive* (31%). To get at what these statistics tell us about the presence of white supremacist ideologies in online games, we can consider these numbers opposite some of the open text responses that were received. Over the years, the open responses on the ADL survey captured a variety of player experiences of these core tenets of white supremacist dogma:

2019: "[I experienced a] player saying whites are superior to other races which made me feel disappointed" (Male, 18–25, white, Jewish, heterosexual game player)

2020: "Person said George Floyd had it coming. They also said whites were superior to blacks cause of our roles in society" (Male, 21–25, Hispanic or Latino and white, Protestant, heterosexual, online multiplayer gamer)

2021: "There were old white men in the voice chat saying how blacks don't deserve rights like white people" (19-year-old female, Hispanic/Latinx, disabled, Protestant, and bisexual gamer)

2022: "I was playing with some random people online and they initiated a conversation about how other races are supposed to be slaves to the supreme white race" (20-year-old male white Protestant heterosexual disabled gamer, playing *Call of Duty*)

These four examples are typical of the open text responses ADL received over the last four years. The explicit white supremacist extremist responses have several characteristics:

1 They do not appear to be targeted at any individual. What the players describe in these instances is overhearing discussions or being engaged in conversation, but not being targeted themselves by the white supremacist ideologies. This differs from other open text responses for more general identity-based hate, where players did speak about their experiences being targeted with slurs and targeted harassment

2 They do not mention recruitment or organizing of extremist activities. While the open text responses do explore white supremacist ideas, they

do not appear to be trying to explicitly convince the listener of their ideology or be related to any kind of coordination of offline activities

3 There is no mention of any pushback from the player, the community who heard these hateful comments or any intervention by the online game platform. This finding was prevalent in the UNOCT survey as well

It is impossible to tell if the players expressing these ideas are white supremacist extremists themselves, on the road to becoming extremists, or merely players flirting with transgressive ideas they may have picked up somewhere online. Similarly, there is a limit to what can be inferred around short open text responses in an online survey. The trends in these comments do seem to align with the idea of online games as spaces in which players feel comfortable expressing these kinds of hateful ideology because they believe they will receive no pushback from the community that plays these games or from the platforms that operate them.

Following the 2019 white supremacist mass shooting in Christchurch, New Zealand, the government of New Zealand produced a report that chronicled the journey of radicalization of the shooter (Royal Commission of Inquiry into the Terrorist Attack on Christchurch Mosque on 15 March 2019, 2020; Veilleux-Lepage *et al.*, 2020). While the shooter's formal radicalization into white supremacist ideologies happened in traditional social media spaces such as *YouTube* and *Facebook*, his first online experiences were in online games. The report details how the shooter was able to "openly express racist and far right views" without pushback from the community or the platform.

The conditions that made that possible – and that made possible the experiences detailed in the open-text responses from ADL's surveys and the frighteningly high number of adults who reported those kinds of experience – must change. To push for change in a manner that is grounded in evidence, however, the industry needs to open up ways for researchers and journalists to understand the scope and nature of the problem and collaborate on novel solutions to the problem of extremism in online multiplayer games.

Public Discourse around Extremism in Games

Following the release of the most recent ADL survey in December 2022, members of US congress engaged in oversight actions regarding how the game industry is addressing issues of hate, harassment, and extremism in online games. A coalition of lawmakers led by Rep. Lori Trahan of Massachusetts wrote letters to 14 major game companies asking for information on how they were addressing these issues (Trahan, 2023).

Other congress people also took oversight action as a result of the 2022 ADL survey. Senator Maggie Hassan of New Hampshire wrote to the game company Valve about the presence of extremist content on its *Steam* platform. Senator Dick Durbin of Illinois wrote to seven major game companies, inquiring about their approaches to extremist content in their online games.

Additionally and notably Rep. Trahan also published summaries of the responses she received from the companies. This document is an important record of what the game industry is doing and not doing in terms of its efforts to address extremism as of early 2023. For example, as Rep. Trahan notes in her summary, nine out of the 14 companies that were asked about their approach to extremism failed to mention any policies or actions they take to address extremist content in their online games. The document is also notable for likely being the first time that the dedicated extremism team at *Roblox* (https://www.roblox.com/) has been acknowledged publicly. The fact that *Roblox* has a team with domain knowledge about extremism dedicated to addressing this issue across their platform is a model that other game companies should follow.

Conclusion

Despite the massive scale and importance of online multiplayer games and gaming (-adjacent) platforms, it remains difficult for researchers and journalists to study and investigate the kinds of interaction players are so frequently having in these digital spaces, let alone to understand the relationship between extremism and online gaming spaces. There is no gaming corollary to *Reddit*, a social media platform that provides near total access to platform data for researchers to study the kinds of interaction that occur there. Additionally, while social media companies have adopted transparency reporting around their content moderation efforts as industry standard practice for a decade (Trust & Safety Professional Association, 2021), 2022 was the first year where gaming companies (one small, Wildlife Studios, and one large, Xbox) provided any kind of transparency reporting (Wildlife Studios, 2022; Xbox, 2022). Even those efforts left much to be desired: For example, Xbox provided no clear data in this transparency report on how they addressed extremist content. More galling is the fact that Microsoft clearly has done the work putting together this data as it is included as part of the aggregate of TVEC (terrorism and violent extremist content) data that it shares in its Digital Safety Content Report, which spans *Xbox* alongside other Microsoft services such as *OneDrive*, *Skype*, and *Outlook* (Corporate Social Responsibility, 2022).

In addition to not sharing data and not producing meaningful trans-parency reports, many game platforms are also not broadly searchable in the way most social media platforms are. With the name of an extremist group or a phrase of the coded language they use to spread their hateful ideologies, it is possible to search platforms such as *Facebook*, *Reddit*, *Twitter*, or *YouTube* to see what kinds of content may appear. The results may not be total or may not be relevant or may be filtered by the platform, but many times it is possible to use a keyword search to find relevant content on these platforms. With many online games – even the largest and most popular with hundreds of millions of players – these kinds of cursory search are not possible.

To determine the activities of various extremists, extremism researchers and investigators often spend time in online spaces where extremists and extremism takes root. That makes sense in spaces that have some level of persistence, such as social media platforms and online forums. A Discord channel's content doesn't disappear and change its membership every 20 minutes. With many online games, while they are, in general, persistent as services, the amount of time that individual spaces persist can be fairly limited, especially for match-based games. A match in *Call of Duty* typi-cally runs for only a limited amount of time and consists of a limited number of players. After that time, players are pulled out of that space and randomly rematched with other players. The communications that hap-pened in that match are not available at all for any journalist or researcher to investigate after the match is completed. In terms of intelligence gath-ering, this means the level of effort to record behaviors and follow any potential threads of information in an online games space is exponentially greater than it is on social media platforms.

An exception here is the game platform *Roblox*, which has come under scrutiny from journalists and researchers for the forms of extremism that have been discovered on the platform. *Roblox* is searchable. *Roblox* is also notable as the first online game platform with an explicit extremism policy and with a team that is explicitly dedicated to addressing terrorist and extremist content on the platform (Roblox, n.d.).

These facts are not unrelated. The search bar at the top of *Roblox*'s web and mobile interface allows users to search the variety of experiences, users, groups, and items present on the platform. This feature allows for researchers and journalists to do certain kinds of investigation on the platform, albeit not as robust as they could have with full API data access such as is available on *Reddit*. That being said, this level of searchability was enough for journalists such as Cecilia D'Anastasio to do the kind of investigative journalism that is present in her piece for *Wired*, "How Roblox Became a Playground for Virtual Fascists," which was published in July 2021 (D'Anastasio, 2021). It was also enough for ADL's Center for Technology and Society to uncover Holocaust denial (ADL, 2022a), other forms of anti-Semitism (ADL Center for Technology and Society, 2022c), and multiple *Roblox* recreations of the white supremacist extremist Christchurch Mosque shooting of 2019 (Gelineau & Gambrell, 2019). Niantic is another exception and has publicly announced its use of "red teams" and enlisting a safety by design approach when it comes to mitigating various harms that may occur in gaming spaces (Francois, 2023).

Public dialogue between industry, media, civil society, and academia about critical issues like how extremism functions is important. Since the end of 2021, the ADL team has not found a single recreation of the Christchurch Mosque shooting on *Roblox*. However, until more online gaming platforms see this relationship as good and healthy and provide ways for researchers and journalists to see what is happening on their platforms, whether that's through developing a search capacity or providing data access to researchers, it is incumbent on researchers and journalists to find other ways to investigate important digital spaces such as online games.

References

ADL Center on Extremism (n.d.a). White Nationalism. ADL. https://extremismterms.adl.org/glossary/white-nationalism.

ADL Center on Extremism (n.d.b). White Supremacy. ADL. https://extremismterms.adl.org/glossary/white-supremacy.

ADL Center for Technology and Society (2019). Free to Play? Hate, Harassment, and Positive Social Experiences in Online Games. ADL. https://www.adl.org/resources/report/free-play-hate-harassment-and-positive-social-experiences-online-games.

ADL Center for Technology and Society (2020). Free to Play? Hate, Harassment and Positive Social Experience in Online Games 2020. ADL. https://www.adl.org/resources/report/free-play-hate-harassment-and-positive-social-experience-online-games-2020.

ADL Center for Technology and Society (2022a) 2021 Online Antisemitism Report Card. ADL. https://www.adl.org/resources/report/2021-online-antisemitism-report-card.

ADL Center for Technology and Society (2022b). Hate is No Game: Harassment and Positive Social Experiences in Online Games 2021. ADL. https://www.adl.org/resources/.report/hate-no-game-harassment-and-positive-social-experiences-online-games-2021.

ADL Center For Technology and Society (2022c, May 3). Online Holocaust Denial Report Card: An Investigation of Online Platforms' Policies and Enforcement. https://www.adl.org/resources/report/online-holocaust-denial-report-card-investigation-online-platforms-policies.

ADL Center for Technology and Society (2022d). Hate Is No Game: Hate and Harassment in Online Games 2022. ADL. https://www.adl.org/resources/report/hate-no-game-hate-and-harassment-online-games-2022.

ADL Center on Extremism (2023). Murder and Extremism in the United States in 2022. ADL. https://www.adl.org/resources/report/murder-and-extremism-united-states-2022.

Amarasingam, A., Argentino, M.-A., & Macklin, G. (2022, July). The Buffalo Attack: The Cumulative Momentum of Far-Right Terror. *CTC Sentinel, 15*(7). https://ctc.westpoint.edu/the-buffalo-attack-the-cumulative-momentum-of-far-right-terror/.

American Psychological Association (APA) (2020, March 3). APA Reaffirms Position on Violent Video Games and Violent Behavior. https://www.apa.org/news/press/releases/2020/03/violent-video-games-behavior.

Anderson, C.A. (2003). Video Games and Aggressive Behavior. In *Kid Stuff: Marketing Sex and Violence to America's Children*. JHU Press.

Anderson, C.A. & Bushman, B. (2001). Effects of Violent Video Games on Aggressive Behavior, Aggressive Cognition, Aggressive Affect, Physiological Arousal, and Prosocial Behavior: A Meta-Analytic Review of the Scientific Literature. *Psychological Science, 12*(5), 353–359. 10.1111/1467-9280.00366.

Anderson, C.A. & Dill, K.E. (2000). Video Games and Aggressive Thoughts, Feelings, and Behavior in the Laboratory and in Life. *Journal of Personality and Social Psychology, 78*(4), 772–790. 10.1037/0022-3514.78.4.772.

Anderson, C.A. & Murphy, C.R. (2003). Violent Video Games and Aggressive Behavior in Young Women. *Aggressive Behavior, 29*(5), 423–429. 10.1002/ab.10042.

Barnett, J. & Coulson, M. (2010). Virtually Real: A Psychological Perspective on Massively Multiplayer Online Games. *Review of General Psychology, 14*(2), 167–179. 10.1037/a0019442.

Bensley, L. & van Eenwyk, J. (2001). Video Games and Real-Life Aggression: Review of the Literature. *Journal of Adolescent Health, 29*(4), 244–257. 10.1016/S1054-139X(01)00239-7.

Brandom, R. (2021, August 17). Roblox is Struggling to Moderate Re-Creations of Mass Shootings. The Verge. https://www.theverge.com/2021/8/17/22628624/roblox-moderation-trust-and-safety-terrorist-content-christchurch.

Breuer, J., Vogelgesang, J., Quandt, T., & Festl, R. (2015). Violent Video Games and Physical Aggression: Evidence for a Selection Effect Among Adolescents. *Psychology of Popular Media Culture, 4*(4), 305–328. 10.1037/ppm0000035.

Campbell, C. (2018, March 10). A Brief History of Blaming Video Games for Mass Murder. *Polygon Analysis*. https://www.polygon.com/2018/3/10/17101232/a-brief-history-of-video-game-violence-blame.

Carnagey, N.L., Anderson, C.A., & Bushman, B.J. (2007). The Effect of Video Game Violence on Physiological Desensitization to Real-Life Violence. *Journal of Experimental Social Psychology, 43*(3), 489–496. 10.1016/ j.jesp.2006.05.003.

Colwell, J. & Kato, M. (2003). Investigation of the Relationship Between Social Isolation, Self-Esteem, Aggression and Computer Game Play in Japanese Adolescents. *Asian Journal of Social Psychology, 6*(2), 149–158. 10.1111/1467-839X.t01-1-00017.

Corporate Social Responsibility (2022). Digital Safety Content Report. Microsoft. https://www.microsoft.com/en-us/corporate-responsibility/digital-safety-content-report.

D'Anastasio, C. (2021, June 10). How "Roblox" Became a Playground for Virtual Fascists. Wired. https://www.wired.com/story/roblox-online-games-irl-fascism-roman-empire/.

Elson, M., Ferguson, C.J., Gregerson, M., Hogg, J.L., Ivory, J., Klisanin, D., Markey, P.M., Nichols, D., Siddiqui, S., & Wilson, J. (2019). Do Policy Statements on Media Effects Faithfully Represent the Science? *Advances in Methods and Practices in Psychological Science*, 2(1), 12–25. 10.1177/2515245918811301.

Ferguson, C.J. (2008). The School Shooting/Violent Video Game Link: Causal Relationship or Moral Panic? *Journal of Investigative Psychology and Offender Profiling*, 5(1–2), 25–37. 10.1002/jip.76.

Ferguson, C.J. (2019). A Preregistered Longitudinal Analysis of Aggressive Video Games and Aggressive Behavior in Chinese Youth. *Psychiatric Quarterly*, 90(4), 843–847. 10.1007/s11126-019-09669-6.

Ferguson, C.J. & Wang, J.C.K. (2019). Aggressive Video Games are Not a Risk Factor for Future Aggression in Youth: A Longitudinal Study. *Journal of Youth & Adolescence*, 48(8), 1439–1451. 10.1007/s10964-019-01069-0.

Francois, C. (2023, June 27). Our Approach to Safety. Niantic Labs. https://nianticlabs.com/news/trustandsafety?hl=en.

Freedman, J.L. (2002). *Media Violence and its Effect on Aggression: Assessing the Scientific Evidence*. University of Toronto Press.

Gelineau, K. & Gambrell, J. (2019, March 15). New Zealand Mosque Shooter is a White Nationalist who Hates Immigrants, Documents and Video Reveal. Chicago Tribune. https://web.archive.org/web/20200602054023/. https:/www.chicagotribune.com/nation-world/ct-mosque-killer-white-supremacy-20190315-story.html.

Gentile, D.A., Lynch, P.J., Linder, J.R., & Walsh, D.A. (2004). The Effects of Violent Video Game Habits on Adolescent Hostility, Aggressive Behaviors, and School Performance. *Journal of Adolescence*, 27(1), 5–22. 10.1016/ j.adolescence.2003. 10.002.

Greitemeyer, T. & McLatchie, N. (2011). Denying Humanness to Others: A Newly Discovered Mechanism by Which Violent Video Games Increase Aggressive Behavior. *Psychological Science*, 22(5), 659–665. 10.1177/0956797611403320.

Hilgard, J., Engelhardt, C.R., & Rouder, J.N. (2017). Overstated Evidence for Short-Term Effects of Violent Games on Affect and Behavior: A Reanalysis of Anderson et al. (2010). *Psychological Bulletin*, 143(7), 757–774. 10.1037/ bul0000074.

Kelley, D. [@danieljkelley] (2021, August 13). I swear to God, I would like one time to search for "Christchurch" on Roblox and not find a new recreation of the 2019 Christchurch mosque shooting on a game platform aimed at very young children. https://t.co/0BvRtGYZHE [Tweet]. Twitter. https://twitter.com/danieljkelley/status/1426209012815704068.

Kowert, R., Martel, A., & Swann, W.B. (2022). Not Just a Game: Identity Fusion and Extremism in Gaming Cultures. *Frontiers in Communication*, 7. https://www.frontiersin.org/articles/10.3389/fcomm.2022.1007128/full.

Kowert, R. & Quandt, T. (Eds.) (2016). *The Video Game Debate: Unraveling the physical, social, and psychological effects of video games.* Routledge.

Lobel, A., Engels, R.C.M.E., Stone, L.L., Burk, W.J., & Granic, I. (2017). Video Gaming and Children's Psychosocial Wellbeing: A Longitudinal Study. *Journal of Youth and Adolescence,* 46(4), 884–897. 10.1007/s10964-017-0646-z.

Mackintosh, E. & Mezzofiore, G. (2019, October 10). How the Extreme Right Gamified Terror. CNN. https://www.cnn.com/2019/10/10/europe/germany-synagogue-attack-extremism-gamified-grm-intl/index.html.

Mojang Studios (2011). *Minecraft.* [Videogame]

Moore, J. (2021, August 18). A Number of Mass Shooting Recreations Have Been Found on Roblox. IGN. https://www.ign.com/articles/roblox-mass-shooting-recreations.

Roblox. (n.d.). Roblox Community Standards. Roblox Support. https://en.help.roblox.com/hc/en-us/articles/203313410-Roblox-Community-Standards.

Rosenblat, M.O. & Barrett, P.M. (2023). Gaming the System: How Extremists Exploit Gaming Sites and What Can Be Done to Counter Them. NYU Stern Center for Business and Human Rights Report. https://bhr.stern.nyu.edu/tech-gaming-report.

Royal Commission of Inquiry into the Terrorist Attack on Christchurch Mosque on 15 March 2019 (2020). *Kō tō tātou kāinga tēnei* (p. 166). https://christchurchattack.royalcommission.nz/the-report/firearms-licensing/the-firearms-licensing-process/.

Schlegel, L. (2018, July 5). Playing Jihad: The Gamification of Radicalization. The Defense Post. https://www.thedefensepost.com/2018/07/05/gamification-of-radicalization-opinion/.

Schlegel, L. (2020). Jumanji Extremism? How Games and Gamification Could Facilitate Radicalization Processes. *Journal for Deradicalization,* 23, 1–44.

Schlegel, L. & Amarasingam, A. (2022). Examining the Intersection Between Gaming and Violent Extremism. United Nations Office of Counter-Terrorism. https://www.un.org/counterterrorism/sites/www.un.org.counterterrorism/files/221005_research_launch_on_gaming_ve.pdf.

Trahan, L. (2023). Summary of Responses from Gaming Companies. U.S. House of Representatives. https://trahan.house.gov/uploadedfiles/summary_responses_to_letter_game_companies_online_harassment_extremism.pdf.

Trust & Safety Professional Association (2021, July 7). History of Transparency Reports. Trust & Safety Professional Association. https://www.tspa.org/curriculum/ts-fundamentals/transparency-report/history-transparency-reports/.

Unsworth, G., Devilly, G.J., & Ward, T. (2007). The Effect of Playing Violent Video Games on Adolescents: Should Parents be Quaking in Their Boots? *Psychology, Crime & Law,* 13(4), 383–394. 10.1080/10683160601060655.

Valve Corporation (2012). *Counterstrike: Global Offensive.* [Videogame]

Veilleux-Lepage, Y., Daymon, C., & Amarasingam, A. (2020). The Christchurch Attack Report: Key Takeaways on Tarrant's Radicalization and Attack Planning. ICCT Perspective. https://www.icct.nl/publication/christchurch-attack-report-key-takeaways-tarrants-radicalization-and-attack-planning.

von Salisch, M., Vogelgesang, J., Kristen, A., & Oppl, C. (2011). Preference for Violent Electronic Games and Aggressive Behavior among Children: The Beginning of the Downward Spiral? *Media Psychology*, *14*(3), 233–258. 10. 1080/ 15213269.2011.596468.

Wayt, T. (2021, August 18). Roblox Players Keep Recreating Mass Shootings in Video Game. New York Post. https://nypost.com/2021/08/18/roblox-players-keep-recreating-mass-shootings-in-video-game/.

Wells, G., Romhanyi, A., Reitman, J.G., Gardner, R., Squire, K., & Steinkuehler, C. (2023). Right-Wing Extremism in Mainstream Games: A Review of the Literature. Games and Culture. Online first. https://journals.sagepub.com/doi/full/ 10.1177/15554120231167214.

Wildlife Studios (2022). Transparency Report. Wildlife Studios. https://wildlifestudios.com/transparency-report/.

Williams, D. & Skoric, M. (2005). Internet Fantasy Violence: A Test of Aggression in an Online Game. *Communication Monographs*, *72*(2), 217–233. 10.1080/ 03637750500111781.

7

BEAUTY IS POWER

The Use of Gaming References and Gaming Aesthetics in Extremist Propaganda

Ashton Kingdon

What we know about extremist and terrorist groups and movements is often what they want us to see. Over the past decade, extremists have not only orchestrated and performed attacks, but have developed as professional storytellers, seeking to hijack the popular culture of the West (i.e., pop culture) as a means of seducing recruits. This is not only a successful tactic, but a relatively easy one to enlist as acts of terrorism have been a recurrent theme within popular culture. For example, many popular television shows and films are already loosely related to genuine events in the headlines. Whether the audience is watching the blockbuster movie *World Trade Centre*, the American spy thriller television series *Homeland*, or reading Richard Preston's *The Cobra Event*, popular culture plays a critical role in shaping attitudes towards terrorism and provides a nearly neverending repository of visuals and narratives for propagandists to draw from to shape their own narratives. The aesthetics drawn from popular culture is of particular importance in this context. First used in the 18th century by German philosopher Alexander Baumgarten, and deriving from the Greek word for perception (*aisthesis*), the term aesthetics most commonly refers to the philosophical study and appreciation of beauty and taste – especially visual art (Johnson, 1969; Eagleton, 1988). It is important to recognize, however, that the origins of artistic worth do not necessarily reside in the artworks themselves, but in the social institutions in which they are produced and consumed (Carrabine, 2012). The power of propaganda is not only in the way it looks, but also in how it makes the audience feel, as images are designed in specific ways to evoke emotion.

DOI: 10.4324/9781003388371-8

Late modernity has borne witness to a progressive expansion of visual culture, encompassing advertising, film, television, social media, and videogames all of which, over the last two decades, have become a major focus, both as the subjects of study and methods of research (Kingdon, 2021). Extremist groups increasingly flourish online, which has created new avenues for radicalization and has had a profound impact on both the speed and scale in which propaganda can be disseminated (O'Shaughnessy, 2004). Consequently, academic research has focussed on the expanding use of the technology employed by extremists to gain support, raise capital, recruit members, engage in psychological warfare, and create and disseminate propaganda (Conway, 2017; Veilleux-Lepage, 2020; Kingdon & Krause, 2021;Winter, 2022).

The aftermath of the "Great Meme War", the internet-based warfare campaigns waged by supporters of various political candidates in the 2016 American Presidential election, saw an increase in research focussed on the use of the aesthetic of memes as a form of disinformation (Piata, 2016; Ross & Rivers, 2017; Mayer, 2018; McKew, 2018; Meyer, 2018; Moody-Ramirez & Church, 2019). The term "meme" was coined by evolutionary biologist Richard Dawkins (1976) to refer to units of cultural information spread by imitation, replicating in a similar way to genes, with cultural ideas passing from parent to child in the same way as biological traits are passed. It is important to note that when defining memes, Dawkins was alluding not specifically to images and videos, but to any unit of culture that had the potential to be replicated and transmitted between individuals, arguing that memes spread like viruses, but instead of carrying diseases that infect the body, they convey ideas that infiltrate the mind. Exploring memes that are taking a central role in extremists' modus operandi is becoming increasingly important.

More recently, videogame aesthetics have become a recurrent and identifiable staple of extremist propaganda and emblematic of a virtual and political culture war. Over the course of videogame history, the capacity to render visual and audio environments has continually improved and videogames have become an art form that can be evaluated from a range of aesthetic perspectives (Atkinson & Parsayi, 2021). Research on the relationship between videogames and extremist propaganda has been increasing over the last few years, focussing on three primary areas: The use of gaming imagery in producing propaganda (El Ghamari, 2017; Dauber, 2019; Kingdon, 2023); gamification as an emergent technique for circulating propaganda and producing radicalizing effects (Lakhani, 2021; Mattheis, 2021); and the relationship between ideology and videogames, and the ways in which they can be used in extremist recruitment (Selepak, 2010; Daniels & LaLone, 2012; Kingdon,

2019; Brett, 2021; O'Connor, 2021; Koehler, Fiebig, & Jugl, 2022). There is also a significant toxicity issue around video games, as evidenced through "Gamergate" – a coordinated misogynistic social media harassment campaign, predominantly in 2014 and 2015, that targeted women associated with the videogame industry – which was considered by many to be a key event in the ascendancy of extremist personalities and tactics to online prominence (for a more detailed overview on Gamergate, see Condis, 2020; Bezio, 2018; Salter, 2018; Emery, 2022). It seems apparent, from the above discussion, that it is vital to research further the hypothesis that gamification in propaganda employs the aesthetic sensibilities and visual rhetoric of gaming to expose specific audiences online to violent and radicalizing materials (Mattheis, 2021).

The video-gaming industry is considered to be one of the fastest growing sectors (Lakhani, 2021); exacerbated by the Covid-19 pandemic during which global lockdown measures constrained millions within their homes, and the amount of time people spent gaming increased (Barr & Copeland-Stewart, 2022). In 2022 alone, it is estimated that there were over 3 billion gamers globally, amounting to approximately 40% of the world's population (Clements, 2022). Predictably, the number of gamers around the world is set to rise steadily over the next few years and by 2027 the user number is estimated to be 3.1 billion (Clements, 2023). As videogames continue to be major components of popular culture, it is no surprise that they are, and will increasingly be, employed by extremist propagandists for recruitment purposes. Videogames as a cultural artifact have aesthetic value and remain a strong form of propaganda, transmitting messages that create powerful emotions. Gaming propaganda is particularly persuasive because it can create cyber-communities that transcend national and regional boundaries and language barriers. Memes, in particular, are successfully rhetorical tools in two ways: They create collectives, while also dividing people through antagonistic methods, both of which can foster notions of in-groups and out-groups (Daymon, 2020; Woods & Hahner, 2020). Gaming propaganda can also be used to circulate extremist content in ways that subvert technological content moderation techniques by making the imagery difficult for machines to concretely categorize as prohibited.

This chapter will use visual empirical data to illustrate how and why jihadist and far-right groups and movements have utilized gaming aesthetics and cultural references within their propaganda, and the ways in which such organizations have developed their own videogames, or modified existing ones, as a means of attracting potential recruits. The chapter will argue that videogame propaganda cannot be understood without considering the role played by aesthetics, as gaming aesthetics revoke the modern boundaries between modes of cognition, experience, and expression. It is thus of paramount importance that research considers the complexity of the extremist/social media nexus as, repeatedly, propagandists borrow aesthetics from video games, turning their purpose, as a specific interactive medium, from one solely to entertain, to one also encompassing socialization, education, and the communication of ideas, opinion, and ideology.

Video Games as Jihadist Propaganda

Bespoke Games

One of the first jihadist groups to utilize gaming aesthetics was Al Qaeda (a Sunni pan-Islamist militant organization), whose propaganda organization released *Quest for Bush* (Global Islamic Media Front) in 2006, a first-person shooter (FPS) videogame that tasked players with fighting American soldiers through six levels to kill "The Boss"[1] – George W. Bush, 43rd president of the United States. The game is a reskinning (remodeling) of the video game *Quest for Saddam* (Petrilla Entertainment), released by the US military in 2003, in which the goal is to overcome Iraqi soldiers to kill "The Boss" – Saddam Hussein (Snowdon, 2014). Much of the propaganda centered on *Quest for Bush* features screenshots from the game that include pictures of George W. Bush, Donald Rumsfeld (Secretary of Defense under President Bush), and Tony Blair (former Prime Minister of the United Kingdom), that adorn the walls of the American military camp featured in the game. All were key figures involved with the War on Terror, the American-led international counterterrorism campaign launched in response to the terrorist attacks of September 11, 2001. Other significant propaganda images depict players brandishing the iconic Avtomat Kalashnikova, referred to more colloquially as the AK-47 (a reference to the date the weapon moved from developmental trials to production). With over 100 million made, the rifle has been the backbone of many insurgencies and is considered the weapon of choice for a revolution due to its cheap manufacture, ample availability, durability, and simplicity of operation; it is as popular in videogames as it is in modern-day warfare (Chapple, 2020).

In addition to Al Qaeda, the Lebanese, militant Shia group Hezbollah has also released videogames as part of its recruitment strategy. Its first, *Special Force* (Hezbollah, 2003), focused on Israel's withdrawal from Southern Lebanon, followed by *Special Force 2: The Tale of the Truthful Pledge* (Central Internet Bureau, 2007), centring on the 2006 Hezbollah-Israel war. Arguably, the group's most valuable videogame in terms of propaganda potential, is *Holy Defense* (Hezbollah), released in 2018, which re-enacts key strategic battles in Syria and Lebanon. Players take on the role of Ahmad, who has recently enlisted with Hezbollah following an Islamic State attack on the Sayyeda Zeinab Shrine in Damascus. As Rose (2018) highlights, the videogame can be considered propaganda designed to legitimize the Iranian-backed group's intervention in the Syrian Civil War by promoting the narrative that Hezbollah is fighting insurgencies and not supporting the Assad regime, or threatening the Western world. More specifically, the game is portrayed as more than merely glorifying victories in warfare – it is a call to arms for young people to emulate the game and take pride in joining the fight (Rose, 2018). On social media platforms such as *Twitter* (twitter.com), the use of artwork and screenshots from *Holy Defense* featuring weapons have been used to show support for Hezbollah from nonaffiliated followers, demonstrating how the game can potentially benefit recruitment (Sherlock, 2018).

The use of weaponry in jihadist propaganda is an example of what Katz (1988) would term "Badass" iconography (individuals who overtly embrace symbols of deviance). The inclusion of violent symbolism coalesces with the phenomenon of "Jihadi Cool," the process whereby terrorist recruiters manipulate illusions of terror, transforming them into something current and fashionable for online audiences (Huey, 2015; Hegghammer, 2017). These types of aesthetic feed into propagandists' attempts to emphatically provide answers to certain youths' visceral desires, with promises of excitement, adventure, and unrestrained violence (Kingdon, 2017). Moreover, the frequent inclusion of the AK-47 in propaganda can be considered a way of communicating masculinity, heroic identity, and capacity for violence – the aesthetic not conjuring the drill-step order of a formal state army, but the revolutionary chic of the freedom fighter (Sunde, Ilan, & Sandberg, 2020). Crucially, propagandists use weapons that have aesthetic value – they are highly compelling, emotive, and breed familiarity. These weapons have the ability to become a proxy and abstract from real-world violence as a semiotic association can be placed immediately on the games and fictional elements.

Videogames can be an effective medium to attract youth as previous research has noted that they have been an extremely successful recruiting tool for the US army (Cowan, 2009; Zyda, 2022). A particularly powerful example is *America's Army* (United States Army) a series of first-person shooter (FPS) videogames developed and published by the US army, launched in 2002, intended to inform, educate, and recruit perspective soldiers, events including accurate rules of engagement encouraging players to view the US military in a particular way. In this sense, it is useful to think of videogames as a strategic part of the "Military Entertainment Complex," which describes the relationship between the United States

Department of Defense and the entertainment industries to their mutual benefit, especially in the fields of cinema, multimedia, and virtual reality (Lenoir & Caldwell, 2018). The example set by *America's Army* may be why, at least partially, extremist and terrorist organizations are choosing to follow suit with the creation of bespoke games for recruitment. It is also worth noting that creating digital games for recruitment and propaganda purposes is a particularly feasible method now that digital technology is easily available and games are cheaper to manufacture.

The Manipulation of Existing Games

In 2017, the video game *Syrian Warfare* (Cats who Play), was released for PC via *Steam* (https://store.steampowered.com/). It is a real-time strategy game that puts players in charge of soldiers, tanks, missiles, and aircrafts (Anderson, 2016). The game is played as a Syrian police officer who is tasked with defending his hometown from the Islamic State and Jabhat al-Nusra. The game developers wanted *Syrian Warfare* to have a degree of realism, lifelike graphics, detailed simulations of modern weapons, and realistic tactical gameplay (Havis, 2016), using these aesthetics of war to divert attention from the reality of destruction. Importantly, these aesthetics have been co-opted by terrorist organizations, most notably by the Islamic State, which has included gameplay footage from *Syrian Warfare* in its propaganda – particularly people being killed by suicide bombers or in vehicle-ramming attacks – as a way of attracting new members. Moreover, one of the most recognizable and racialized taglines within the game *What Kind of Arab Would I Be if I Didn't Have an RPG* has been used by Islamic State propagandists alongside imagery of players in the game using rocket-propelled grenades, uncomplicated but powerful explosives widely associated with militias, insurgents, and terrorists across the world (Rottman, 2010). Often these weapons are used not only against the targets for which they were designed – armored fighting vehicles – but against personnel, fortifications, buildings, and civilians (Cengiz, 2019) – a versatility that makes them a popular staple of Islamic State propaganda.

Islamic State's consistent use of aesthetics from popular games as part of its recruitment strategy is an important illustration of the relationship between jihadist groups and videogames. In addition to drawing on the aesthetics of popular games for its own original material, Islamic State has also directly copied and employed the visual imagery of FPS games such as *Call of Duty: Black Ops* (Treyarch), in its videos as a way of sanitizing violence, making it seem more acceptable to the technologically savvy young men Islamic State wishes to recruit (Dauber, 2019). One example of this motif is the well-known meme depicting two jihadists with bright spots covering their faces and the group's black standard flag. One man is holding the AK-47 rifle and making the "Tawhid[2]" gesture with the text "THIS IS OUR CALL OF DUTY, AND WE RESPAWN[3] IN JANNAH."[4] The suggestion being that to become an Islamic State fighter is to respond to the "duty" of all "real men" to fight for righteousness, and that just like in videogames, death is not permanent and thus not to be feared; similarly to the game avatars, Islamic State fighters will revive.

Research has also discussed the use of *Grand Theft Auto 5* (Rockstar North) in propaganda (Al-Rawi, 2018), a game that is instantly recognisable and thus appeals to potential recruits. A popular image disseminated by Islamic State is an adapted version of the original artwork of the game, with a printed-over image of the Islamic State logo and monochrome flag, aesthetics that are instantly recognizable. This is part of the strategy urging young men to get out from behind their video controllers to join the "real games" by partaking in jihad. In the hijacked video, the Islamic State Western narrator states: "Your games which are producing you, we do the same actions in the battlefields." Robinson and Whittaker (2021) argue that videogames, and the culture that surrounds them, are an important aspect of the group's recruitment strategy because they tap into the global youth demographic.

A large focus for popular games has been photorealism – making games look as indistinguishable from reality as possible. Game developers have had great success in this endeavor, particularly as technology has improved, and propagandists have also benefited. The manipulation of pre-existing footage from games to create a jihadist narrative, rather than having a playable physical version of the game, is an example of "machinima," a portmanteau word of "machine" and "cinema." Machinima is the use of real-time computer graphics engines to create a cinematic production, most frequently utilizing videogames to generate computer animation (Kelland, 2011). Many channels, on encrypted social media platforms such as *Telegram*, are dedicated to distributing *YouTube* links to machinima video clips created from the real-time 3D engines of popular videogames such as *Arma3* (Bohemia Interactive), *Grand Theft Auto*, and *Call of Duty*.

These games are manipulated to create characters that resemble Islamic State militants, depicting scenes that feature the Islamic State flag, as well as the recreation of violent scenes including executions, suicide bombings, and plane hijackings (see Figure 7.1 for an example). The machinima videos that are produced imitate, or are shot in the style of official Islamic State propaganda, with *nasheeds*[5] in the background, often recreating famous attacks such as the 2015 Bataclan Theatre attack in Paris, or the 2016 attacks in Nice and Brussels. Moreover, propaganda images will

FIGURE 7.1   Screenshot from a YouTube machinima video of the video
game Arma 3 title *Islamic State Attack on US Base.*

often depict scenes of armed men pulling police officers from their cars and
shooting them to death, explosive attacks on military convoys and civilians, or shooting the enemy with assault rifles; all of these clips being
interspersed with Islamic State iconography, the visual and audio game
effects making the viewing experience feel even more real. Having discussed various ways in which jihadist groups and movements have utilized
gaming aesthetics, this chapter will now turn to the exploitation of gaming
by the far right.

Videogames as Far-Right Propaganda

Bespoke Games

Videogames created by extremist groups and individuals seeking to spread
violent ideologies pose a unique challenge to those working to prevent and
combat radicalization (Fisher-Birch, 2020). The creation of videogames by
the far right is not a new phenomenon and includes, for example, the
following titles: *KZ Manager* (The Missionaries, 1990), which puts
players in charge of the running of a Nazi concentration camp where
resources have to be managed, including poison gas supplies, money, and
equipment, as well as public opinion about the productivity of the camp;
White Law (Resistance Records, 2003), based on the 1978 racist dystopian novel *The Turner Diaries*, users play as an Irish-American police

officer taking up arms to protect his territory from racial minorities; *Ethnic Cleansing* (Resistance Records, 2002), an FPS in which you play as either a white skinhead or a Klansman and are tasked with killing people of color and Jews to beat "The Boss" – Ariel Sharon who served as the 11th Prime Minister of Israel 2000–2006; *Zog's Nightmare*[6] (The National Socialist Movement, 2006) and *Zog's Nightmare 2: The War Continues* (The National Socialist Movement, 2007), which encourage players to fight for a white country and defeat Jewish soldiers and a police agency controlled by Jews. These games allow for extremist groups to advertise, and encourage the dehumanization of their perceived opponents, while portraying violence as a positive mechanism (Khosravi, 2017). While extremist games are not novel, they are becoming easier to produce due to the democratization of technology; the barriers to game creation are lowering as new development software is released, and the skills necessary to build games become widespread. Games developed by or on behalf of groups and individuals that promote extremism, racism, anti-Semitism, Islamophobia, and transphobia need to be treated as propaganda tools, and, the section below will provide some examples as to how aesthetics contributes to this.

The Manipulation of Existing Games

Far-right propagandists have increasingly adopted videogame aesthetics to make their propaganda more appealing to young Western audiences. Games set in historical recreations of the past have proved immensely popular (Chapman, 2016). One of the most recognizable, the *Assassins Creed* (Ubisoft) franchise, immerses players in incredibly detailed re-enactments of historical eras in various civilizations around the world, from ancient Greece and Egypt to revolutionary Russia. A key component of far-right propaganda is the invocation and creation of a glorious and utopian – albeit mythical – past. Just as Nazi Germany drew selectively from the pre-Weimar years for inspiration on how things "should be," and Italian fascists were nostalgic for a romanticized version of the fallen Roman Empire, present-day far-right movements, such as the pan-European Identitarian Movement (a transnational far-right network of activists mobilizing against globalization, immigration, and Islam), look to an imagined past in which Europe was ethnically "pure," as the basis on which to reconstruct an idealized future in which a white ethno-state can flourish (Valencia-Garcia, 2020).

Far-right propagandists frequently utilize the aesthetics of ancient Greece and Rome to provide support for their imagined idea of Western civilization, by offering a unified cultural narrative for the audience to draw from that is customarily regarded in the popular imagination as the apex of classical artistic and cultural achievement. So history, or rather its manipulation into an artificial historical construction, becomes a means for glorifying masculinity and whiteness, ideals that far-right ideologies conceive as synonyms with their aspirations for Western civilization. For example, the Identitarian Movement has increasingly been exploiting artifacts, texts, and historical figures evocative of ancient Greece to lend cultural weight to its reactionary vision of ideal masculinity in a bid to perpetuate the idea that white men are the guardians of intellectual authority and advertise itself as a movement that has the potential to return to the cultural achievements of ancient Greece and Rome (Zuckerberg, 2018). Figure 7.2 is an example of imagery disseminated by Europa Invicta – a visual propaganda arm of the Identitarian Movement – utilizing artwork from the video game *Assassins Creed Odyssey* (Ubisoft). The game relates a mythological history of the Peloponnesian War between Athens and Sparta (431–422 BCE), in which the protagonist is a Spartan-born *misthios* (wandering mercenary) who has the option of siding with either Athens and its Delian League allies, or Sparta and its Peloponnesian League city states.

Figure 7.2 incorporates not only artwork from *Assassins Creed Odyssey* but also the phrase "Back to the Warmth of Rome"– a play on words of one of the main songs in the game's soundtrack, "The Flight," which contains the lyrics "Back to the Warmth of Home." The image clearly depicts ancient Athens, identifiable by its famous landmarks, most notably the Acropolis and the Parthenon, although the figure is dressed in the traditional Spartan armor – the *aspis* (shield), crimson tunic, and large bronze helmet. This discrepancy demonstrates that the creators of such images are more concerned with the overall aesthetic of ancient Greece, and what this conjures in the audience's imagination, than with being historically accurate.

FIGURE 7.2 Propaganda image disseminated on the Europea Invicta Facebook page showing artwork of the game *Assassins Creed Odyssey*.

The gameplay allows audiences to identify Greek history as their own and, by acting out fantasies, such persuasive participation could strongly influence players' ideology in the physical world. The aesthetic of ancient Greece has further historical connotations: the Greeks resisted two Persian invasions, at the Battle of Marathon in 490 BCE and the Battle of Thermopylae a decade later. Such resistance to an invasion from the East is lauded by the far right, who interpret modern multicultural Europe as a defeated land, subject to the creeping invasion of nonwhite peoples – a narrative termed the Great Replacement Theory (Davey & Ebner, 2019) and a version of history that sees only centuries of Eastern conquest and conflict, but which overlooks integration, collaboration, and cohabitation. The appropriation of ancient Greece epitomizes a fundamental feature of the far right: the presumption that the ancient world serves as a source of inspiration for the white racial consciousness, which it is believed must be restored if the white race is to survive. This core belief is sustained by erroneous interpretations and distortions of the historical record, that convey certain ancient culture as wholly admirable, timeless, and, most importantly, white.

Videogames, especially those with violent themes and gameplay have tended to avoid any recognizable settings or direct correlation with real-life foreign policy (Gagnon, 2010; Schulzke, 2013). In March 2018, *Far Cry 5* (Ubisoft) attracted global media attention by setting its scenes within the fictional "Hope County," a region located within the real-world state of Montana. The provocative decision to use the modern USA as a backdrop can be considered a direct response to the politically polarized climate of that time (Marsh, 2018). Capitalizing on religious symbolism, the cover art of *Far Cry 5* on the game's box, the promotional posters, and the online imagery in the virtual stores and the game's home screen resemble one of the most recognizable pieces of art in history, Leonardo da Vinci's *Last Supper*, which instituted the bread and wine of the Eucharist, the heart of Christian worship. The manipulation of this image by the far right has provided powerful and much used propaganda, designed to emphasize the intricate connections between religion, politics, and gun control, and portraying the fictitious members of the Caucasian Christian doomsday cult in the game *Eden's Gate* as a powerful militant organization (Kingdon, 2019). More specifically, variations of this artwork have appeared in *Instagram* (instagram.com) posts with accounts affiliated with the religious right, a strategically organized minority that gained influence under former President Trump (Marcotte, 2020). This is a clear example of far-right narratives utilizing artwork from games to promote the need for a more avowedly religious and explicitly Christian country, a message reinforced by the use of religious concepts and scriptures to justify threats and violence;

their incorporation of widely recognized gaming elements helps them connect even more effectively with target audiences.

Although the cult of *Eden's Gate* may be unique in its detail, the underlying concept has a precedent based in reality, drawing from the *Bundy Stand-Offs* in Bunkerville, Nevada, in 2015 and the Malheur National Wildlife Refuge in Oregon in 2016 (Walker, 2018). The Bundys' opposition to the federal government promoted radical libertarian utopian ideas and the illusion that they were saviors of the American West, by tapping into anti-government sentiment and creating an image of a patriotic cowboy around whom people could rally, they both justified violence and resonated with their audience (Kingdon, 2021). In anti-government groups on the social media platform *Gab* (https://gab.com/), screenshots from the game are used symbolically to represent the "Old West," a testament of how America ought to be, these traditional masculine values being exemplified within the scenes selected from the game. As Robinson and Whittaker (2021) argue, seeing videogames as sources of propaganda working to reinforce the views of those already emphatic to an organization's messages, significantly assists the understanding of the interrelationship between audiences and propagandists. As the manipulation of *Far Cry 5* highlights, all videogames have a story to tell, but when used for propaganda, narratives are usually shaped and manipulated by the players, rather than being embedded in the game itself.

The aesthetics encompass the theme and style of the game, and those that create unique and recognizable art styles are likely to be more attractive to potential recruits. For example, because the narratives of *Far Cry 5* are resonant of the current political climate in the USA, the utilization of artwork from this specific game are strategically utilized in propaganda to reflect the political uncertainty that has emerged within the USA, which, aggravated by the socioeconomic issues such as recession and mass migration has led to an increase in ethnic tensions. As this chapter has illustrated, videogames are becoming ever more adept at interweaving fictional elements of popular culture and political activism. What has become clear is that no matter how escapist in design or intent videogames may be, they are the products of, and therefore reflect, the political, social, and cultural frameworks from which they emerge (Kingdon, 2019). Generating fear and interweaving it with elements of truth, even if only partial, makes for compelling propaganda, and videogames such as *Far Cry 5*, rooted in the complex politics of the modern USA, are thus particularly persuasive.

Conclusion

When it comes to aesthetics, technology has expanded the canvas on which propagandists are able to create and tell their stories. As an art form that only exists in digital space, videogames are truly a collision of art and science that has promoted the evolution of many new forms of artistic expression (Melissinos, 2015). It is in this way that gaming aesthetics revoke the modern boundaries between modes of cognition, experience, and expression. The imagery included in this chapter has demonstrated that videogame propaganda cannot be as comprehensively understood without considering the role played by aesthetics, as increasingly, propaganda is infused with political ideology to transform narratives into a unified work of art. Examination of the historical and subcultural elements contained within videogame-related imagery provides an opportunity to analyze how ideologies of extremism become intertwined with cultural representations, and demonstrates the importance of the contribution of visual analysis in making research more integrated and significant. Videogames are not just reflections of the historical period that they seek to recreate, but also products of the time in which they are created (Fuller, 2022). Future research should therefore focus on the utilization of internet memes featuring videogame aesthetics as a distinctly powerful medium with the capability of conveying ideologies easily and seamlessly between groups and locations.

One of the key messages of this chapter has been to convey the importance of looking beyond the immediately apparent impact of imagery to reveal the underlying force and power that visual culture can have. It is of paramount importance for future research to take into account the complexity of the extremist/social media nexus as, repeatedly, propagandists borrow aesthetics from videogames, turning their purpose, as a specific interactive medium, from one solely to entertain, to one also encompassing socialization, education, and communication of ideas, ideology and opinion. Increased attention must also be placed on the aesthetic and subcultural elements of propaganda, and the ways in which the content of videogames could be resonating with the individual, as well as with the wider audience. In the contemporary world of ever increasing digital spectacle, narratives of extremism are promulgated as much through the image as through the word; consequently, researchers need to utilize the visual evidence used by propagandists within their imagery, to gain an understanding of the power of imagery in shaping popular opinion and the social perception of extremism and radicalization.

Notes

1 "Boss" battles generally occur at the climax of a particular section of the game, usually at the end of a level or stage, or guarding a specific object. The enemy Boss is generally far stronger than the opponents the player has faced up until that point, and it usually faced solo.

2 A single, raised index finger as a symbol of their cause and a well-known sign of power and victory around the world.
3 Respawn is a gaming term used to describe a situation where a computer or human-controlled character in a video game comes back to life after dying or being killed.
4 In Islam, Jannah is the final abode of the righteous and it often used symbolically to refer to paradise.
5 A *nasheed* is a song without musical instruments with lyrics that resemble hymns praising Allah.
6 Zionist Occupied Government (ZOG) refers to the US federal government, which, adherents contend, is controlled or manipulated by international Jewish interests.

References

Al-Rawi, A. (2018). Video Games, Terrorism, and ISIS's Jihad 3.0. *Terrorism and Political Violence, 30*(4), 740–760.
Anderson, C. (2016). Syrian Warfare Set for Steam Green Light. https://www.keengamer.com/articles/news/syrian-warfare-set-for-steam-greenlight/.
Atkinson, P. & Parsayi, F. (2021). Video Games and Aesthetic Contemplation. *Games and Culture, 16*(5), 519–537.
Barr, M. & Copeland-Stewart, A. (2022). Playing Video Games During the COVID-19 Pandemic and Effects on Players' Well-Being. *Games and Culture, 17*(1), 122–139.
Bezio, K. (2018). Ctrl-Alt-Del: GamerGate as a Precursor to the Rise of the Alt-Right. *Leadership, 14*(5), 556–566.
Brett, N. (2021). Moments of Political Gameplay: Game Design as a Mobilisation Tool for Far-Right Action. In M. Devries, J. Bessant, & R. Watts (Eds.), *Rise of the Far Right: Technologies of Recruitment and Mobilisation* (pp. 215–237). Rowman & Littlefield Publishers.
Bohemia Interactive (2013). *Arma 3*. [Videogame]
Carrabine, E. (2012). Just Images: Aesthetics, Ethics and Visual Criminology. *British Journal of Criminology, 52*(1), 463–489.
Cats who Play (2017). *Syrian Warfare*. [Videogame]
Cengiz, M. (2019). Prevention of the Procurement of Arms and Explosives by Terrorists. In A. Schmid (Ed.), *The Handbook of Terrorism Prevention and Preparedness* (pp.508–532). ICCT.
Chapman, A. (2016). *Digital Games as History: How videogames represent the past and offer access to historical practice*. Routledge.
Chapple, A. (2020). That Gun! Lukashenka Chooses Weapon Favored By Osama Bin Laden, Islamic State Leader. https://www.rferl.org/a/30801778.html.
Clements, J. (2022). Online Gaming – Statistics & Facts. https://www.statista.com/topics/1551/online-gaming/#dossierKeyfigures.
Clements, J. (2023). Number of Users of Video Games Worldwide 2017–2027. https://www.statista.com/statistics/748044/number-video-gamers-world/.
Condis, M. (2020). Hateful Games: Why White Supremacist Recruiters Target Gamers. In J. Reyman & E.M. Sparby (Eds.), *Digital Ethics: Rhetoric and responsibility in online aggression* (pp. 143–159). Routledge.

Conway, M. (2017). Determining the Role of the Internet in Violent Extremism and Terrorism: Six Suggestions for Progressing Research. *Studies in Conflict and Terrorism, 40*(1), 77–98.

Cowan, D. (2009, November 19). America's Army Most Effective Recruitment Tool for US Army. [Weblog]. https://www.gamedeveloper.com/pc/-i-america-s-army-i-most-effective-recruitment-tool-for-u-s-army.

Daniels, J. & Lalone, N. (2012). Racism in Video Gaming: Connecting Extremist and Mainstream Expressions of White Supremacy. *Social Exclusion, Power, and Video Game Play: New Research in Digital Media and Technology,* 85–99.

Dauber, C.E. (2019). Call of Duty: Jihad – How the Video Game Motif Has Migrated Downstream from Islamic State Propaganda Videos. *Perspectives on Terrorism, 13*(3), 17–27.

Davey, J. & Ebner, J. (2019). "The Great Replacement": The Violent Consequences of Mainstreamed Extremism. https://www.isdglobal.org/isd-publications/the-great-replacement-the-violent-consequences-of-mainstreamed-extremism/.

Dawkins, R. (1976). *The Selfish Gene.* Oxford University Press.

Daymon, C. (2020). LOL Extremism: Humour in Online Extremist Content. https://gnet-research.org/2020/10/26/lol-extremism-humour-in-online-extremist-content/.

Eagleton, T. (1988). The Ideology of the Aesthetic. *Poetics Today, 9*(2), 327–338.

El Ghamari, M. (2017). Pro-Daesh Jihadist Propaganda A Study of Social Media and Video Games. *Security and Defence Quarterly, 14*(1), 69–90.

Emery, D. (2022). Snopestionary: What Was "Gamergate"? https://www.snopes.com/articles/402899/what-was-gamergate/.

Fisher-Birch, J. (2020). The Emerging Threat of Extremist-Made Video Games. https://www.counterextremism.com/blog/emerging-threat-extremist-made-video-games.

Fuller, C. (2022). Playing at Digital Soldiers. *Art Quarterly.*

Gagnon, F. (2010). "Invading Your Hearts and Minds": *Call of Duty®* and the (Re)Writing of Militarism in US Digital Games and Popular Culture. *European Journal of American Studies, 5*(3).

Havis, M. (2016). Sick Video Game that Lets Players kill Syrians is "a Gift to ISIS". https://www.dailystar.co.uk/news/latest-news/syrian-warfare-video-game-russia-19176575.

Hegghammer, T. (2017). *Jihadi Culture: The art and social practices of militant Islamists.* Cambridge University Press.

Huey, L. (2015). This is Not Your Mother's Terrorism: Social Media, Online Radicalization and the Practice of Political Jamming. *Journal of Terrorism Research, 6*(2). http://jtr.st-andrews.ac.uk/articles/10.15664/jtr.1159/.

Johnson, R.V. (1969). *Aestheticism.* Routledge.

Katz, J. (1988). *Seductions of Crime: A chilling exploration of the criminal mind – from juvenile delinquency to cold-blooded murder.* Basic Books.

Kelland, M. (2011). From Game Mod to Low-Budget Film: The Evolution of Machinima. In H. Lowood & M. Nitsche (Eds.), *The Machinima Reader* (pp. 23–37). MIT Press.

Kellner, D. (2016). *Guys and Guns Amok: Domestic terrorism and school shootings from the Oklahoma City bombing to the Virginia Tech massacre.* Routledge.

Khosravi, R. (2017). Neo-Nazis are Making their Own Video Games—and They're just as Horrifying as You'd Think. https://www.mic.com/articles/174705/neo-nazis-are-making-their-own-video-games-and-they-re-just-as-horrifying-as-you-d-think.

Kingdon, A. (2017). Seductions of the Caliphate: A Cultural Criminological Analysis of Online Islamic State Propaganda. *Internet Journal of Criminology.* https://docs.wixstatic.com/ugd/b93dd4_990f66a56f064179990215b0f7238b5d.pdf.

Kingdon, A. (2019). Framing *Far Cry 5*: The Gamification of White Separatist Propaganda. In E. Leidig (Ed.), *Mainstreaming the Global Radical Right* (pp. 257–262). Ibidem-Verlag.

Kingdon, A. (2021). The Meme Is the Method: Examining the Power of the Image Within Extremist Propaganda. In A. Lavorgna & T. Holt (Eds.), *Researching Cybercrimes: Methodologies, ethics, and critical approaches* (pp. 301–322). Palgrave Macmillan.

Kingdon, A. (2023). God of Race War: The Utilisation of Viking-Themed Video Games in Far-Right Propaganda. https://gnet-research.org/2023/02/06/god-of-race-war-the-utilisation-of-viking-themed-video-games-in-far-right-propaganda/.

Kingdon, A. & Krause, J. (2021). Dark Tech Futures: The Far Right and the Quantum Arms Race. *Centre for Analysis of the Radical Right.* https://rantt.com/radical-right-extremists-and-the-quantum-arms-race.

Koehler, D, Fiebig, V. & Jugl, I. (2022). From Gaming to Hating: Extreme-Right Ideological Indoctrination and Mobilization for Violence of Children on Online Gaming Platforms. *Political Psychology*, 1–16.

Lakhani, S. (2021). Video Gaming and Violent Extremism: An Exploration of the Current Landscape, Trends, and Threats. https://home-affairs.ec.europa.eu/system/files/2022-02/EUIF%20Technical%20Meeting%20on%20Video%20Gaming%20October%202021%20RAN%20Policy%20Support%20paper_en.pdf.

Lenoir, T. & Caldwell, L. (2018). *The Military Entertainment Complex.* Harvard University Press.

Marcotte, A. (2020). Trump's Christian Right Worships Power More than they Worship God. https://www.salon.com/2020/03/03/trump-christian-right-power-worshippers-katherine-stewart/.

Marsh, C. (2018). When it Comes to Controversy, *Far Cry 5* will be on the Right Side of History. https://www.gamesradar.com/when-it-comes-to-controversy-far-cry-5-will-be-on-the-right-side-of-history/.

Mattheis, A. (2021). Beyond the "LULZ": Memifying Murder as "Meaningful" Gamification in Far-Right Content. https://gnet-research.org/2021/01/18/beyond-the-lulz-memifying-murder-as-meaningful-gamification-in-far-right-content/.

Mayer, J. (2018). How Russia Helped Swing the Election for Trump. https://www.newyorker.com/magazine/2018/10/01/how-russia-helped-to-swing-the-election-for-trump.

Mckew, M. (2018). Brett Kavanaugh and the Information Terrorists Trying to Reshape America. https://www.wired.com/story/information-terrorists-trying-to-reshape-america/.

Melissinos, C. (2015). Video Games Are One of the Most Important Art Forms in History. https://time.com/collection-post/4038820/chris-melissinos-are-video-games-art/#:~:text=As%20an%20art%20form%20that,that%20transcends%20any%20one%20type.

Meyer, R. (2018). The Grim Conclusions of the Largest-Ever Study of Fake News. https://www.theatlantic.com/technology/archive/2018/03/largest-study-ever-fake-news-mit-twitter/555104/.

Moody-Ramirez, M. & Church, A.B. (2019). Analysis of Facebook Meme Groups Used During the 2016 US Presidential Election. *Social Media & Society*, *1*(1), 1–11.

O'Connor, C. (2021). The Extreme Right on Twitch. https://www.isdglobal.org/wp-content/uploads/2021/08/05-gaming-report-twitch.pdf.

O'Shaughnessy, N. (2004). *Politics and Propaganda: Weapons of Mass Seduction*. Manchester University Press.

Petrilla Entertainment (2003). *Quest for Saddam*. [Videogame]

Piata, A. (2016). When Metaphor Becomes a Joke: Metaphor Journeys from Political Ads to Internet Memes. *Journal of Pragmatics*, *106*(1), 39–56.

Robinson, N. & Whittaker, J. (2021). Playing for Hate? Extremism, Terrorism, and Videogames. *Studies in Conflict & Terrorism*.

Rockstar North (2013). *Grand Theft Auto 5*. [Videogame]

Rose, S. (2018). "Holy Defence": Hezbollah Issues Call of Duty to Video Gamers. https://www.middleeasteye.net/news/holy-defence-hezbollah-issues-call-duty-video-gamers.

Ross, A. & Rivers, D. (2017). Digital Cultures of Political Participation: Internet Memes and the Discursive Delegitimization of the 2016 US Presidential Candidates. *Discourse, Context & Media*, *16*(1), 1–11.

Rottman, G.L. (2010). *The Rocket Propelled Grenade*. Osprey Publishing.

Salter, M. (2018). From Geek Masculinity to Gamergate: The Technological Rationality of Online Abuse. *Crime Media Culture*, *14*(2), 247–264.

Schulzke, M. (2013). Being a Terrorist: Video Game Simulations of the Other Side of the War on Terror. *Media, War & Conflict*, *6*(3), 207–220.

Selepak, A. (2010). Skinhead Super Mario Brothers: An Examination of Racist and Violent Games on White Supremacist Web Sites. *Journal of Criminal Justice and Popular Culture*, *17*(1), 1–47.

Sherlock, R. (2018). Hezbollah Designed A Video Game To Appeal To The US. https://www.npr.org/2018/07/16/629588453/hezbollah-designed-a-video-game-to-appeal-to-the-u-s.

Snowdon, P. (2014). "Game over Mubarak": The Arab Revolutions and the Gamification of Everyday Life. *Fast Capitalism*, *11*(1), 23–29.

Sunde, H.M., Ilan, J., & Sandberg, S. (2020). A Cultural Criminology of "New" Jihad: Insights from Propaganda Magazines. *Crime, Media, Culture*, *17*(2).

Treyarch (2010). *Call of Duty: Black Ops*. [Videogame]

Ubisoft (2007). *Assassins Creed*. [Videogame]

Ubisoft (2018). *Assassins Creed Odyssey*. [Videogame]

Ubisoft (2018). *Far Cry 5*. [Videogame]

Valencia-Garcia, L. (2020). *Far Right Revisionism and the End of History*. Routledge.

Veilleux-Lepage, Y. (2020). *How Terror Evolves: The emergence and spread of terrorist techniques*. Rowman & Littlefield Publishers.

Walker, A. (2018). Talking Cults and Culture with the Developers of *Far Cry 5*. https://www.vice.com/en/article/d3wjyv/far-cry-5-interview-talking-cults-and-culture-with-the-developers.

Winter, C. (2022). *The Terrorist Image: Decoding the Islamic State's photo propaganda*. Hurst & Co.

Woods, H.S. & Hahner, L.A. (2020). *Make America Meme Again: The rhetoric of the Alt-Right*. Peter Lang Publishing.

Zuckerberg, D. (2018). *Not All Dead White Men: Classics and misogyny in the digital age*. Harvard University Press.

Zyda, M. (2022). *Weapons of Mass Distraction: The America's army game at 20*. Computer, 55(1), 112–122.

8

A IS FOR APPLE, B IS FOR BULLET

The Gamification of (Violent) Extremism

Suraj Lakhani

Christchurch, 2019

"Remember lads, subscribe to PewDiePie" were the words uttered by 28-year-old Australian national, Brenton Tarrant, as he calmly drove through the streets of Christchurch, New Zealand, towards his first target, the Al Noor Mosque. Within a mere 36 minutes, using numerous weapons, Tarrant had committed the deadliest mass shooting New Zealand had witnessed in 30 years (Macklin, 2019). In total, 51 Muslim worshippers were gunned down in cold blood across two locations on that Friday afternoon in March 2019, including a three-year-old child. But what did PewDiePie, one of the most subscribed to YouTubers, have to do with the attack? The answer is both simple in some regards, yet exceptionally complicated in others. Only those with comprehension of fast-moving internet subcultures could help to translate this and other decisions taken by the perpetrator. At the time of writing, PewDiePie, real name Felix Arvid Ulf Kjellberg, a Swedish-born video-gamer and YouTuber, has over 111,000,000 "subs" (or subscribers, i.e., those who have specifically chosen to follow a channel and receive its content) and is the fifth most subscribed to channel on the social media platform. However, back in 2019, the term "subscribe to PewDiePie" was considered to be a "meme," a term used to "shitpost"[1] and to identify to others that you were an internet insider, someone who not only understood online subcultures, but were firmly entrenched within that culture. If you got the "joke," you were one of them. It appears that this may well have been the intention of Tarrant, to declare to other *8Chan* users – a now banned imageboard frequented by far-right violent extremists – that he was one of *them*.

DOI: 10.4324/9781003388371-9

The fact that Kjellberg was a video-gamer – one who regularly produced videos of himself playing games, reviewing games, or navigating often murky and "edgy" subcultures associated with gaming – is no coincidence. Videogames and gaming-related considerations played a big part in Tarrant's attack and formed a dominant part of Tarrant's identity; he was described in the official Royal Commission of Inquiry (2020) into the terrorist attack on Christchurch as an "avid internet user and online gamer." One of his relatives went even further and described Tarrant as having a "severe addiction" to videogames (Macklin, 2019). From mentions of obscure gaming-related references in his manifesto, to "'jokes" made by those responding on an *8Chan* thread initiated by the perpetrator moments before his attack that corresponded to classic videogames, to the "subscribe to PewDiePie" expression picked up on the video he was livestreaming on *Facebook*, this attack was complicatedly entwined with video-gaming. It was his livestream that caught the interest of many around the world, particularly as it felt that the attack resembled a videogame in the style of the prevalent first-player shooter (FPS) genre. There are wider parallels here with popular "Let's Play" videos, which document the play through of a section or entirety of a videogame watched by an audience either live or as a recording afterwards (Lakhani, 2021). When analyzing other parts of Tarrant's attack – as undertaken by Lakhani and Wiedlitzka (2022) – including his 74-page manifesto, and the *8Chan* thread he initiated, and subsequent replies, it can be argued it had distinct similarities with "gamification."

This chapter focusses on the growing threat associated with the gamification of violent extremism. It does so, first, by defining the term and conceptualizing it more broadly. Considerations of how gamification can intersect with violent extremism using real-world examples then follow. The chapter is focussed towards far-right extremism rather than other threats, including jihadism. This does not mean that the gamification of violent extremism in relation to the latter is not important, more so it reflects the current state of research. The section thereafter critiques the concept of the gamification of violent extremism and considers whether alone it can be responsible for radicalization or as the sole motivator to undertake acts of terrorism. This section also considers the wider value and usefulness of gamification. A short conclusion then follows summarizing the chapter and briefly outlining considerations for future threats.

Conceptualizing Gamification

Gamification "feeds on an environment" of numerous people globally playing videogames on computers, consoles, phones, and tablets (Kim &

Werbach, 2016). In 2022 alone, it was estimated that there were over 3 billion gamers, amounting to roughly 40% of the world's population (Clement, 2022). Primarily due to this increasing popularity with gaming, those implementing gamified strategies believe that "since video games are designed with the primary purpose of entertainment, and since they can demonstrably motivate users to engage with them with unparalleled intensity and duration, game elements should be able to make other, non-game products and services more enjoyable and engaging as well." (Deterding et al., 2011, p. 10) One of the inaccuracies or misinterpretations when considering the gamification of (violent) extremism, however, is the conflation with the production of bespoke and modified violent extremist videogames; "although they have overlaps, they are distinct phenomena" (RAN, 2020, p. 2). These issues have also manifested within gamified approaches to business, with academics feeling the need to point out that "what distinguishes 'gamification' from 'regular' entertainment games and serious games is that they are built with the intention of a system that includes elements from games, not a full 'game proper' ... We therefore suggest restricting 'gamification' to the description of elements that are characteristic to games – elements that are found in most (but not necessarily all) games, readily associated with games, and found to play a significant role in gameplay" (Deterding et al., 2011, p. 12).

How, though, can the term "gamification" specifically begin to be defined and conceptualized? Unsurprisingly, as is frequently the case when taking academic approaches to defining key terms, gamification – at least definitionally – is contested. As with the terms "terrorism" (Hoffman, 2017), "extremism" (Lakhani, 2014), and "radicalization" (Schmid, 2013), there is no universally accepted definition of gamification (Sailer et al., 2017), regardless of the rapidly increasing number of gamified approaches and applications. There is a plethora of varying definitions (Deterding et al., 2011). When analyzing the literature, the "majority of scholars do, however, agree upon some general aspects of its being" (Lakhani & Wiedlitzka, 2022, p. 3). Gamification, as charted above, is about harnessing the motivational potential associated with videogames and gaming, and, at its very core, "is the use of game design elements in non-game contexts" (Deterding et al., 2011, p. 10).

Asking where the bakery is in French in Paris has never been so much fun to learn for language seekers around the world with the emergence of gamified learning techniques – at least according to app developers, such as *Duolingo*. Companies including McDonald's also regularly implement gamification with product sales – teaming up with one of the best-known board games of all time, *Monopoly* (Parker Brothers). Customers who purchase products at the global food franchise during the gamified period find *Monopoly*-themed stickers attached, stickers that when peeled reveal prizes consisting of food, cash, holidays or other winnings. As with the basic premise of the original *Monopoly* game – including its various editions – special prizes are available for those committed (and, likely, fortunate) customers who collect full sets of stickers, e.g., all the railways (Lakhani *et al.*, 2022).

McDonald's and *Duolingo* are by no means alone. Increasing numbers of businesses are realizing the potential of gamification to achieve various objectives and address different challenges including solidifying user commitment and loyalty to their brand, customer satisfaction, generating and increasing spending on products, improving employee satisfaction, motivation, and performance (Kim & Werbach, 2016), and the actual value it holds for employees themselves (Mitchell *et al.*, 2020). Brands such as Nike, Coca-Cola, Starbucks, among countless others, and even rap brands like Jay-Z, have successfully gamified products or parts of their businesses to these ends. Due to these seemingly successful experimentations with gamified approaches as business solutions, the "implementation of gamification or gamified applications and systems have diversified into numerous sectors, including finance, education, government, health, news, entertainment, marketing and advertising, public engagement, environmental protection, amongst others" (Lakhani & Wiedlitzka, 2022, p. 3).

The idea of using game design principles to affect motivation (and, as part of this, behavior change) in nongaming contexts appear to underpin organizations' strategic implementation of gamified applications (Robson *et al.*, 2016). Gamification is "considered to be a motivating force as it provides competition, an element of fun, positive reinforcement as rewards are offered (in the form of points, for example), and a social aspect where people have opportunities to connect with friends and others" (Lakhani, 2023, p. 114). It is an approach that "establishes objectives addressed ostensibly to the hedonic desires of the individual" including fun or compulsion, through the implementation of "psychological levers such as social comparison or rewards" (Kim & Werbach, 2016, p. 160). Broadly speaking, as outlined by Lakhani and Wiedlitzka (2022), motivation can be considered as "intrinsic" or "extrinsic," with intrinsic motivation relating to those activities for the purposes of personal satisfaction, and extrinsic motivation being "external to the behavior ... usually derived from the outcomes of the behavior, such as rewards, punishments, or social pressure" (Mitchell *et al.*, 2020, p. 324). The latter is primarily about offering the reward of points, badges, or climbing up leaderboards (PBLs) with competition being a dominant driving force (Kim & Werbach, 2016; Sailer *et al.*, 2017; Mitchell *et al.*, 2020); something "that give[s] consumers information about their achievements, progress and high scores" (Bittner & Shipper, 2014, p. 391). Work on gamification of violent extremism tends to focus on extrinsic motivation, although academics have argued a deeper exploration of the value of intrinsic motivation should also be considered (Mattheis, 2021). Similarly, many assert that either of these motivations (intrinsic or extrinsic) alone is not enough and should be considered combined (Bittner & Shipper, 2014).

A for Apple, B for Bomb: Gamification and (Violent) Extremism

Over the years, (violent) extremists have also either realized the potential of gamification or have more organically implemented these types of approach into their activities as some of them are gamers themselves and there is some alignment with the particular subcultures they are part of. Whether in the digital realm, actions in the physical world, or a blending of both, gamification has played a prominent role in various strategies or acts of terrorism implemented by violent extremist organizations or individuals affiliated (ideologically or otherwise) to violent extremism. Numerous instances exemplifying the gamification of (violent) extremism exist, from Islamic State's use of gamification within propaganda videos (Wicks, 2020), some of which have displayed the "familiar imagery of FPS [First Player Shooter] games … by using HD helmet cameras" (Schlegel, 2020a, p. 9), to the supporters of Al Qaeda building "reputation points" and rankings into forums (Brachman & Levine, 2011). Far-right and jihadist forums in the early 2000s also featured ranks or levels for posting comments, reputation meters, and virtual badges as rewards, with other rewards for those considered to be committed included being invited to participate in certain "secret" groups online (Schlegel, 2021). In terms of physical world actions, one of the most prominent and widely discussed examples holding distinct parallels to gamification is the Christchurch attack that was recounted at the start of this chapter. It is important, when considering these examples, to apply some sort of structure.

Within the context of (violent) extremism, researchers have loosely conceptualized gamification as either being "top down" or "bottom up" (Schlegel, 2021). Top-down gamification "refers to the strategic use of gamification by extremist organizations, such as the use of apps which offer points for undertaking various tasks, in order to recruit, disseminate propaganda, or encourage engagement and commitment, for example" (Lakhani & Wiedlitzka, 2022, p. 2), whereas bottom-up gamification is far more organic and frequently occurs with small groups of individuals, or individuals themselves, within both online and offline communities (Schlegel, 2021). Researchers have argued for the existence of bottom-up gamification within three broad examples: "[G]amification driven by perpetrators of attacks, gamification within online communities, and gamification in radicalization processes of individuals and small groups" (Schlegel, 2021, p. 5).

Top-Down Gamification

M is for missile and T is for tank. Developed for both desktop computers/ laptops and as a mobile phone application (app) on the Android mobile operating system, Islamic State's *Huroof* app took the traditional "A is for apple" method popular across the world to teach young children a particular alphabet as its approach to teach its youth Arabic; although in this instance using distinct symbols affiliated to violence and war. Publicized through various wide-ranging and wide-reaching official Islamic State outlets, the app "combines bright colors, pictures of grass, trees, clouds, trains, balloons, as well other 'classic' graphics used in books for children, with 'militaristic vocabulary' ... and illustrations of guns, bullets, rockets, cannons, or tanks" (Lakomy, 2019, p. 394). The value and effect of gamification in terms of (violent) extremism is relatively unknown and somewhat contested (Lakhani *et al.*, 2022), as will be discussed later, although it is reasonable to suggest that the app was developed "arguably in a bid to reinforce commitment to Islamic State ideologies, aims, and objectives" (Lakhani, 2022).

The production of an app as demonstration of top-down gamification is not necessarily reserved for Islamic State, with the Identitarian Movement[2] also having an app that was apparently in development at one point, although (at the time of writing) never completed or released. *Patriot Peer* was set to bring together numerous gamified elements within one app with the aim of motivating its users to not only deepen their commitment to the cause, but to be more social and (as numerous unsolicited junk folder emails promise) to connect users with like-minded individuals. A large part of it was, thus, about "facilitating networking within the movement" (Schlegel, 2020a, p. 13). At its core, however, developers of the app planned to turn "resistance into a game" (Schlegel, 2020a, p. 14). Resting on the notion of extrinsic motivation as detailed in the previous section, "[u]sers of the app would attain points and move up the rankings and leaderboard by undertaking various tasks which included networking (connecting with others on the app and in person – facilitated through the app), [and] visiting sites deemed to be of cultural heritage" (Lakhani *et al.*, 2022, p. 10), with points also potentially awarded for taking action deemed beneficial to Identitarian Movement causes, including "disrupting cultural or political events of adversaries or by disturbing the operation of boats used to rescue refugees in the Mediterranean Sea" (Schlegel, 2020a, p. 13).

Bottom-Up Gamification

Bottom-up gamification describes a more organic approach with the emphasis on the individual or small group(s) of individuals. Alongside the aforementioned Christchurch attacks (and subsequent attacks of a similar nature),[3] other examples of gamifying violent extremism can be found littered across recent years. In 2018, as one particular example, British white supremacist David Parnham was sentenced to 12 1/2 years in prison for distributing flyers that called for various actions to be taken on 3 April 2018 (Dearden, 2019). As recounted and shared online by the numerous mosques and individual Muslims Parnham sent the flyers to, people would be "rewarded" with a points-based system for engaging in abusive and violent acts towards Muslims, Islamic symbols, and places of worship, including: "Verbally abuse a Muslim" (10 points); "Pull the head-scarf off a Muslim 'woman'" (25 points); "Throw acid in the face of a Muslim" (50 points); "Beat up a Muslim" (100 points); "Torture a Muslim using electrocution, skinning, use of a rack" (250 points); "Butcher a Muslim using gun, knife, vehicle or otherwise" (500 points); "Burn or bomb a mosque" (1,000 points)'; and "Nuke Mecca" (2,500 points).

Parnham was by no means the only person to implement this type of gamified approach towards enacting hate and violent extremism. After failing to gain access to a synagogue to undertake a massacre in 2019, Stephen Balliet proceeded to murder two people on the streets of Halle, Germany. Alongside the similarities to the Christchurch attack including the FPS-like visual choreography of the livestream (as will be mentioned later), numerous other indications of gamification could be detected, such as outlining in his manifesto a range of "objectives" and "achievements" that he intended to "unlock" (Lakhani et al., 2022; Lakhani & Wiedlitzka, 2022). With the overt overlaps with objectives and achievements found within numerous videogames, Balliet's manifesto outlined that as part of the gamified attack, "[p]oints would be scored, he explained, for killing Jews, Muslims, Christians, blacks, children and communists, as well as through the use of different means, including 3D-printed guns, grenades, swords, a nail-bomb, and his 'secret weapon,' which likely referred to his car. The gunman was doubtless hoping future attackers would tally up his 'high score' – and eventually try to beat it" (Hoffman & Ware, 2020).

Communities of Support and Cultural Scripts

When considering Christchurch, alongside the actual attack which has similarities to either strategic or organic gamification (i.e., purposeful or resembling videogames by chance, or due to the perpetrator being entrenched in gaming subcultures), wider consideration also needs to be given to (often online) communities that become involved. Not necessarily in the physical act itself, but as communities of support. After Christchurch – and, in fact, after Anders Breivik's 2011 Oslo attack and various mass school shootings including Columbine (Lakhani & Wiedlitzka, 2022) – countless forums in visible and more obscure online spaces were replete with people celebrating these types of mass atrocity and at the same time (purposefully and/or organically) gamifying the attacks. *Telegram*, imageboards such as *4Chan/8Chan*, and other online spaces contained gamification-related expressions including "Game over for this person" and "Beat that score" – referring to the high body count "achieved" by Tarrant and encouraging others to better this (RAN, 2020). Even during the attack and afterwards, users on *8Chan* asked, "So what's the fucking highscore?", urging others to "GUESS THE BODY COUNT" (Lakhani & Wiedlitzka, 2022). Virtual leaderboards then become relevant in these communities. After Christchurch, a user on *8Chan* shared a picture of a gamified chart – originally posted on *4Chan* and updated over the years every time a relevant incident took place – which included various mass shooters (or shooters who intended mass casualties) like incel Elliot Roger and asked "where will he fit in[?]" (Lakhani & Wiedlitzka, 2022), referring, of course, to where the assailant would rank on the leaderboard. After this – as with the attacks that occurred prior – came encouragement. Users asked, "will you make it onto the leader board … in the fight for white survival?" (Macklin, 2022).

As Tarrant did, John T. Earnest also frequented *8Chan* and outlined on the thread he initiated moments before his attack on the synagogue, Chabad of Poway (USA), that he had been "lurking for a year and a half" and "what I've learned here is priceless. It's been an honor" (Macklin, 2019). The attack, which took place mere weeks after Christchurch, was met on that thread with people urging Earnest to "get the high score." He fortunately did not achieve this and, in the opinion of many who were in support of these attacks, he had failed in his objective and at the game and was even widely criticized and ridiculed. Earnest was not the only one who followed Tarrant's modus operandi. In fact, several did, many of whom were open about their admiration of Tarrant and outlined how he had in some way influenced them (Macklin, 2022). Alongside ideological nuance Tarrant's "propaganda of the deed" seems to have been particularly inspirational to others. "Tarrant was a catalyst for me personally. He showed me that it could be done. And that it needed to be done," stated Earnest in a document discovered by law enforcement (together with a copy of a web posting written by Tarrant). Highlighting the self-referential nature of these kinds of act, he added "Brenton Tarrant inspired me. I hope to inspire many more" (Macklin, 2019, p. 25). This affinity to

Tarrant, or at least the nature of his attack, was witnessed through the various similarities in how these attacks were undertaken and, importantly, gamified (Lakhani *et al.*, 2022). Several attackers attempted to or successfully livestreamed their attacks, used gamified language within manifestos, and included other aspects of gamification. The Halle attacker – as did the Buffalo shooter who came after (Lamphere-Englund & White, 2022) – livestreamed his attack to *Twitch* (www.twitch.tv), an Amazon-owned (primarily) gaming adjacent platform that is extremely popular with gamers (Lakhani, 2021), one on which people can engage with "Let's Play" videos (as mentioned earlier). The Poway attacker even included a playlist of songs, which included the Pokémon theme song. For some, Christchurch was considered to be a blueprint, a loose framework, referring to the incidents that came after as "copycat attacks." Others, such as Macklin (2022), have more accurately suggested that thinking about them as following the same "cultural script" is a more useful approach.

Gamification of Violent Extremism: A Critique

Gamification has its critics, ranging from those who assert that "gamification is not effective per se, but that specific game design elements have specific psychological effects" (Sailer *et al.*, 2017, p. 371), to the contestation of the underlying mechanisms of gamification where there is some assumption that its effects could be overestimated (Schlegel, 2020a). Gamification cannot be thought of as a "magic bullet" that has some causal effect on behavior, simply by introducing points, rewards, or a virtual leaderboard (Schlegel, 2021). Within studies of business alone these arguments resonate widely (Sailer *et al.*, 2017; Mitchell *et al.*, 2020), although when considering the use of gamification to motivate acts of violent extremism particular caution must be considered. Motivating someone to purchase their lunch from McDonald's rather than another fast food venue due to a gamified promotion is one thing, but motivating someone to undertake a massacre of human beings is another completely. As with videogames and violence more generally, gamification is not a causal factor of violence or extremism. Even from a basic approach, i.e., considering the control group, important questions need to be asked about why only an extremely small number of those who are exposed to gamified acts of violent extremism partake in their own. Much of this relates to the literature on radicalization, which posits it as a process or processes that – although there will be natural overlaps – are individual to each person and contingent on numerous micro-, macro-, and meso-level factors that are dependent on people's own life courses and experiences (Lakhani, 2014). This is a complicated multifaceted area concerning human actors with individual and overlapping motivations, conditions, needs and desires. Naturally, then, a "debate remains as to how exactly this is achieved … [with] one of the most common criticisms of gamification research [being] its focus on whether – to the exclusion of how – gamification can modify behavior" (Mitchell *et al.*, 2020, p. 324).

What then can be reasonably deduced about the use of gamification and its "value" within these types of attack? Although gamification alone more than likely will not be enough to motivate people to engage in violent extremism, it can play some, possibly quite important, role. Through a psychological and social psychological lens, ideas around pleasure, positive reinforcement, empowerment of users, peer competition, and social relatedness can be useful for extremists to capitalize on (Schlegel, 2021). This is particularly pertinent when considering the cultural aspects and value of games (Kowert & Newhouse, 2022). Across the literature, there are various broader aspects of gamification that can have an effect on (violent) extremism. It can enable a blurring of boundaries between the real and virtual world, and can be a way for some to structure reality (Schlegel, 2020b). Livestreams of attacks can also appeal to those within gaming communities due to "a familiarity in the form of messaging" (Schlegel, 2020a, p. 16). It can have subcultural appeal to people (Schlegel, 2021), including other gamers. This is about coolness, being edgy, excitement, and other existential attractions (Cottee & Hayward, 2011; Lakhani & Hardie-Bick, 2020). In his seminal book, Jack Katz (1988) argued that when studying criminality and deviance in general, there is a propensity to overly focus on background factors without properly considering the emotional, seductive, and sensual subjective phenomenological foreground. Gamifying violent extremism reinvigorates these arguments where it can be reasonably asserted that the literature needs to consider the experiential "foreground" in greater depth, as demonstrated in wider studies on violent extremism (cf. Cottee & Hayward, 2011; Lakhani & Hardie-Bick, 2020).

Gamification also publicizes the attack to a wider audience, blurs the line between "shitposting" and violent extremism, and appeals to wider and potentially younger groups of individuals, subcultures, or communities (Lakhani & Wiedlitzka, 2022). In this regard, gamification has the ability to build communities and deepen bonds within existing ones. Overall, as Schlegel (2020a, p. 29) argues:

> Games and gamified elements do not by themselves give rise to radicalization processes, but both can draw players in, immerse them more tightly within extremist communities, cause increased engagement and identification with extremist content and, like Jumanji, provide a

gateway or "a game for those who seek to find a way to leave their world behind." Some have argued that gamification even has the potential to increase engagement and identification with (violent) extremist content (RAN, 2020).

Others have discussed it within the context of violence, at least as contributing towards displaying "a socially inappropriate degree of moral indifference ... to fundamental human values such as the sanctity of life" (Kim & Werbach, 2016, p. 167); a process by which such violent acts are reframed as "worthy, just, necessary, or inconsequential" (Hartmann et al., 2014, p. 312).

Of course, wider parallels can be drawn here with established criminological theories, particularly Sykes and Matza's (1957) "techniques of neutralization," which describes how people neutralize moral concerns around conducting deviant acts based on denial of responsibility of the victim, or condemning the condemners, for example. Macklin (2019, 2022) develops these contemplations by arguing that it might serve better to consider these types of attack not as isolated acts, but as part of a cumulative continuum of "collective" extreme right violence. Thresholds of violence can then potentially be decreased each time an act of violence takes place. Subsequent attacks can also be inspired to be more devastating than the last, regardless of whether implementing gamification alone motivates people to participate in violent extremism. In other words, while these attacks "were the work of individual actors unconnected with one another, they were not 'random': their violence gained a cumulative momentum from this online milieu, which actively encouraged and glorified each successive act of violence in the hope of generating more terror" (Macklin, 2022, p. 216).

Conclusion

The study of gamification within the context of violent extremism is in its infancy and more research and resources need to be dedicated to illuminate this contemporary phenomenon. Through methodologically rigorous research, core questions need to be addressed or at least begin to be explored within these approaches. This includes determining the implications of the question posed earlier in this chapter, i.e., whether gamification is an intentional or purposeful strategy used by violent extremists (for recruitment, radicalization, behavior change, etc.) or whether its inclusion is more organic, due to these people being gamers themselves (or a blend of both). Of course, this will not be simple to determine, although beginning to better understand this question can help to shape future counterterrorism approaches (see Chapter 10 in this volume). These questions will only be sufficiently illuminated as this under-researched and new area of study continues to grow and relevant data is collected and analyzed. Researchers also need to consider where future threats lie, alongside dealing with current ones. Studying violent extremism is generally a fast moving landscape, something that is particularly exacerbated by the evolution of technology. Since the early use of murals to disseminate propaganda and ideologies to current uses of the internet, violent extremists have, of course unfortunately, been at the forefront of utilizing emerging technologies (Scrivens & Conway, 2019). These individuals and organizations need to be early adopters and innovators of technology in order to ensure growth (and arguably survival). Thus, looking to the future, decentralization is an aspect that should be closely monitored, with Web 3.0 and associated aspects likely being a prominent issue in the near to long-term future. In this regard, Lakhani (2023) contemplates possible scenarios of the gamification of violent extremism within the metaverse in this regard.

Considering the narrative of this chapter more broadly, there is no indication that the intersection between video-gaming and (violent) extremism is beginning to subside and, actually, it appears to only be strengthening; something the increasing popularity of gaming will only contribute to (Lakhani & Wiedlitzka, 2022). Gamification, which forms a critical part of this framework, is no different and, in fact, can be linked to numerous devastating attacks of violent extremism around the world. Although the consideration of results from studies pertaining to the application of gamification in the business world are useful, when applying them to the study of (violent) extremism there naturally needs to be some caution. This does not mean that considering gamification in this context is not useful, quite the contrary. The point here is that it cannot be forgotten that violent extremism generally, and acts of this nature, are often complicated and multifaceted – particularly when contemplating important questions around "how and "why." Gamification alone cannot provide answers to these questions, but it can form a dominant part of the narrative, particularly as wider research has found that prior experience with digital games has significant influence on investment in gamified products (Bittner & Shipper, 2014).

Notes

1 Shitposting "is the act of throwing out huge amounts of content, most of it ironic, low-quality trolling, for the purpose of provoking an emotional reaction in less Internet-savvy viewers. The ultimate goal is to derail productive discussion and distract readers" (Evans, 2019).

2 A right-wing Austrian "movement" led by Martin Sellner. Sellner has admitted involvement with neo-Nazi networks in his youth. Notably, he was sent a 1,500 Euro donation in 2018 from Brenton Tarrant, the Christchurch assailant (Wilson, 2019).
3 These include "an attack in April 2019 on a synagogue in Poway, California; two attacks in August 2019 inside a Wal-Mart in El Paso, Texas; a mosque in Bærum, Norway; an attempted attack in October 2019 on a synagogue in Halle, Germany; and more recently an attack in May 2022 in a store in Buffalo, New York" (Lakhani et al., 2022, p. 9).

References

Bittner, J.V. & Shipper, J. (2014). Motivational Effects and Age Differences of Gamification in Product Advertising. *Journal of Consumer Marketing*, 31(5), 391–400. 10.1108/JCM-04-2014-0945.

Brachman, J. & Levine, A. (2011, April 13). The World of Holy Warcraft: How Al Qaeda Is Using Online Game Theory to Recruit the Masses. *Foreign Policy*. https://foreignpolicy.com/2011/04/13/the-world-of-holy-warcraft/.

Clement, J. (2022, October 25). Number of Video Gamers Worldwide in 2021, by region. *Statista*. https://www.statista.com/statistics/293304/number-video-gamers/.

Cottee, S. & Hayward, K. (2011). Terrorist (E)motives: The Existential Attractions of Terrorism. *Studies in Conflict and Terrorism*, 34, 963–986.

Dearden, L. (2019, September 3). White Supremacist Behind "Punish a Muslim Day" Jailed for 12 Years. *Independent*. https://www.independent.co.uk/news/uk/crime/david-parnham-court-punish-muslim-day-sentence-white-supremacist-trial-a9090186.html.

Deterding, S., Dixon, D., Khaled, R., & Nacke, L. (2011). From Game Design Elements to Gamefulness: Defining "Gamification". *MindTrek*, 11, 9–15.

Evans, R. (2019). Shitposting, Inspirational Terrorism, and the Christchurch Mosque Massacre. *Bellingcat*. https://www.bellingcat.com/news/rest-of-world/2019/03/15/shitposting-inspirational-terrorism-and-the-christchurch-mosque-massacre/

Hartmann, T., Krakowiak, K.M., & Tsay-Vogel, M. (2014). How Violent Video Games Communicate Violence: A Literature Review and Content Analysis of Moral Disengagement Factors. *Communication Monographs*, 81(3), 310–332. 10.1080/03637751.2014.922206.

Hoffman, B. (2017). *Defining Terrorism*. Columbia University Press.

Hoffman, B. & Ware, J. (2020, June 21). The Challenges of Effective Counterterrorism Intelligence in the 2020s. *Lawfare*. https://www.lawfareblog.com/challenges-effective-counterterrorism-intelligence-2020s.

Katz, J. (1988). *Seductions of Crime: Moral and sensual attractions in doing evil*. Basic Books.

Kim, T.W. & Werbach, K. (2016). More Than Just a Game: Ethical Issues in Gamification. *Ethics and Information Technology*, 18(2), 157–173. 10.1007/s10676-016-9401-5.

Kowert, R. & Newhouse, A. (2022). *Landscape of Extremist Behaviour in Games [Conference Presentation]*. Game Developers Conference (GDC). San Francisco, CA, United States.

Lakhani, S. (2014). *Radicalisation as a Moral Career: A qualitative study of how people become terrorists in the United Kingdom*. Cardiff University Press.

Lakhani, S. (2021). *Video Gaming and (Violent) Extremism: An Exploration of the Current Landscape, Trends, and Threats*. Radicalisation Awareness Network *(Policy Support)*, European Commission. https://ec.europa.eu/home-affairs/system/files/2022-02/EUIF%20Technical%20Meeting%20on%20Video%20Gaming%20October%202021%20RAN%20Policy%20Support%20paper_en.pdf.

Lakhani, S. (2022, June 10). The Gamification of Violent Extremism: An Empirical Exploration of the Christchurch Attack. *GNET Insights*. https://gnet-research.org/2022/06/10/the-gamification-of-violent-extremism-an-empirical-exploration-of-the-christchurch-attack/.

Lakhani, S. (2023). When Digital and Physical Worlds Combine: The Metaverse and the Gamification of Violent Extremism. *Perspectives on Terrorism, XVII* (2), 108–125.

Lakhani, S. & Hardie-Bick, J. (2020). "There's a chance for adventure …": Exploring Excitement as an Existential Attraction of Violent Extremism", in D. Polizzi (Ed.), *Jack Katz: Seduction, the Streets and Emotion*. Emerald.

Lakhani, S., White, J., & Wallner, C. (2022). *The Gamification of (Violent) Extremism: An Exploration of Emerging Trends, Future Threat Scenarios, and Potential P/CVE Solutions*. Radicalisation Awareness Network *(Policy Support)*, European Commission. https://home-affairs.ec.europa.eu/system/files/2022-09/RAN%20Policy%20Support-%20gamification%20of%20violent%20extremism_en.pdf.

Lakhani, S. & Wiedlitzka, S. (2022). "Press F to Pay Respects": An Empirical Exploration of the Mechanics of Gamification in Relation to the Christchurch Attack. *Terrorism and Political Violence*, 1–18. 10.1080/09546553.2022.2064746.

Lakomy, M. (2019). Let's Play a Video Game: *Jihadi* Propaganda in the World of Electronic Entertainment. *Studies in Conflict & Terrorism, 42*(4), 383–406. 10.1080/1057610X.2017.1385903.

Lamphere-Englund, G. & White, J. (2022, May 16). The Buffalo Attack and the Gamification of Violence. *RUSI Commentary*. https://www.rusi.org/explore-our-research/publications/commentary/buffalo-attack-and-gamification-violence.

Macklin, G. (2019). The Christchurch Attacks: Livestream Terror in the Viral Video Age – Combating Terrorism Center at West Point. *CTC Sentinel, 12*(6), 18–29.

Macklin, G. (2022). "Praise the Saints". In J. Dafinger & M. Florin, *A Transnational History of Right-Wing Terrorism* (1st ed., pp. 215–240). Routledge.

Mattheis, A. (2021, January 18). Beyond the "LULZ": Memifying Murder as "Meaningful" Gamification in Far-Right Content. GNET Insights. https://gnet-research.org/2021/01/18/beyond-the-lulz-memifying-murder-as-meaningful-gamification-in-far-right-content/.

Mitchell, R., Schuster, L., & Jin, H. S. (2020). Gamification and the Impact of Extrinsic Motivation on Needs Satisfaction: Making Work Fun? *Journal of Business Research, 106*, 323–330. 10.1016/j.jbusres.2018.11.022.

RAN (2020). "Extremists" Use of Video Gaming – Strategies and Narratives. *Radicalisation Awareness Network (Policy Support), European Commission.* https://ec.europa.eu/home-affairs/networks/radicalisation-awareness-network-ran/publications/ran-cn-extremists-use-video-gaming-strategies-and-narratives-online-meeting-15-17-september-2020_en.

Robson, K., Plangger, K., Kietzmann, J.H., McCarthy, I., & Pitt, L. (2016). Game On: Engaging Customers and Employees Through Gamification. *Business Horizons*, 59(1), 29–36. 10.1016/j.bushor.2015.08.002.

Royal Commission of Inquiry (2020). Ko Tō Tātou Kāinga Tēnei—Report: Royal Commission of Inquiry into the Terrorist Attack on Christchurch Masjidain on March 15, 2019.

Sailer, M., Hense, J.U., Mayr, S.K., & Mandl, H. (2017). How Gamification Motivates: An Experimental Study of the Effects of Specific Game Design Elements on Psychological Need Satisfaction. *Computers in Human Behavior*, 69, 371–380.

Schlegel, L. (2020a). Jumanji Extremism? How Games and Gamification Could Facilitate Radicalization Processes. *Journal for Deradicalization*, 23, 1–44.

Schlegel, L. (2020b, March 17). Can You Hear Your Call of Duty? The Gamification of Radicalization and Extremist Violence. *European Eye on Radicalization.* https://eeradicalization.com/can-you-hear-your-call-of-duty-the-gamification-of-radicalization-and-extremist-violence/.

Schlegel, L. (2021). The Role of Gamification in Radicalization Processes. *Moduslzad.* https://modus-zad.de/wp-content/uploads/2021/01/modus-working-paper-12021.pdf.

Schmid, A. (2013). Radicalisation, De-Radicalisation, Counter-Radicalisation: A Conceptual Discussion and Literature Review. *Terrorism and Counter-Terrorism Studies*. 10.19165/2013.1.02.

Scrivens, R. & Conway, M. (2019). The Roles of "Old" and "New" Media Tools and Technologies in the Facilitation of Violent Extremism and Terrorism. In R. Leukfeldt & T.J. Holt (Eds.), *The Human Factor of Cybercrime* (1st ed., pp. 286–309). Routledge.

Sykes, G.M. & Matza, D. (1957). Techniques of Neutralization: A Theory of Delinquency. *American Sociological Review*, 22(6), 664. 10.2307/2089195.

Wicks, S. (2020, September 2). Islamic State's Use of Gamification and Low-Tech Terror Tactics. *GNET Insights.* https://gnet-research.org/2020/09/02/iss-use-of-gamification-and-low-tech-terror-tactics/.

Wilson, J. (2019). Christchurch Shooter's Links to Austrian Far Right "More Extensive Than Thought." *The Guardian.* https://www.theguardian.com/world/2019/may/16/christchurch-shooters-links-to-austrian-far-right-more-extensive-than-thought.

9

LEVEL UP

Policies, Practices, and Positive Interventions to Counter Terrorism and Violent Extremism in Gaming Spaces

Erin Saltman and Nagham El Karhili

There is no evidence to correlate higher use of gaming with higher rates of participation in, or sympathy towards, violent extremism or terrorism (APA Task Force on Violent Media, 2015; Tielemans, 2021; Lamphere-Englund & White, 2023). However, terrorists and violent extremists have always exploited new technologies, seeking to optimize their efforts in the most effective way. This can include efforts to reach new audiences for potential recruitment, consolidate and communicate with existing core supporters or members, fundraise, disseminate propaganda, operationalize an attack, and further enhance terror through the exploitation of an attack online. While terrorist and violent extremist (TVE) actors are a minority in the online space, these low prevalence, high-risk scenarios are worthy of preventive efforts that must evolve alongside the constant evolution of adversarial shifts.

While more research has come out in recent years analyzing the potential for games and gaming infrastructure to be used in the recruitment and radicalization of especially younger audiences, little attention has been paid to platform tooling and safety-by-design elements. This chapter reviews existing literature before looking at gaming and gaming (-adjacent) platform architecture, policies, and moderation tools in how they provide outlets or blockers for TVE activities, including a review of potential approaches for positive interventions. Reviewing positive intervention strategies includes a deeper look at online *surfaces*, meaning the specific user-facing part of a platform where an intervention might appear (e.g., within a direct message, ads targeted content in a newsfeed, a pop-up of information tied to an action on the platform, or redirected information

DOI: 10.4324/9781003388371-10

from a search query). The authors review safety-by-design practices and approaches within gaming, gaming (-adjacent), and virtual-reality platforms, highlighting tools that can be introduced for baseline and advanced interventions. The chapter reviews real cases of relevant Global Internet Forum to Counter Terrorism (GIFCT) member companies *XBox*, *Niantic*, *Discord*, *Twitch*, and *Oculus* that represent these three gaming typologies.

The aim of this analysis is to be practical in highlighting potential surfaces that extremist actors look to exploit across online gaming surfaces, showcase where advancements have been made in efforts to ensure safe environments for users, and provide actionable recommendations for platforms across the gaming spectrum. Significant advances have been made in large part by social media companies in the last five years and many of the lessons learned can be reappropriated for the gaming industry. The evolution of safety-by-design takes many forms. Policies let a user know what is or is not allowed on a platform. Remediation tooling allows a user to flag to the platform something that is wrong or allows a platform to take automated actions when violating content or activities are proactively identified. User-flagging pipelines allow concerns from users to triage to in-house generalist or specialist reviewers in order to take actions. Lastly, intervention models go beyond the removal of violative behavior to allow for an educational moment or dialogue with the user to target the root cause of an issue, rather than simply tackling the symptom. Each one of these safety-by-design features takes separate areas of development with often different teams within a tech platform. If the aim is to facilitate gaming- related companies to better prevent and counter terrorism and violent extremism on their platforms, it will take an acute understanding of current trends alongside both cross-platform and cross-sector collaboration models.

Research to date

Studies focussing on better understanding terrorist actors' online activities and behaviors have exponentially evolved over the past two decades (Conway, 2006; Innes, 2021; Trauthig & Bodo, 2022) with a significant focus on social media platforms as propaganda tools (Dean & Bell, 2012; Rapoport, 2021; Khosravinik & Amer, 2022) as well as more recent work analyzing broader violent extremist ideologies on diversified platforms across the tech stack (Nuraniyah, 2019; Conway & Macdonald, 2020; Allington, 2021; Mustaffa, 2022). Overall, the research outlines a complex and dynamic threat landscape with bad actors whose use of and presence on digital spaces is as varied and strategic as regular online users globally.

As one of the largest financially valued popular culture sectors (World Economic Forum, 2022), the online gaming industry has great allure to users globally as well as to a range of nefarious actors. To better understand those spaces, research analyzing extremist actors' use of the various gaming, gaming (-adjacent) platforms, and augmented and virtual reality (AR/VR) has ranged widely. On the one end, studies point to video games' usage as tools for recruitment or propaganda by extremist groups (Al-Rawi, 2018; Anti-Defamation League, 2019, 2020; Schlegel, 2020). Historically, there has been evidence of terrorist groups producing their own videogames, such as Hezbollah's production of *Special Force* in 2003 and *Special Force* 2 in 2007 (Souri, 2007). However, there has never been a significant uptake in the production of videogames by terrorist or violent extremist groups due to their inability to match the production of complex high-quality games paired with the lower cost and ease of modifying pre-existing games (Robinson & Whittaker, 2020). Ultimately, these tactical shifts in the behavior of terrorist actors on gaming platforms allow them to reach broader publics and embed themselves with the larger popular gaming culture.

In parallel, terrorist and violent extremist organizations have exploited gaming (-adjacent) platforms and culture. Studies point to terrorist groups' use of various references to gaming culture, and gaming aesthetics, within their organizational propaganda materials such as ISIS's meme "This is our Call of Duty" and "we Respawn in Jannah" (Selepak, 2010; Lakomy, 2019).[1] Additionally, further research showcases terrorist groups' use of strategic communication tactics and distribution of propaganda materials housed on various gaming (-adjacent) platforms such as *Steam* (store.steampowered.com; Vaux, Gallagher, & Davey, 2021). More recent research efforts critique previous analysis for their simplistic reading of in-game representations "at the expense of attention to the central role of interactive game play" (Robinson & Whittaker, 2020). Most significantly, this recent development in the research points to a wide and active presence across the ideologically extremist spectrums that continues to exploit gaming (-adjacent) platforms, while attempting to keep up with the latest development such as AR/VR.

While being a relatively newer space, research on the exploitation of augmented and virtual reality by extremist actors recognizes the various challenges and opportunities that the technology provides. It is important to note that these new technologies have had many positive usages such as the assistance of investigative efforts in terrorism trials (Ajah et al., 2020). Furthermore, the numerous usages of virtual reality are being explored as potential tools to counter violent extremism (United Nations, 2021), to treat victims of terrorist attacks (Roy, 2016), and overall contribute to better deradicalization efforts (Pelletier & Drozda-Senkowska, 2020).

However, augmented and virtual reality used by terrorist actors also poses a pervasive and omnipresent threat due to the ways in which these environments can allow terrorist groups to create virtual training camps (Office of the Director of National Intelligence, 2021), and ultimately reinvent themselves and rebrand. More specifically, research points to the dangers of terrorist use of the metaverse (d'Argenlieu, 2022) as one of the fastest growing public virtual reality products. In particular, studies highlight external uses around recruitment, coordination, new targets, and training, along with more internally facing usage for extremist leaders and in-group community building (Elson, Doctor, & Hunter, 2022).

By reflecting on the research themes and approaches in studying this fast growing sector and its use by malign actors, our lack of knowledge around platform responses to threats becomes apparent. While the term platform can refer to any user-facing interface online, this chapter specifically focusses on game-play spaces online, AR/VR game-play spaces, and gaming (-adjacent) spaces where users primarily go to engage with other gamers and talk about games and gaming. Some case studies by the Institute on Strategic Dialogue showcase a few moderation efforts on platforms such as *Twitch* (twitch.tv; a gaming-adjacent livestreaming platform), *Steam* (a video-gaming distribution service), and *DLive* (dlive.tv; a video livestreaming service) (O'Connor, 2021; Thomas, 2021; Vaux *et al.*, 2021). However, the research is limited to gathering data of online terrorist activity, while little is known about content or accounts that have been suspended or removed by platform providers. More comparative analyses of these platforms' efforts, paired with practical and actionable recommendations that can guide moderation teams to implementing educated and impactful moderation policies while they attempt to manage this dynamic threat landscape are needed. This chapter attempts to fill part of this knowledge gap.

Platform Policies, Pipelines, and Tools

In looking towards preventive measures and safety-by-design to prevent and counter terrorist and violent extremist exploitation of gaming and gaming (-adjacent) platforms, it is important to understand what policies, pipelines, and tools have been developed, can be expanded, or need to be created. Safety-by-design is a term used to refer to technical developments that consciously focus on minimizing potential exploitation or harms to users or the wider public, integrating methods for identifying risk early in design processes. The capacity for a platform to develop nuanced policies or tooling to facilitate policy actions depends greatly on four things (Saltman & Hunt, 2023):

1 The human resources with subject matter expertise that a platform is able to hire
2 The engineering and tooling support a platform is able to give to any particular threat type (e.g., game modifications, bespoke games, propaganda dissemination)
3 The awareness or prevalence of a certain threat or type on the platform (e.g., spam, bullying, account hacking, violent extremism)
4 The external pressures by government, media and civil society pressuring a company to prioritize focus on a certain online harm issue

Most global technology companies, including gaming industries, must consider online parameters for acceptable behavior within a platform and consequences for users if they cross those lines. While this is similar to government considerations around legal parameters for citizens, the scale and global nature of online users and content present a different set of trade-offs between human and technical resources in relation to which policy areas demand prioritization. Terrorist and violent extremist exploitation on gaming-related platforms is a low prevalence violating activity with high risk for real world harm. Most companies will not have an in-house, specialized counterterrorism team. However, there are basic ways to signal a platform is not hospitable to TVE actors. The first step in ensuring proactive oversight is to make policies clear to users.

To join GIFCT, for example, companies must meet a six-point list of membership criteria (GIFCT, 2023). The first criterion dictates that companies must have public platform standards that explicitly prohibit the promotion of terrorism and/or violent extremism in their terms of service, community guidelines, or other publicly available content policies. A further criterion dictates that companies must have the ability to receive and act on reports of illegal activity or activity violating their terms of service from their users. There are a number of platforms that have adequate policies but have little to no ability or will to act on those policies at scale, meaning that policies must be paired with pathways to vary out actions against policy-violating users. This can be done proactively, through internal teams (such as specific abuse type investigation or moderation teams) or tooling available to a company (such as photo- and video- matching detection or keyword linguistic detection discussed later in the chapter). This can also be done reactively, through reports from users and third parties. While reporting capabilities and mechanisms can vary across platforms, they generally include internal flagging tools, reporting portals, or outreach emails. Whatever form it takes, it is important to ensure that the community using a platform understands how to highlight abuses to the company. Additionally, companies often make policies and relevant tooling known to users (be they players or participants) through guidelines alongside safety portals where wider safety information can be easily found and understood.

The next section reviews the policies and tooling for remedial actions taken the global gaming companies *Xbox* and *Niantic* (a software company that has produced augmented reality games such as *Pokémon Go*), alongside the popular gaming-adjacent platforms *Discord* (social platform for private and communal messaging) and *Twitch* (videogame livestreaming platform), and virtual-reality gaming on *Oculus* (oculus.com). Reviewing these five companies gives an idea of the range of policy approaches and remedial tooling available to gaming-related platforms in more nascent development stages.

Policies and Tooling of Larger Gaming Companies

As well-established companies, *Xbox* and *Niantic* benefit from having larger resource pools and infrastructure to support thorough policies and enforcement tools. *Niantic* is a parent company hosting a range of games to access through its platform, including augmented-reality games such as *Pokémon Go*. Similarly, *Xbox* is a console hosting a range of games, but benefits from a robust policy and oversight team from parent company, Microsoft, which owns a range of brands and platforms that go above and beyond gaming. Microsoft had a revenue of $198.3 billion in 2022 (Zippia, 2023) with a 2021 estimate that there were 57.1 million *Xbox* console users globally (Gitnux, 2023). In 2022 *Niantic* had a revenue of $885.07 million (Statista, 2023) with around 79 million monthly users of their most famous AR game, *Pokémon Go*, as of June 2023 (Krawanski, 2023). Reviewing larger companies allows for a better idea of what the idealized operationalization for enforcement may look like. Both companies have community standards paired with a range of settings that allows for the customization to adhere to age ratings and appropriate conduct. This allows families to customize with various roles, settings, permissions, and even time restrictions (Xbox, Manage Xbox Privacy Settings 2023; Niantic, Kids support – PokémonGo help center 2023). These two companies are examples of larger, well-resourced gaming entities, which can show us what expanded resources can lend to safety approaches and tooling solutions.

"Content" can take on many different forms in online spaces and in interactive gameplay. In a game-play space, content might be reviewed in terms of the choices a player makes in choosing how its avatar looks. Content might also be discourse if a game allows for numerous players with communication in text or audio between two or more people in different locations. Content might also be actions a player takes. Examples of how these can be abused by terrorist or violent extremist entities include a player making a character that is dressed in the iconography or logos of a hate-based group (such as an ISIS logo or swastika being brandished). Recruitment, hate speech, or abuse can take place if a game space allows for dialogue between platers. Even the actions a player takes could be interpreted as a signal to wider extremist ideologies – for example, if a character is able to make "Heil Hitler" salutes. In all cases, it is important to have options where a user or player can report, or "flag," to the platform instances of abuse or violations of the platform's policy that are witnessed. Online abuse and TVE activities more specifically, take on different guises depending on the surface where the exploitation occurs and oftentimes the cultural nuance of how violations might manifest in different languages or settings. Given the size and scale of user bases a platform might have, there will always be a significant challenge in ensuring moderators understand how abuse or violative content appears around the world, particularly with nuanced symbols and coded language used by violent and nonviolent hate-based groups online (Richardson, 2020).

On these larger gaming platforms, there are options for users to report pieces of content, a player's profile, a player's message, a player's in-game voice chat, or an activity that takes place from players within the playing space, which could be content or a screen capture of something witnessed. There are also a range of remedial actions on players for inappropriate, community standards violating conduct or content listed in Table 9.1. Understanding how to flag content or other players can sometimes be the

TABLE 9.1 Punitive measures on larger gaming platforms for violating policies

Punitive measures	Examples
Restrictions	• Restrictions on uploading or sharing content • Restrictions on the use of online multiplayer gaming or group spaces • Restricting access to share content across other social media platforms
Blocking capacities	• Blocking the ability to upload game clips or screenshots • Blocking real-time voice/text interactions • Blocking the ability to broadcast live game play
Removals/suspensions	• Removal of certain abilities to interact with others, such as to send text and voice messages • Removal of inappropriate content • Removal of editing capacities • Removal of mods • Account suspension, banning or removal • Device suspension, banning or removal

most challenging aspect within interactive gaming spaces. In addition to going directly to a player's profile to flag an account, *Xbox* gives players options to fill in a contact form, speak through a web chat 24 hours a day, or receive support over the phone at certain hours of the day. *Niantic* deploys multiple technology detection systems to flag, hide, or block potentially dangerous or harmful content (Niantic, Kids support – PokémonGo help center, 2023). The table maps out punitive measures that larger gaming platforms have developed to take action against users who violate their terms of service or policies. The more a platform has clear policies that prohibit terrorism and violent extremist activities combined with clear punitive measures for violations, and the resources to carry out those punitive measures, the more a platform creates a naturally hostile environment to bad actors.

While the table looks at individual company actions, there is also increasing benefit to ensure cross-platform solutions can be operationalized. Both companies speak openly about the deployment of photo- and video hash-matching technologies to proactively mitigate risk of spreading content related to child exploitation or terrorist and violent extremist content, discussed later in the chapter.

Policies and Tooling of Gaming-Adjacent Companies

Gaming (-adjacent) platforms take many forms but are largely used as a space for gamers to (1) share their gameplay in real time, (2) record and share their game play after they game to create a discussion, or (3) to discuss game trends, tips, and news with a wider online network of like-minded gamers and enthusiasts. *Discord* and *Twitch* are both platforms that have increased in popularity as "gaming-adjacent" platforms, although their social media and networking platforms can be used for myriad nongame related purposes. *Discord* is a voice, video, and text chat app with over 140 million active monthly users and 300 million registered accounts as of January 2023 (Curry, 2023). Users can send media or files in private or group communities called "servers" (Discord, 2022). *Twitch* is a video livestreaming service developed for videogame streaming in real time, including esports competitions, music broadcasts, and wider creative content (Twitch, 2023). Twitch has 140 million active users as of April 2023 (Wise, 2023) with a monthly average of 7.2 million channels streaming each month and 2.46 million channels streaming at any one point in time as of May 2023 (Twitchtracker, 2023). These gaming-adjacent apps are largely used to solve a longtime problem for gamers on how to talk to each other, how to organize people long enough to get a game started with a group (Hornshaw, 2022), and how to bring audiences into virtual game play as fans or participants. These newer platforms can learn from the many years of policy and tooling trials and tribulations of more traditional social media outlets like *Facebook* (facebook.com) and *YouTube* (youtube.com).

Both *Discord* and *Twitch* have a range of tools for restricting or re-moving content, accounts, or servers. *Discord* has a minimum age requirement of 13, like many social media platforms. *Discord* also allows for parental or educator settings to restrict or limit certain permissions. Discord has a range of online training videos and resources for parents, educators, and wider users through safety policies, tools, and settings (Discord, 2023). *Twitch*'s policy includes warnings and suspensions combined with temporary or indefinite bans as noted in their safety center enforcement levels (see Figure 9.1). Establishing age criteria for certain online spaces is another way to prevent certain types of exploitation among children. *Twitch* has a list of "prohibited games" listed transparently. The platform also lays out how their policies dictate wider safety enforcement across servers, channels, and users.

For both gaming and gaming-adjacent platforms the main focus of counterterrorism and counter-extremism measures to date has been the proactive deployment of a combination of internal safety teams focussed on specific harm types (both human resource and engineering teams to deploy proactive detection where possible) and reactive reviews of content that users have flagged to better understand how on-platform violations manifest. Violations in terrorism and violent extremism on gaming-adjacent platforms have included the livestreaming of attacks such as in

Viewer-Level Safety
Blocking, Chat Filters, Content Warnings

Channel-Level Safety
Moderators, Mod View, Auto Mod

Service-Level Safety
Review and Enforcement, User Reporting, Machine Detection

Community Guidelines
Content and Behavior Policies

FIGURE 9.1   Twitch Safety Center Enforcement Levels.

Christchurch, New Zealand (2019); Halle, Germany (2019); Glendale, Arizona, USA (2020); Buffalo, New York, USA (2022); and Memphis, Tennessee, USA (2022). Cases have also included broader recruitment of younger individuals and coordination around events, including examples such as Unite the Right rallies. Understanding nuanced signals and the behavior of bad actors is key to being able to carry out the necessary punitive measures against a platform's policies. Understanding a situation and being able to interpret it quickly is key, particularly in cases of incident response when a real-world, ongoing threat, has online assets intrinsically tied to the real-world harm.

Augmented- and Virtual-Reality Game Play

For online gaming and gaming-adjacent platforms there is a lot in the counterterrorism and counter-extremism space that can be advanced by reviewing how larger social media companies have progressed efforts in the last ten years, and how those strategies can be implemented in gaming surfaces. However, for augmented- and virtual-reality game spaces, there are new levels of complexity for safety-by-design, user flagging, and proactive tooling efforts. Online gaming audiences are increasingly aware of augmented-reality (AR) and virtual-reality (VR) game play. In 2022 there were an estimated 1.1 billion mobile AR app users (Alsop, 2022) and 171 million VR users (Petrov, 2023). Augmented reality adds audiovisual content to an existing environment and layering immersive experiences onto real surroundings during game play. Virtual reality describes a process by which a gaming system takes over the user's audio and visual environment to place the player into an entirely virtual world for full immersion. Both experiences to date are largely done through headsets or, in the case of *Pokémon Go* and other well-known apps, can be accessed through a smartphone where the added visuals can be seen through your phone camera and app.

Games like *Pokémon Go* are probably the most well-known popular AR games. Most of the attention around safety for such games has been placed on ensuring parental consent for games that prompt younger audiences to engage with real-world environments. For example, in the *Pokémon Go* Safety FAQs, the language on safety focusses almost entirely on paying attention to one's surroundings with risks keying in on avoiding inappropriate areas and basic traffic avoidance (Pokémon Go, 2023). These technologies are still in their early adoption phases, with few concrete examples of overt terrorist and violent extremist exploitation. Most exploitation has taken place in user-built spaces, where a user can build a world or an aesthetic. However, safety-by-design is meant to prevent exploitation in advance of it becoming a wider issue.

While VR gaming tends to take place either at home using personal consoles, or within VR game spaces, the future concern for terrorism and violent extremism is perhaps less about the physical environment. The main concern remains how to adapt what is known about safety and tooling in traditional 2D game play, and how these measures can be evolved as fit-for-purpose in fully immersive online spaces. *Oculus* has some of the more advanced VR safety settings since the parent company, Meta, is one of the better resourced companies developing VR games within the "metaverse." The term metaverse came from a 1992 near-future science fiction novel, *Snow Crash*, whereby people could dial into a fully immersive virtual world, taking on an avatar character form and existing in a parallel world to the real world. Similarly, today's metaverse and VR spaces refer to fully immersive digital spaces, traditionally accessed through headsets, that create a fully augmented visual and auditory alternative reality.

In fully virtual-reality spaces, there are some traditional safety measures such as a 13+ age limitation and punitive measures that can be user controlled or flagged to moderators, somewhat dependent on the VR game or space being engaged with (Oculus, 2023). A user is usually able to block or mute other players in a VR space in most cases, however, more complex flagging or self-protection can sometimes be difficult or non-existent to users. There have been a number of documented cases of negative experiences in multiplayer VR spaces including, hate speech, bullying, harassment, and virtual unwanted sexual advances, whereby users were ill equipped to know how to best respond (Allen & McIntosh, 2022).

While part of the responsibility will remain on the user to understand how to keep safe in virtual gaming spaces with available resources, there remains a gap in understanding how to flag complex abuse, particularly when looking at potential exploitation by terrorist and violent extremist users. If a group of players begin doing Nazi salutes, how can other users flag behaviors of other players in real-time immersive multiplayer games? How can tools such as logo detection be modified to understand 3D builds of logos whether that is depicting a swastika or ISIS logo? How can better real-time natural language processing understand slogans and slurs both in text and audio? Here, evolving tools to fit the future threat will be crucial. Ensuring user-facing tools are easy to find, understand, and use by players that do witness or experience online abuse are equally important.

Solution Building: Knowledge Sharing, Cross platform Moderation, and Positive Interventions

There is a wealth of policy, tooling and safety-by-design knowledge developed by traditional social media platforms that can be reappropriated and adapted to gaming surfaces. Some of these efforts will need individual platforms to adapt tools to fit platform-specific needs and effectively connect it to sensitive user data, pipelines, and moderation efforts. Other efforts can be leveraged as cross-platform solutions, so that particularly smaller and less resourced platforms can benefit from shared signals with other vetted platforms, like in the case of GIFCT Hash Sharing efforts (GIFCT, 2023). Finally, game spaces are nascent in thinking through what positive interventions, friction building, and preventing/countering violent extremism (PVE/CVE) initiatives could be deployed through partnership models that present innovative opportunities.

Knowledge Sharing and Tooling

There are a range of tools that social media companies have developed in aid of proactively countering terrorism and violent extremism online that gaming spaces could employ in different ways. This includes tools such as logo detection, TVE classifiers, and strategic network disruptions. While each of these tools could be developed in-house to a platform or company, knowledge sharing of tactics, source data for training algorithms, and understanding of adversarial shifts to better deploy these tools in gaming spaces would have an amplifying effect of their utility.

Logo detection, also known as "object detection," can be a powerful image recognition technology that localizes and identifies objects in a given image (Solawetz, 2021). It is a subcategory of computer vision, a field of artificial intelligence, that uses deep learning algorithms to train computers to interpret and understand the visual world and react to the input (Statistical Analysis System, 2023). Training the algorithm involves giving it a series of annotated images indicating those objects you want it to identify, such as a corpus of images with the logos of a designated terrorist organization. The ability for gaming spaces to understand if a player uses terrorist or violent extremist logos in their profile picture, to modify a game space, or dress its virtual player in an outfit with identifiable logos are all ways logo detection could be deployed in proactive detection models for gaming.

Many gaming spaces also have built-in chat for paired or multiplayer gaming, as do gaming (-adjacent) platforms. Most user-generated content published on the internet is in text format. It is impossible for human analysts to read everything that is written online in real time; therefore, the detection and analysis of terrorist and violent extremist activities online can greatly benefit from computerized linguistic tools (Johansson & Kaati, 2016). Terrorist or violent extremist activity can be detected by identifying signs of certain warning behaviors in a written text known as "linguistic markers." **Natural language processing** (NLP) algorithms enable machines to read, understand, and derive meaning from human languages (UNOCT, 2021) and have been instrumental in the study of extremist discourse. These, too, could be deployed across game related chat threads internal or adjacent to games.

Lastly, a final methodology currently deployed individually by platforms for disrupting terrorist and violent extremist exploitation is **strategic network disruptions** (SNDs) (Lewis, 2020; Saltman, 2020). These take the form of targeted actions against networks of dangerous organizations, groups, or individuals that are on a specific platform by developing a behavior-focussed approach of mapping a network of bad actors and shutting them down all at once to cripple a network. Again, once a trend or group is initially identified within a game-play space, SNDs could allow the platform to further identify terrorist and violent extremist users related to the initial identification to better assess and remove the network. While it sounds like SNDs would lend themselves to cross-platform solutions, potential solutions often find limitations put forward by privacy and data-sharing regulations such as the General Data Protection Regulation (GDPR) pr E-Privacy regulations in Europe.

Cross-Platform Solutions

Hash-sharing sits at the forefront of cross-platform signal sharing. There are various methods for image and video matching but most tech companies use artificial intelligence (AI) as well as locality sensitive hashing (LSH) algorithms such as PhotoDNA and VideoDNA or PDQ and TMK +PDQF to prevent users from uploading photos or videos that match content previously identified as terrorist and violent extremist content. These various forms of photo and video matching algorithms turn content into "hashes." Hashes are numerical representations, or digital fingerprints, of content, such as images, videos or PDFs, and are difficult to reverse engineer. The hash can help a company proactively find when a known violating piece of content is shared on a given platform. Companies including *Facebook* have openly discussed their usage of PDQ and TMK+PDQF to combat a range of different online harms including child sexual exploitation and violent extremism (Davis & Rosen, 2019). These technologies are designed to operate at a high scale and allow for the automation of processes that could otherwise require tens of thousands of highly specialized human moderators.

In 2017, the founding members of GIFCT spearheaded a shared, safe, and secure industry database to house "perceptual hashes" of known terrorist-produced images and videos. This means visually similar content creates hashes that are mathematically close to each other. Recognizing that there was not one agreed on international definition of terrorism, the parameters of the hash-sharing database were founded with the limitation to hashes of content (images and videos) that GIFCT members had removed from their services for being terrorist content and that were also produced by terrorist entities on the United Nations Security Council's Consolidated Sanctions List. Subsequently, this has grown to include taxonomy labels for content associated with GIFCT's Content Incident Protocol (when an attack is livestreamed), for attacker manifestos, and branded terrorist and violent extremist content (GIFCT, 2021). When a hash-sharing database member identifies an image or video on its platform that has violated its terms of service and is associated with the GIFCT taxonomy, it can produce a hash of the content and upload the hash to the hash-sharing database. The process first converts the picture to grayscale and resizes it so that all images are identically formatted before being hashed.

Hashes allow GIFCT members to quickly identify visually similar content on their own platform which has been removed by one member, enabling them to review (or re-review) such content to see if it breaches their terms and conditions (without sharing any user data between companies). When GIFCT members review the content that has been identified by matching it against hashes, they also have the option to give feedback to the system and tell other members whether they agree or disagree that any one hash relates to terrorist activity and rate its severity. GIFCT respects that each member has different policies, corporate purposes, and terms and conditions. As a result, there is not a one-size-fits-all approach to how companies use hashes to support their platforms or how member companies apply their policies to the material surfaced from matches against hashes in the hash-sharing database.

Members can share signals about terrorist or violent extremist content they have identified on their platform so that other members can quickly identify if the same content is shared on their platform and assess it in line with their policies and terms of service. All without sharing any user data between companies. As GIFCT efforts increasingly include gaming and gaming (-adjacent) platforms, ensuring that different forms of content can be hashed to be of utility to the widest types of platform will be important. Today, the ability to hash different forms of terrorist and violent extremist content has increased from just image and video to include PDFs and URLs (GIFCT, 2022). Future content hashing should evolve to include audio and 3D visual formatting to face future threats in gaming spaces. As gaming and gaming (-adjacent) platforms might become the source of terrorist and violent extremist activities or have related content filter into game play spaces (such as profile pictures or shared within multi-gamer chat threads) being optimized in networks for hash sharing will be key.

Potentials for Positive Interventions

Much of the preventive and safety measures mentioned so far are aimed at identifying when and where violating actors are operating or violating activity is taking place. These present good baseline best practices for preventing the exploitation of terrorist and violent extremist activity when these policies, tools, and remedial actions are aligned and active. However, content removal alone addresses a symptom and not the root causes of radicalization leading to violence. Gaming and gaming (-adjacent) platforms have myriad surfaces that are prime for positive interventions and strategic communication, learning from models that have been deployed and measured on larger social media platforms. Over the last ten years, there have been many lessons learned through international counter-narrative programs and tooling to help activists and NGOs scale and optimize their voices online as part of wider efforts to push back on hate speech and extremism online. These include lessons about how to work with local and regional partners, how to deliver messages accurately, and how to treat at-risk audiences sensitively (CAPPI Working Group, 2021; Saltman *et al.*, 2021; Harjani *et al.*, 2022; Zamir, 2022).

To date, positive intervention models have primarily been launched on the same three to four platforms (*Facebook, Instagram, YouTube, Twitter*) yet target audiences and wider youth audiences that may be vulnerable to violent extremist messaging are on a much wider array of platforms, including gaming spaces. Tactics and approaches for preventing and countering violent extremist messaging through gaming spaces has vast opportunity to innovate and grow. Learning from social media case studies, any gaming space (in-game or adjacent) that has a search functionality to find specific games, teams, or individuals can benefit from potential redirection, looking at the **redirect method** (Moonshot, 2023). While this method was originally piloted through advertised targeting of intervention content, this can also be adapted when partnering with a platform. In these cases, a pipeline can be created whereby when a user searches for specified terrorist or violent extremist terms, groups, individuals, or even phrases the platform can automatically surface a redirected friction message or lead the user to helpful alternative groups or resources (Saltman *et al.*, 2021). This intervention strategy on Facebook was piloted in the USA and Australia with local disengagement partners redirecting white supremacy and neo-Nazi search terms towards the NGO partner sites with outreach off-ramps showing significant increases in traffic towards the intervention providers, including cases of sustained engagement with individuals looking to leave hate-based groups (Moonshot, 2020). In gaming, as an individual or group creates team names, looks for other games (some on prohibited lists), or searches for other groups this sort of positive intervention friction poses new potentials for user safety.

In gaming-adjacent or in-game chat spaces there are also potentials to build out better guidance for moderators, activists and practitioners to have counter-conversations to intervene and off-ramp users facing violent extremist content or indicators. The methodology for **counter-conversations** highlights tactics and off-ramp techniques to have active human interactions in the online space for preventing and countering extremism and hate (Davy *et al.*, 2018). While there are myriad different approaches to build positive interventions into gaming spaces, the tactics, considerations, and challenges of deploying various methods highlight the need for interventions to be based on process and insight-driven stages, phases, and pathways. The more thought and insights given to the planning processes, the greater the likelihood an intervention will yield positive results for the overall project's objectives. As illustrated by Zamir (2022) from work conducted with the GIFCT Positive Interventions Working group, the processes and phases shown in Figure 9.2 are key components of an effective positive intervention. Whether it is a gaming or gaming-adjacent platform, there has been little testing of intervention strategies to date, meaning the terrain is ripe for exploration partnerships and testing.

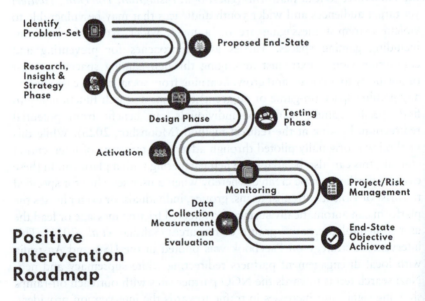

Positive Intervention Roadmap

- Identify Problem-Set
- Proposed End-State
- Research, Insight & Strategy Phase
- Design Phase
- Testing Phase
- Activation
- Monitoring
- Project/Risk Management
- Data Collection Measurement and Evaluation
- End-State Objective Achieved

FIGURE 9.2 GIFCT's positive interventions roadmap.

Conclusion

This chapter has looked to add to the literature on the nexus of gaming and extremism by focussing on a practical analysis of where policies, tooling, and partnerships can help in countering terrorism and violent extremism in gaming, gaming-adjacent, and AR/VR game play spaces. The findings have highlighted the significant role that both human and tooling resources play in creating a strong set of safety mechanisms across gaming-related platforms. There are a range of tools for remedial actions against users that violate platforms' community guidelines explicitly stated in most gaming spaces. It remains the case that larger global companies benefit from well-funded resource pools and infrastructure, which support their ability to update and enforce thorough policies and tools, which, in turn, creates a naturally more hostile environment for bad actors. In contrast, smaller platforms can reappropriate and adapt solutions, policies, and tools from larger social media platforms.

Opportunities in policy and tooling advancements range from tools such as logo detection technologies and natural language processing, to cross-platform solutions such as hash sharing. The more companies can work together across platforms and across sectors, the more knowledge sharing can directly benefit proactive awareness and implementation of counter-terrorism and counter-extremism measures. Game-play spaces are particularly nascent in thinking through how to encourage or develop partnership models for positive interventions. Positive intervention models deployed on platforms such as *Facebook* and *YouTube* over the past decade can also be replicated by smaller gaming and gaming-adjacent platforms. Applying lessons learned from previously tested interventions, such as the redirect method or directly training players and disengagement experts in intervention strategies within gaming surfaces has yet to be tested but has great potential for measurable innovation. Where and how best to create interventions in a nuanced and sensitive way will take close collaboration between private platform partnerships with experts and practitioners.

There remain a string of challenges in implementing effective proactive detection models looking at the nuanced and adversarial manner in which terrorist and violent extremist signals appear, and it is important to recognize game-play spaces are not heterogeneous in their structures. Some types of abuse signal will remain harder to capture than others. For example, it remains difficult to catch signal in audio-only formats to police live voice-based gaming or gaming-adjacent abuses, or to train users how to effectively flag abuses taking place in real-time, multi-player game spaces that might be visible actions by players, rather than voice or text evidence – such as a player making "Heil Hitler" salutes. The more nuanced user flagging tools are to capture different abuse types, the better a platform is able to track what adversarial shifts look like.

The debate about what to do with "borderline content" will also continue. There are a range of online abuses related to hate-based extremist groups that brush up against country laws and platform policies but purposefully do not cross policy lines. It is in this space that positive intervention strategies will be most effective; developing positive alternative content, education points, and friction options into play instead of relying on content moderation and censorship.

Moving forward, research should continue to explore the evolving landscape of online gaming and its potential risks and opportunities for violent extremist and terrorist entities. As other experts in this field have discussed in this book, prevalence of overt terrorist and violent extremist exploitation on these platforms is low, and many smaller and medium companies do not have the in-house expertise to adequately identify and tackle this low prevalence but high-risk abuse type. Future research should focus on the continued development of effective and efficient tools and policies for ensuring the safety and security of all users on these platforms.

Note

1 "Respawn" is gamer language and refers to restarting a level after dying while "jannah" is a religious term referring to paradise.

References

ADL (2019). Free to Play? Hate, Harassment, and Positive Social Experiences in Online Games. https://www.adl.org/resources/report/free-play-hate-harassment-and-positive-social-experiences-online-games.

ADL (2020). This is Not a Game: How Steam Harbors Extremists. https://www.adl.org/resources/report/not-game-how-steam-harbors-extremists.

Ajah, B.O., Ajah, I.A., & Obasi, C.O. (2020). Application of Virtual Reality (VR) and Augmented Reality (AR) in the Investigation and Trial of Herdsmen Terrorism in Nigeria. *International Journal of Criminal Justice Sciences*, 15(1), 1–20.

Allen, C. & McIntosh, V. (2022). Safeguarding the Metaverse. *The Institution of Engineering and Technology*. https://www.theiet.org/media/9836/safeguarding-the-metaverse.pdf.

Allington, D. (2021, February 8). Conspiracy Theories, Radicalisation and Digital Media – GNET. *Global Network on Extremism and Technology*. https://gnet-research.org/wp-content/uploads/2021/02/GNET-Conspiracy-Theories-Radicalisation-Digital-Media.pdf.

Al-Rawi, A. (2018). Video Games, Terrorism, and ISIS's Jihad 3.0. *Terrorism and Political Violence*, 30(4).

Alsop, T. (2022, December 1). Global Mobile Augmented Reality (AR) User Devices 2024. Statista. https://www.statista.com/statistics/1098630/global-mobile-augmented-reality-ar-users/.

APA Task Force on Violent Media (2015). Technical Report on the Review of Violent Video Game Literature. https://www.apa.org/pi/families/review-video-games.pdf.

Content Sharing Algorithms, Processes, and Positive Interventions (CAPPI) GIFCT Working Group (2021). Positive Interventions. https://gifct.org/wp-content/uploads/2021/07/GIFCT-CAPI2-2021.pdf.

Conway, M. (2006). Terrorism and the Internet: New Media – New Threat? *Parliamentary Affairs*, 59(2), 283–298.

Conway, M. & Macdonald, S. (2020). Introduction to the Special Issue: Extremism and Terrorism Online – Widening the Research Base. *Studies in Conflict & Terrorism*, 1–7.

Curry, D. (2023). Discord Revenue and Usage Statistics (2023). *Business of Apps*. https://www.businessofapps.com/data/discord-statistics/

d'Argenlieu, E. (2022). Terrorist Use of the Metaverse: New Opportunities and New Challenges. *Technology*.

Davis, A. & Rosen, G. (2019, August 1). Open-Sourcing Photo- and Video-Matching Technology to Make the Internet Safer | Meta. *Meta*. https://about.fb.com/news/2019/08/open-source-photo-video-matching/.

Davy, J., Birdwell, J., & Skellett, R. (2018). Counter Conversations. *ISD*. https://www.isdglobal.org/wp-content/uploads/2018/03/Counter-Conversations_FINAL.pdf

Dean, G. & Bell, P. (2012). The Dark Side of Social Media: Review of Online Terrorism. *Pakistan Journal of Criminology*, 3(4), 191–210.

Discord (2022, May 31). Beginner's Guide to Discord – Discord. *Discord Support*. https://support.discord.com/hc/en-us/articles/360045138571-Beginner-s-Guide-to-Discord.

Elson, J.S., Doctor, A.C., Hunter, S. (2022). The Metaverse Offers a Future Full of Potential – For Terrorists and Extremists, Too. https://theconversation.com/the-metaverse-offers-a-future-full-of-potential-for-terrorists-and-extremists-too-173622.

Gitnux (2023). The Most Surprising Xbox Statistics And Trends in 2023. *Gitnux*. https://blog.gitnux.com/xbox-statistics/.

Global Internet Forum to Counter Terrorism (2019, May 15). Actions to Address the Abuse of Technology to Spread Terrorist and Violent Extremist Content. *GIFCT*. https://gifct.org/2019/05/15/actions-to-address-the-abuse-of-technology-to-spread-terrorist-and-violent-extremist-content/.

Global Internet Forum to Counter Terrorism (2022, December 15). 2022 GIFCT Transparency Report. *Global Internet Forum to Counter Terrorism*. https://gifct.org/wp-content/uploads/2022/12/GIFCT-Transparency-Report-2022.pdf.

Global Internet Forum to Counter Terrorism (2023). GIFCT's Hash-Sharing Database. *GIFCT*. https://gifct.org/hsdb/.

Global Internet Forum to Counter Terrorism (2023). Membership. *GIFCT*. https://gifct.org/membership/.

Harjani, T., Roozenbeek, J., Biddlestone, M., van der Linden, S., Stuart, A., Iwahara, M. et al. (2022). A Practical Guide to Prebunking Misinformation. https://interventions.withgoogle.com/static/pdf/A_Practical_Guide_to_Prebunking_Misinformation.pdf.

Hornshaw, P. (2022, September 17). What is Discord? *Digital Trends.* https://www.digitaltrends.com/gaming/what-is-discord/.

Innes, M. (2021, November). "Fogging" and "Flooding": Countering Extremist Mis/Disinformation After Terror Attacks. *Global Network on Extremism and Technology.* https://gnet-research.org/wp-content/uploads/2021/11/GNET-Report-Fogging-And-Flooding-Countering-Extremist-MisDisinformation-After-Terror-Attacks.pdf.

Johansson, F. & Kaati, L. (2016). Detecting Linguistic Markers of Violent Extremism in Online Environments. In M. Sahlgren (Ed.), *Combating Violent Extremism and Radicalization in the Digital Era. Advances in Religious and Cultural Studies.* (p. 375). IGI Global. 10.4018/978-1-5225-0156-5.

Khosravinik, M. & Amer, M. (2022). Social Media and Terrorism Discourse: The Islamic State's (IS) Social Media Discursive Content and Practices. *Critical Discourse Studies, 19*(2), 124–143.

Krawanski, F. (2023). How Many People Play Pokemon Go? Pokemon Go Player Count. *Dexerto.* https://www.dexerto.com/pokemon/how-many-people-play-pokemon-go-pokemon-go-player-count-2132719/.

Lakomy, M. (2019). Let's Play a Video Game: Jihadi Propaganda in the World of Electronic Entertainment. *Studies in Conflict & Terrorism, 42*(4), 383–406.

Lamphere-Englund, G. & White, J. (2023). The Online Gaming Ecosystem: Assessing Digital Socialisation, Extremism Risks and Harms Mitigation Efforts. *Global Network on Extremism and Technology (GNET).* https://gnet-research.org/wp-content/uploads/2023/05/GNET-37-Extremism-and-Gaming_web.pdf.

Lewis, J. (2020). Facebook's Disruption of the Boogaloo Network. *GNET (blog).* https://gnet-research.org/2020/08/05/facebooks-disruption-of-the-boogaloo-network/.

Macdonald, S. (2018, June 26). How Tech Companies Are Trying to Disrupt Terrorist Social Media Activity. *Scientific American.* https://www.scientificamerican.com/article/how-tech-companies-are-trying-to-disrupt-terrorist-social-media-activity/.

Moonshot (2020). From Passive Search to Active Conversation: An Evaluation of the Facebook Redirect Programme. *Moonshot.* https://counterspeech.fb.com/en/wp-content/uploads/sites/2/2020/11/Facebook-Redirect-Evaluation_Final-Report_Moonshot-1.pdf.

Moonshot (2023). The Redirect Method. *Moonshot.* https://moonshotteam.com/the-redirect-method/.

Mustaffa, M. (2022, April). Radical Right Activities in Nusantara's Digital Landscape: A Snapshot. *Global Network on Extremism and Technology.* https://gnet-research.org/wp-content/uploads/2022/04/GNET-Report-Radical-Right-Activities-in-Nusantaras-Digital-Landscape.pdf.

Niantic (2023). Niantic Kids Support — Pokémon GO Help Center. *Niantic Support.* https://niantic.helpshift.com/hc/en/6-pokemon-go/faq/36-niantic-kids-support/.

Niantic Labs (2023). Niantic Player Guidelines – Niantic Labs. *Niantic Labs.* https://nianticlabs.com/guidelines.

Nuraniyah, N. (2019, July 11). The Evolution of Online Violent Extremism in Indonesia and the Philippines. *Royal United Services Institute.* https://gnet-research.org/wp-content/uploads/2019/12/5.pdf.

O'Connor, C. (2021). The Extreme Right on Twitch. https://www.isdglobal.org/isd-publications/gaming-and-extremism-the-extreme-right-on-twitch/.

Oculus (2023). Oculus Safety Center | Oculus. *Meta Quest VR Headsets, Accessories & Equipment*. https://www.oculus.com/safety-center/.

Office of the Director of National Intelligence (2021, March). The Future of Terrorism: Diverse Actors, Fraying International Efforts. https://www.dni.gov/index.php/gt2040-home/emerging-dynamics/international-dynamics/the-future-of-terrorism.

Pelletier, P. & Drozda-Senkowska, E. (2020). Virtual Reality as a Tool for Deradicalizing the Terrorist Mind: Conceptual and Methodological Insights from Intergroup Conflict Resolution and Perspective-Taking Research. *Peace and Conflict: Journal of Peace Psychology*, 26(4), 449.

Petrov, C. (2023, January 26). 45 Virtual Reality Statistics That Rock the Market in 2023. *Techjury*. https://techjury.net/blog/virtual-reality-statistics/#gref.

Pokémon Go (2023). Safety FAQs — Pokémon GO Help Center. *Niantic Support*. https://niantic.helpshift.com/hc/en/6-pokemon-go/faq/114-safety-faqs/.

Rapoport, D.C. (2021). The Capitol Attack and the 5th Terrorism Wave. *Terrorism and Political Violence*, 33(5), 912–916.

Richardson, J. (2020). A Guide to Online Radical-Right Symbols, Slogans and Slurs. *Centre for Analysis of the Radical Right (CARR)*. https://www.radicalrightanalysis.com/wp-content/uploads/2020/05/CARR-A-Guide-to-Online-Radical-Right-Symbols-Slogan-and-Slurs.pdf.

Robinson, N. & Whittaker, J. (2020). Playing for Hate? Extremism, Terrorism, and Videogames. *Studies in Conflict & Terrorism*, 1–36.

Roy, M.J. (2016). Virtual Reality in the Treatment of Survivors of Terrorism in Israel. *Novel Approaches to the Diagnosis and Treatment of Posttraumatic Stress Disorder*, 6, 196.

Saltman, E. (2020). Countering Terrorism and Violent Extremism at Facebook: Technology, Expertise and Partnerships. *ORF*. https://www.orfonline.org/expert-speak/countering-terrorism-and-violent-extremism-at-facebook/.

Saltman, E., Farshad, K., & Vockery, K. (2021). New Models for Deploying Counterspeech: Measuring Behavioral Change and Sentiment Analysis. *Studies in Conflict & Terrorism*. 10.1080/1057610X.2021.1888404.

Saltman, E., and Hunt, M. (2023). Borderline Content: Understanding the Gray Zone. *European Union Internet Forum Handbook on Borderline Content*.

Schlegel, L. (2020). Can You Hear Your Call of Duty? The Gamification of Radicalization and Extremist Violence. https://eeradicalization.com/can-you-hear-your-call-of-duty-the-gamification-of-radicalization-and-extremist-violence/.

Selepak, A. (2010). Skinhead Super Mario Brothers: An Examination of Racist and Violent Games on White Supremacist Websites. *Journal of Criminal Justice and Popular Culture*, 17(1), 1–47.

Solawetz, J. (2021, February 1). Object Detection for Computer Vision. *Roboflow Blog*. https://blog.roboflow.com/object-detection/.

Souri, H.T. (2007). The Political Battlefield of Pro-Arab Video Games on Palestinian Screens. *Comparative Studies of South Asia, Africa and the Middle East*, 27(3), 536–551.

Statista (2022). Annual Mobile Revenue Generated by Niantic Worldwide from 2015 to 2022. *Statista*. https://www.statista.com/statistics/1255744/niantic-annual-app-revenue/.

Statistical Analysis System (SAS) (2023). Computer Vision: What it Is and why it Matters. *SAS*. https://www.sas.com/en_us/insights/analytics/computer-vision.html.

Tielemans, A. (2021, June 28). A Survey of Violent Extremist and Terrorist Activities Across the Gaming Environment – GNET. *Global Network on Extremism and Technology*. https://gnet-research.org/2021/06/28/a-survey-of-violent-extremist-and-terrorist-activities-across-the-gaming-environment/.

Thomas, E. (2021). The Extreme Right on DLive. https://www.isdglobal.org/isd-publications/gaming-and-extremism-the-extreme-right-on-dlive/.

Trauthig, I. & Bodo, L. (2022, August). Emergent Technologies and Extremists: The DWeb as a New Internet Reality? *Global Network on Extremism and Technology*. https://gnet-research.org/wp-content/uploads/2022/07/GNET-Report-Emergent-Technologies-Extremists-Web.pdf.

Twitch (2023). About Twitch. https://www.twitch.tv/p/en/about/.

Twitch (2023). Twitch Safety Center. https://safety.twitch.tv/s/?language=en_US.

Twitch Tracker (2023). https://twitchtracker.com/statistics.

United Nations (2021, July 8). The application of Augmented Reality and Virtual Reality Technologies in Countering Terrorism and Preventing and Countering Violent Extremism. *United Nations*. https://media.un.org/en/asset/k1m/k1m7xgrgx4.

UNOCT & UNICRI (2021). Countering Terrorism Online with Artificial Intelligence: An Overview for Law Enforcement and Counter-Terrorism Agencies in South Asia and South-East Asia. *New York*. https://www.un.org/counterterrorism/sites/; www.un.org.counterterrorism/files/countering-terrorism-online-with-ai-uncct-unicri-report-web.pdf.

Vaux, P., Gallagher, A. & Davey, J. (2021). The Extreme Right on Steam. https://www.isdglobal.org/isd-publications/gaming-and-extremism-the-extreme-right-on-steam/.

Wise, J. (2023). Twitch Statistics 2023: How Many People Use Twitch? *EarthWeb*. https://earthweb.com/twitch-statistics/.

World Economic Forum (2022, July 28). https://www.weforum.org/agenda/2022/07/gaming-pandemic-lockdowns-pwc-growth/.

Xbox (2023). Xbox Community Standards. *Xbox*. https://www.xbox.com/en-US/legal/community-standards?xr=footnav#consequences.

Xbox (2023). Manage Xbox online safety and privacy settings. *Xbox Support*. https://support.xbox.com/en-GB/help/family-online-safety/online-safety/manage-online-safety-and-privacy-settings-xbox-one.

Zamir, M. (2022). Active Strategic Communications: Measuring Impact and Audience Engagement. *GIFCT Working Group Outputs 2022*. https://gifct.org/wp-content/uploads/2022/09/GIFCT-22WG-Combined-US-Sizing2. 1-2.pdf.

Zippia (2023). Annual Mobile Revenue Generated by Niantic Eorldwide from 2015 to 2022. *Zippia*. https://www.zippia.com/microsoft-careers-7480/revenue/.

10
PREVENTING AND COUNTERING EXTREMISM IN GAMING SPACES

Linda Schlegel

Considering the various ways extremists are seeking to exploit gaming and gaming culture, it is unsurprising that the nexus between gaming and extremism has become a serious concern for policymakers, tech companies, civil society organizations, and other actors working on preventing and countering (violent) extremism (P/CVE). Although research regarding this issue is still in its infancy and, as we have seen in previous chapters, important knowledge gaps remain, it is nevertheless important to discuss, develop, and implement P/CVE efforts aimed at curbing extremists' influence in the gaming sphere in parallel to the unfolding research efforts. The evidence accumulated so far clearly suggests that extremist actors are currently present and active in gaming spaces. Extremists are utilizing gaming at this very moment and, consequently, countermeasures in the gaming realm need to be developed promptly.

This need for gaming-related P/CVE efforts has been recognized by a number of organizations, including the European Commission's Radicalization Awareness Network (RAN), which commissioned a number of publications focussed on gaming-related P/CVE efforts (RAN, 2021a, 2021b, 2022), the United Nations Office of Counter-Terrorism (UNOCT), which recently published a study partially concerned with the positive outcomes of gaming and the potential use of gaming to prevent or counter extremism (Schlegel & Amarasingam, 2022), and the Extremism and Gaming Research Network (EGRN), which identified the question "How can gaming, gaming-related spaces, and gamers themselves help prevent extremism?" as one of its key areas of concern (EGRN, n.d.).

DOI: 10.4324/9781003388371-11

This chapter reviews current P/CVE measures in the gaming sphere. It focusses on positive, proactive P/CVE measures, i.e., on measures aimed at preventing and mitigating radicalization and other harmful activities *before* they occur. Reactive measures, such as content moderation, removal, or blocking of extremist content, deplatforming of certain users, and GIFCT's hash-sharing database[1] are undeniably crucial for counter-extremism. However, such reactive measures are not sufficient to curb extremism. For instance, a considerable amount of extremist content does not violate the terms and conditions of platforms and tech companies, who often focus on the removal of explicitly violent or unambiguously hateful posts. Extremists may often post their narratives in the form of "soft pill" memes, codes, or (dark) jokes, which are not overtly violent or extremist and, hence, may not be subjected to content removal (Schlegel & Amarasingam, 2022; see also Lakhani, 2021). Additionally, seeking to reduce the *supply* of extremist content online by removing it, may not be sufficient in and of itself to address digital extremist activities (Neumann, 2012). Rather, P/CVE measures are required to reduce the *demand* for extremist content, curb extremist influence over digital discourses, and provide positive alternatives to extremist narratives.

Hence, a holistic approach to countering extremism in gaming spaces necessitates the development of proactive, positive P/CVE measures and cannot solely rely on reactive approaches. This chapter will discuss how we can leverage the positive effects of gaming and gaming-related content to prevent and counter extremists' influence in digital gaming spaces by examining gaming-related prevention and counter-extremism measures, gaps in current campaigns, opportunities for future P/CVE projects, and the challenges that we need to overcome to develop and implement effective gaming-related P/CVE measures. The chapter first examines existing, gaming-related P/CVE measures, including the use of bespoke video games, existing videogames, gaming (-adjacent) platforms, gaming aesthetics, and gamification, and discusses the remaining gaps and areas of improvement for each of these types of measure (RAN, 2022). Subsequently, ways forward and unresolved challenges that P/CVE practitioners need to overcome to design and implement effective gaming-related projects, are discussed.

Gaming-Related P/CVE Measures

Generally speaking, many traditional P/CVE measures have not considered games as potential vehicles for prevention and counter-extremism campaigns. This is because digital games, as a technology and cultural art form, had not been considered particularly relevant in the field of extremism and radicalization until 2019, when the right-wing extremist attack in Christchurch, New Zealand, incorporated game-like elements (see Chapter 8 in this volume). At the time of writing, a mere four years have passed since this attack – a very short timeframe in which to adapt P/CVE measures to the gaming realm. Although a number of theoretical discussions on potential opportunities for P/CVE in the digital gaming spaces have been developed since 2019 (e.g., RAN, 2021a, 2021b; Schlegel, 2021), very few P/CVE measures featuring gaming-related elements have been implemented so far. Even fewer have been analyzed and evaluated. Consequently, the amount of projects and practitioners' experiences available for examination in this chapter must be regarded as extremely limited and large gaps in both knowledge and experience persist. As such, this chapter should be read as a preliminary discussion of a field that is rapidly evolving in both theory and practice.

P/CVE approaches within digital gaming spaces can take many forms (RAN, 2020, 2022). P/CVE actors may a) produce bespoke games, b) use existing games either to play with target audiences, to use the in-game communication features, or by modifying them, c) be present and communicate with users on gaming (-adjacent) platforms, d) utilize gaming aesthetics or gaming (cultural) references to make P/CVE content more appealing, or e) employ gamification. Each of these is discussed in more detail below. It should be noted that while games, gaming-related content, and gamification are not limited to the digital sphere, most gaming-related P/CVE measures are realized online. As such, the focus of this chapter will be the current practices, gaps, and areas of improvement of digital P/CVE measures.[2]

Bespoke Games

The production of bespoke (i.e., custom) games is the most popular type of gaming-related P/CVE initiatives. In the last few years, several games have been produced for these purposes (Schlegel, 2022). Examples include:

- *Decount* (Pisoiu & Lippe, 2022) places players in the shoes of individuals, who may be on the path of radicalization. The game is based on the premise that radicalization processes constitute a series of seemingly mundane decisions, which can escalate to radicalization. It offers players four stories to choose from: Two jihadist radicalizations and two right-wing radicalizations. Players have to make binary decisions, e.g., to go to a right-wing concert or not, and the conglomerate of decisions then may lead to a radicalization of the main character. The game was developed by Austrian Institute for International Affairs (oiip), Bloodirony Games, and Subotron in 2020. The declared goal of the chat-based game is to increase the players' critical thinking skills and knowledge about radicalization processes.

- *Hidden Codes* is a mobile game developed by the Bildungsstätte Anne Frank [The Anne Frank Educational Centre] and the game development studio PlayingHistory in 2021. It was created to be played with teenage audiences in educational settings. The goal of the game is to raise awareness about both right-wing and jihadist radicalization processes in the digital sphere. Players scroll through chats, online profiles, and posts in order to gain insights into radicalization processes and prominent codes and narratives used by extremist actors online, develop digital literacy skills, and learn how to identify and react to posts with extremist messages.
- The game *Leon's Identität* [Leon's Identity] is a point-and-click game designed to raise awareness about the dangers of far-right ideology and is one of the few P/CVE games that was developed not by an NGO but by a governmental institution. It was produced in 2020 by the game development studio btf on behalf of the Ministry of Interior of the German state North Rhein-Westfalia. In the game, a young man named Leon has suddenly gone missing after becoming involved in the far-right milieu and the player takes on the role of Leon's brother, who is searching Leon's room trying to find clues about his disappearance. The game was designed to educate teenage audiences about the Identitarian Movement and potential signs of radicalization.[3]

Other examples of P/CVE games include *Klif* (KleineBeerFilm, n.d.), *Gali Fakta* (Moonshot, 2022), several Games for Peace,[4] *Loulu* (onlinetheater.live & HAU Hebbel am Ufer, 2021), and *Call of Prev* (Cultures Interactive, 2021). All these games are serious games, i.e., they are developed with the intention to educate and not (only) to entertain (Jacobs, 2021). The trend to produce bespoke games for P/CVE is likely to continue in the coming years and current projects, such as *GameD – Gaming for Democracy*, are set to produce a second generation of P/CVE games with a larger emphasis on the entertainment quality of the game.[5]

While many bespoke P/CVE games are created as standalone experiences, some P/CVE actors combine the production of bespoke games with more traditional educational approaches. A recent example of this is *Call of Prev*, a project implemented by the German NGO Cultures Interactive. This game was developed for adolescents who are *not* radicalized (i.e., are considered to be in the primary prevention category).[6] The game revolves around gangs, (violent) conflict, and moral dilemmas of wishing to stay out of trouble but needing or wanting to choose sides. In contrast to many other games created for the P/CVE contexts, *Call of Prev* was developed to be utilized exclusively in schools and educational workshops. These settings facilitate conversations around the content between the players of the game and the administrators of the project and the conversations surrounding the gameplay were found to be more impactful than the content of the game itself (Call of Prev team, personal correspondence, January 30, 2023). Interestingly, the creators of *Call of Prev* found that users reported the ability to create modifications (or mods) to the game the most most important feature of the entire experience (Call of Prev team, personal correspondence, January 30, 2023) – that is, the players' ability to create their own worlds, maps, characters, quests, and dialogs. The modding experiences allowed the educators to ask crucial educational questions such as "What does a good world look like for you?," "Why does this map look the way it does?," "Which experiences did you have in your personal life that are similar to the quest or dialogue you made?," or "Why do these characters look the way they do?" The creators of *Call of Prev* reported that the ensuing conversations about these questions opened up meaningful conversations with the young people.[7]

Developing bespoke games has clear advantages for P/CVE efforts, because it allows for complete control over the content and design to ensure that the game matches the needs and preferences of P/CVE actors. However, current P/CVE games do not live up to their full potential. A recent review of existing bespoke P/CVE games found that most of these games are largely limited to audiences in political education and primary prevention settings. That is, they are created with the specific purpose of reaching individuals who are not radicalized. The bespoke games were also found to be largely text-heavy and static single-player games with relatively simple mechanics (e.g., point-and-click), often employing linear, short, and simple narratives that do not afford players a lot of agency. For example, they typically utilize binary decision making to drive the story forward rather than encouraging exploration, and heavily prioritize relaying serious topics and "getting the message across" rather than emphasizing an enjoyable game experience (Schlegel, 2022). In other words, many of these games require players to *read* a substantial amount of text rather than providing the opportunity to *play* the narrative. This is notable, as it indicates that custom- designed games for P/CVE largely are not fully taking advantage of the entertainment value videogames can offer despite the fact that a significant amount of the educational value games provide comes from being engaged and entertained by the material, a phenomenon referred to as "unintentional learning" (Kowert, 2021).

Bespoke games for P/CVE purposes are still a burgeoning area of research and development. Nevertheless, some preliminary insights can be deduced. Most importantly, while some of these game-based interventions have been found to elicit some positive effects (Moonshot, 2022), a lack of emphasis on creating fun and entertaining games has likely limited the effectiveness of these interventions. Future development in this area could focus on modeling P/CVE games less as educational experiences and more as entertainment products – for instance, by reducing the amount of text players have to read, employing exciting mechanics rather than point-and-click, and offering dynamic rather than static gameplay. A more thorough engagement with how to embed and connect these games to existing P/CVE measures and traditional educational formats could create more effective P/CVE intervention work, particularly for those in the primary prevention category.

Existing Games

P/CVE efforts have also employed existing videogames in prevention and counter-extremism efforts. In comparison to the production of bespoke games, using existing videogames has a number of advantages. For example, the development of new videogames requires a considerable amount of funding, technical skills, and game design expertise, while the use of existing games requires fewer resources and offers the opportunity to utilize professionally produced games. Hence, P/CVE actors can benefit from the quality of the existing games without having to spend large sums on game production. The use of pre-existing games also has the advantage of tapping into existing player bases, rather than having to build user communities from the ground up, which can be time consuming and difficult.

The use of existing videogames for P/CVE efforts can take many forms. This can include, but is not limited to, playing games together with target audiences as a way to initiate conversations with young target audiences, modifying pre-existing games to tailor them to P/CVE or other educational content, making use of in-game communication features within existing games, hosting gaming tournaments to facilitate a positive gaming experience, raising awareness on extremists' use of (certain popular) videogames, and engaging the communities surrounding existing games in P/CVE work.

Two successful initiatives using pre-existing games for prevention efforts are *Cops vs. Kids* implemented by the North Yorkshire Police (UK) and *Gamen Met De Politie* [Gaming with the Police] developed by the Dutch Police.[8] Both projects are based on the same premise: By offering to play popular video games such as *Fifa* (EA Sports) or *Rocket League* (Psyonix) with young people in the community, police officers in both of these projects are able to reach, encourage conversations, and facilitate trust in target audiences, who are potentially difficult to reach or considered at risk. While

Gamen Met De Politie is implemented online, *Cops vs. Kids* takes place in offline settings such as youth centers in the style of classical LAN Parties. Both initiatives employ popular existing games and consoles audiences are already familiar with, which considerably lowers the barriers to participation. Playing together serves as a conversation starter, reduces insecurities and breaks down barriers to interacting with the police, allows conversations to flow naturally while focussing on the game, and makes it easier for young people to approach police officers and ask questions. The desired outcome of both projects is that the teenagers are more comfortable to approach police officers and gain enough trust in them to raise concerns they may have.

Another possibility for P/CVE efforts would be to create mods of existing games. Although a number of mods have been produced by extremist actors as well as by civil society actors working in the space of conflict resolution, peace education, and related fields (Darvasi, 2016), mods with the goal of preventing or countering radicalization have not been integrated into P/CVE projects so far. Modifying existing videogames may be especially convenient for P/CVE actors as the development of mods requires fewer resources and technical skills than the creation of bespoke games and projects may benefit from the popular appeal of the original game in seeking to reach target audiences. However, so far, P/CVE actors have not attempted to incorporate modding into their project designs. Therefore, mods are a hitherto unexplored avenue for counter-extremism efforts and present an important gap in the current P/CVE landscape (RAN, 2022). Producing high-quality modifications that can compete with extremist mods of popular videogames and analyzing their effects would be a useful next step for the field.

In addition, in-game communication features have also not (yet) been used in P/CVE work. This is problematic considering that a recent UNOCT study uncovered that many gamers encounter hateful and extremist content when using in-game communication features such as voice- or text-based chats (Schlegel & Amarasingam, 2022). While chats have been used in P/CVE initiatives and digital youth work in other digital spaces such as social media platforms, this has not been transferred to in-game chats and game-based social spaces. The main reason for this is difficulties in accessing relevant chat communications. If P/CVE actors are to meaningfully engage players during in-game communication, they need to do so in real time while the extremist content is being discussed. This would entail becoming embedded in the gaming community and being active in the chats while the conversation is unfolding, which would require P/CVE practitioners to spend (at least part of) their working hours playing videogames and talking to other players (RAN, 2022). In addition, it is currently unclear which games are used by extremist actors to spread their narratives – making it difficult for P/CVE actors to decide which videogames to focus on. Nevertheless, future P/CVE efforts will have to mitigate these issues as UNOCT's study clearly demonstrated the need for counter-extremism measures in in-game chats and other game-based communication features.

Gaming (-Adjacent) Platforms

P/CVE actors have implemented initiatives on various (social) media platforms for years. As millions of people have begun to use gaming and gaming (-adjacent) platforms such as *Steam* (https://store.steampowered.com/), *Discord* (https://discord.com/), *Twitch* (https://www.twitch.tv/), *Roblox* (https://www.roblox.com/), and *DLlive* (https://dlive.tv/), these digital spaces have now also become relevant for both extremists and the P/CVE actors seeking to curb extremists' influence (see Chapter 5 in this volume). While these platforms are often grouped under one label and referred to as "gaming (-adjacent) platforms," they are diverse in their features and main functions and provide a range of different opportunities. As such, there is a significant potential for P/CVE measures across these platforms.

For example, according to the RAN (2021b), P/CVE actors could collaborate with streamers and other influencers on these platforms, support organic counterspeech efforts, implement their own counterspeech initiatives, transfer digital youth work approaches from other social media platforms to forums, chats, and servers on gaming (-adjacent) platforms, engage users in direct conversations on these platforms, establish their own spaces such as Discord servers or forums, employ (live)streaming, or publish Let's Play videos – either of bespoke P/CVE games or of commercial games with relevant narratives such as *Through the Darkest of Times* (Paintbucket Games).

Despite the large variety of possibilities to deliver P/CVE initiatives on gaming (-adjacent) platforms, very few P/CVE projects have actually been implemented in these spaces so far. Although digital P/CVE initiatives are now standard practice, the knowledge among P/CVE practitioners surrounding new digital environments such as gaming-related platforms, is still limited. In order to design effective interventions in gaming spaces, P/CVE actors would need more subcultural knowledge about gaming and acquire a deeper understanding on the platform characteristics, communication standards, and modes of interaction. As this knowledge is lacking, most P/CVE projects implemented so far have not made use of gaming (-adjacent) platforms. However, as extremist actors are present and active on these platforms, it is adamant for P/CVE practitioners to develop the necessary subcultural and platform-specific knowledge to include gaming (-adjacent) platforms in the design of future P/CVE campaigns.

One of the few P/CVE projects that incorporates gaming (-adjacent) platforms is *Good Gaming - Well Played Democracy*.[9] The project is implemented by the German Amadeu Antonio Foundation and consists of two components. First, a monitoring of right-wing extremist, far-right, and fringe activities on gaming and gaming (-adjacent) platforms such as *Steam* and *Discord* is carried out. Second, the information gathered during the monitoring is used to conduct workshops, disseminate information, and develop recommendations for interested P/CVE practitioners. The findings of the monitoring are also the basis for a pilot initiative seeking to implement a digital youth work approach on gaming (-adjacent) platforms. Users who engage with far-right or right-wing extremist content are addressed in a one-to-many approach by the project team and, should the opportunity arise, also in one-to-one conversations. While this is a good starting point, there are many more possible types of intervention P/CVE actors could and should explore on gaming (-adjacent) platforms in the future.

Gaming Aesthetics and Gaming (Cultural) References

As discussed in Chapter 7, there are a range of extremist actors who incorporate gaming aesthetics and gaming (cultural) references in their propaganda (Dauber *et al.*, 2019; Hass im Netz, 2020). Until now, however, P/CVE projects have rarely mirrored this trend. This is surprising as it could be a viable option for P/CVE actors to increase the appeal of their content. The digital sphere is highly competitive and users can choose from an abundance of entertainment options. In this environment, many P/CVE projects struggle to create the necessary visibility and reach for their initiatives and to develop content that can compete with entertainment content for the attention of target audiences. Employing gaming aesthetics and gaming references may be an opportunity to benefit from the popcultural appeal of video games and improve the attractiveness of P/CVE content without having to develop a full video game. By appropriating videogame aesthetics and gaming references in existing P/CVE content formats such as counter- and alternative narrative campaigns, P/CVE actors can make such content more appealing without requiring a large amount of funding or technical expertise. There are myriad possibilities to utilize videogame aesthetics or gaming cultural references. This may include the appropriation of visual styles used in gaming, the use of terms derived from gamer language, incorporating allusions to gaming subculture, making direct references to popular videogames or using stories derived from popular videogames to relay P/CVE content.

A prominent illustrative example of how P/CVE actors can appropriate gaming aesthetics in their narrative projects is *Jamal al-Khatib*, a YouTube and Instagram campaign against jihadism developed and implemented by the Austrian organization TURN.[10] The declared goal of the campaign is to create content that is geared towards the viewing habits of teenagers and adolescents, which explicitly includes camera "shots [akin] to first-person shooter sequences like those in video games" (Reicher & Lippe, 2019; Ali *et al.*, 2020, p. 232). This entails, as depicted in Figures 10.1, 10.2 and 10.3, the use of camera angles such as over-the-shoulder shots

FIGURE 10.1 Screenshot from *Jamal al-Khatib* season 2, episode 3.

FIGURE 10.2 Screenshot from *Jamal al-Khatib* season 2, episode 3.

FIGURE 10.3 Screenshot from *Jamal al-Khatib* season 2, episode 3.

before a fight breaks out, game-inspired fight scenes, and the placement of Quran verses to mirror instructions given in videogame tutorials.[11] "By incorporating the visual style of first-person shooter games into the counter-narrative/alternative narrative video campaign, the project transfers the aesthetic allure and attractiveness of gaming media to a non-gaming context. This presents a subtle yet effective way to employ gaming cultural references in a P/CVE intervention," concludes a review by the Radicalisation Awareness Network (RAN, 2020, p. 12).

Gamification

Gamification may be defined as the "use of game design elements within non-game contexts" (Deterding *et al.*, 2011) and refers to the transfer of game components such as points, leaderboards, or badges to contexts not traditionally regarded as spaces of play. It is often associated with the attempt to motivate a desired behavior (change) in participants, e.g., to recycle their garbage, work out, or take their medication on time (Schlegel, 2021, 2022). Not only extremists, but also civil society organizations and P/CVE actors have begun to use gamified applications (Lakhani *et al.*, 2022). In fact, a recent book by Fleisch (2018) postulates that "gamification4good" will become a "central pillar" of civil society organizations' projects and can be used to address "the biggest challenges of human development" (p. 85, my translation; see also McGonigal, 2012).

This suggests that gamification may also be applied to initiatives to prevent or counter extremism. Indeed, recent theoretical contributions indicate that "gamification4good" could be successfully employed by P/CVE actors in multiple ways (RAN, 2021a; Schlegel, 2021). This includes, but is not limited to, the use of gamified elements to motivate counterspeech efforts, employing concepts such as raids, quests, and narratives in digital P/CVE work to motivate users to learn more about counterextremism, or to integrate gamified elements in existing P/CVE projects, e.g. by introducing caption competitions or similar game elements on existing P/CVE-related Instagram channels. The clear advantage of using gamification rather than developing a whole standalone game is that these gamified elements can be applied in various ways, that gamification is far less resource intensive than the development of a whole videogame, and that it can be incorporated into existing P/CVE measures. However, like many other gaming elements and spaces discussed in this chapter, gamification has rarely been used in P/CVE initiatives. P/CVE practitioners do not (yet) seem comfortable enough and lack the required knowledge to effectively apply gamification in their projects.

One of the few P/CVE projects with a gamification component is *Detect Then Act* (DTCT).[12] The project is run by a consortium of NGOs from across Europe and seeks to encourage "upstanders" – volunteers who have been trained in countering hate speech in the digital sphere – to respond to hateful messages online. The replies of the upstanders can be text based or contain GIFs and humorous memes. The upstanders' experience of engaging in countering hate speech is gamified. They are presented with a dashboard that is tracking hate speech. This dashboard includes progress bars and points for each post's reach, threat level, and degree of hatefulness (see RAN, 2022, p. 14 for images). Furthermore, DTCT organized an online event named #1dayofonlinehappiness. For 24 hours, the upstanders were divided into national teams and held a friendly competition to determine who could respond to more hate speech messages. The teams of upstanders were awarded points for each hateful post they responded to as well as every comment, like, and share of their reply, which were displayed on a scoreboard. Overall, DTCT employed rather simple gamification elements, but this case nevertheless points to the potential gamification may hold for P/CVE initiatives.

Future projects could and should explore gamification in more depth and move beyond "pointification" towards more sophisticated gamified applications in P/CVE.

Conclusion and Ways Forward

Gaming-related P/CVE interventions are still in their infancy – even more so than research on extremists' use of video games, gaming elements, and gaming spaces discussed throughout this book. P/CVE actors are only beginning to explore how different aspects of gaming could aid their goal of preventing and countering extremist actors and their propaganda in digital gaming spaces. Hence, very few projects have been implemented so far and practical experiences, lessons learned, and recommendations for gaming-related P/CVE are extremely limited at this point in time. However, the last few years have seen a stark increase in interest from P/CVE practitioners, NGOs, and international organizations such as the Radicalisation Awareness Network in exploring gaming-related P/CVE measures and enabling P/CVE actors to use the positive appeal of gaming for their efforts against extremism. This suggests that more gaming-related P/CVE interventions will be funded, developed, and implemented in the coming years and that gaming content could become a constant element of the P/CVE "toolbox."

However, if this is to be effective and successful, a more thorough engagement with videogames, gaming-related content, and gaming (-adjacent) platforms is needed. As we have seen above, the conglomerate of existing gaming-related P/CVE interventions is clearly skewed toward the production of bespoke games. Producing videogames is the logical entry point into engagement with gaming, but is only one of many options experts could draw from to incorporate and benefit from the popular appeal of videogames. As shown above, few existing projects have utilized gaming (-adjacent) platforms or gaming (cultural) references, while modifications and in-game chats have not been used at all. Gamification has only been used sparingly and only in simple formats, more akin to "pointification" rather than true gamification. In other words, going forward P/CVE actors can and should utilize a broader, more diverse spectrum of gaming approaches and test their utility for prevention and counter-extremism efforts.

It is not only extremists who have been using gaming content and spaces for their ends. A large body of research has demonstrated that gaming and gamification can serve a number of goals and can have a range of persuasive outcomes and may change attitudes and even behavior. This includes outcomes related to P/CVE such as improved perspective taking, awareness of conflict, or a decrease in skepticism towards out-groups (see Schlegel, 2022 for an overview). Employing gaming and gaming-related elements in P/CVE is therefore a promising avenue for the future. However, as this chapter suggests, P/CVE actors need to overcome a range of challenges related to the development and implementation of gaming-related interventions. According to the RAN (2021a, 2021b, 2022), important challenges include a general lack of knowledge about gaming, gaming spaces, and gamification and how to utilize them effectively in P/CVE projects. P/CVE actors need to explore how to use, for instance, in-game chats or forums on gaming (-adjacent) platforms and understand gaming communities as a new target audience for counter-extremism approaches to be able to successfully transfer existing digital P/CVE measures from social media platforms to gaming spaces. Similarly, employing gaming cultural references or developing a videogame also requires at least basic subcultural knowledge on (popular) videogames, gaming culture, and gaming communities. This subcultural knowledge is the foundation for all gaming-related P/CVE efforts and, hence, needs to be developed by P/CVE actors seeking to implement such campaigns.

Another crucial challenge is the technical and creative expertise needed to develop games and mods, appropriate gaming aesthetics in videos, or design gamified applications. It is unfeasible to expect P/CVE practitioners, who often have backgrounds in social work, pedagogy, political science, criminology, or religious studies, to learn game design. Here cooperation with tech companies, game design studios, and gamification experts (and the funding such cooperations require), will be necessary. However, as a recent RAN paper (2022) postulated, such collaborations between the P/CVE and the gaming sector are currently limited. The success of future gaming-related P/CVE interventions will partially depend on a more in-depth engagement of P/CVE actors with gaming and related fields, but equally on possibilities to build partnerships across sections – similar to existing cooperations between social media companies and P/CVE practitioners and efforts such as the Global Internet Forum to Counter Terrorism (GIFCT).

Overall, more evidence and practical experiences with gaming-related P/CVE interventions need to be accumulated before the practicality, effectiveness, and impact of such interventions can be adequately judged. However, as we have seen, it is encouraging that gaming-related interventions are gaining in prominence and the appeal and effects of a range of gaming-related P/CVE projects is currently being tested. Going forward, more pilot interventions and (bold) trial-and-error approaches will be necessary to accumulate the necessary practical knowledge on how gaming elements may be successfully incorporated into digital P/CVE efforts. Only by embracing gaming as a new element in the P/CVE toolkit and developing and implementing a diverse array of gaming-related approaches will P/CVE actors be able to gauge which types of gaming-related intervention can be expected to have impact, which effects such interventions should be expected to achieved, which types of intervention are most effective, which projects are most suitable to reach desired target audiences, and which lessons and recommendations can be deduced from their pilot interventions in the gaming sphere. Doing so, as the EGRN postulates, is one of the fundamental tasks for future counter-extremism and prevention efforts in the gaming realm.

Notes

1 The hash database allows platforms and tech companies to share information about extremist content they found with other platforms and companies to support cross-platform removal of such content. See https://gifct.org/hsdb/.
2 Nevertheless, an exploration of how gaming-related content could enhance offline P/CVE efforts would be interesting and fruitful in its own right and should be the focus of future studies.
3 The Identitarian Movement is an umbrella organization comprising multiple far-right actors and (sub-) movements in German-speaking Europe, who perceive the European identity to be in danger and seek to protect it.
4 https://mgiep.unesco.org/gamesforpve.
5 https://www.scenor.at/gamed.
6 Audiences in primary prevention are not radicalized, whereas audiences in secondary prevention have already been exposed to extremist propaganda and have begun a process of radicalization, and audiences in tertiary prevention are fully radicalized.
7 This section is based on the author's personal correspondence with members of the Call of Prev project team (January 30, 2023). A project report will be published soon.
8 https://www.youtube.com/watch?v=WIxx9mp8z8M [video on the *Cops vs. Kids* pilot].
https://gamenmetdepolitie.nl/ [*Gamen met de Politie* website in Dutch].
9 https://www.amadeu-antonio-stiftung.de/projekte/good-gaming-well-played-democracy/.
10 https://www.youtube.com/c/JamalalKhatib/videos.
11 The verse depicted in the third image states that mujahideen are those who are fighting against themselves and their own deficiencies – an understanding of jihad that the protagonist of the videos uses as an instruction for his own life and encourages his viewers to do the same.
12 https://dtct.eu/.

References

Ali, R., Sibljakovic, D., Lippe, F., Neuburg, U., & Neuburg, F. (2020). "You're Against Dawla, but You're Listening to their Nasheeds?" Appropriating Jihadi Audiovisualities in the Online Streetwork Project Jamal al-Khatib – My Path! In C. Günther & S. Pfeifer (Eds.), *Jihadi Audiovisuality and its Entanglements: Meanings, aesthetics, appropriations* (pp. 222–246). Edinburgh University Press.
Bildungsstätte Anne Frank (2021). *Hidden Codes*. [Videogame]. https://hidden-codes.de/.
Cultures Interactive (2021). *Call of Prev*. [Videogame]. https://www.cultures-interactive.de/en/the-project.html.
Darvasi, P. (2016). Empathy, Perspective and Complicity: How Digital Games Can Support Peace Education and Conflict Resolution. United Nations Educational, Scientific and Cultural Organization | Mahatma Gandhi Institute of Education for Peace and Sustainable Development. https://unesdoc.unesco.org/ark:/48223/pf0000259928.
Dauber, C., Robinson, M., Baslious, J., & Blair, A. (2019). Call of Duty: Jihad – How the Video Game Motif Has Migrated Downstream from Islamic State Propaganda Videos. *Perspectives on Terrorism*, 13(3), pp. 17–31.

Deterding, S., Dixon, D., Khaled, R., & Nacke, L. (2011). From Game Design Elements to Gamefulness: Defining Gamification. https://www.researchgate. net/publication/230854710_From_Game_Design_Elements_to_Gamefulness_ Defining_Gamification/link/00b7d5315ab1be3c37000000/download.

EA Sports (n.d.). *Fifa*. [Videogame]

EGRN (n.d.). https://extremismandgaming.org/.

Fleisch, H. (2018). *Gamification4Good: Gemeinwohl spielerisch stärken*. Erich Schmidt Verlag.

Hass im Netz (2020). Rechtsextremismus und Gaming: Ein komplexes Verhältnis. https://www.hass-im-netz.info/themen/artikel/rechtsextremismus-und-gaming-ein-komplexes-verhaeltnis.html.

Jacobs, R. (2021). Serious Games: Play for Change. In R. Kowert & T. Quandt (Eds.), *The Video Game Debate 2: Revisiting the physical, social, and psychological effects of video games* (pp. 19–40). Routledge.

KleineBeerFilm (n.d.) *Klif. [Videogame]*. https://www.klif-game.nl/.

Kowert, R. (2021). Unspoken Benefits of Video Game Play. *Entertainment Software Rating Board*. https://www.esrb.org/blog/unspoken-benefits-of-video-game-play/.

Lakhani, S. (2021). Video Gaming and (Violent) Extremism: An Exploration of the Current landscape, trends, and threats. https://homeaffairs.ec.europa.eu/system/ files/2022-02/EUIF%20Technical%20Meeting%20on%20Video%20Gaming %20October%202021%20RAN%20Policy%20Support2paper_en.pdf.

Lakhani, S., White, J., & Wallner, C. (2022). The Gamification of (Violent) Extremism: An Exploration of Emerging Trends, Future Threat Scenarios and Potential P/CVE Solutions. https://home-affairs.ec.europa.eu/system/files/2022-09/RAN%20Policy%20Support-%20gamification%20of%20violent %20extremism_en.pdf.

McGonigal, J. (2012). *Reality is Broken: Why Games Make Us Better and How They Can Change the World*. Vintage Books.

Ministry of Interior of North Rhein-Westfalia (2020). *Leon's Identität*. [Videogame]. btf https://leon.nrw.de/.

Moonshot (2022). Advancing Media Literacy in Indonesia: Building Resilience and Measuring Behavior Change. https://moonshotteam.com/resource/ advancing-media-literacy-in-indonesia-building-resilience-and-measuring-behavior-change/.

Moonshot (2020). *Gali Fakta*. [Videogame]

Neumann, P. (2012). Countering Online Radicalization in America. *Bipartisan Policy Center*. https://bipartisanpolicy.org/download/?file=/wp-content/ uploads/2019/03/BPC-_Online-Radicalization-Report.pdf.

Oiip (2020). *Decount*. [Videogame]. https://www.extremismus.info/decounten.

onlinetheater.live & HAU Hebbel am Ufer (2021). *Loulu*. [Videogame]. https:// onlinetheater.live/project/loulu.

Paintbucket Games (2020). *Through the Darkest of Times*. [Videogame]. https:// paintbucket.de/en/game/through-the-darkest-of-times.

Pisoiu, D. & Lippe, F. (2022). The Name of the Game: Promoting Resilience Against Extremism Through an Online Gaming Campaign. https://firstmonday. org/ojs/index.php/fm/article/view/12600/10632.

Psyonix (n.d.). *Rocket League.* [Videogame]

RAN (2020). Extremists' Use of Video Gaming – Strategies and Narratives. https://home-affairs.ec.europa.eu/system/files/2020-11/ran_cn_conclusion_paper_videogames_15-17092020_en.pdf.

RAN (2021a). The Gamification of Violent Extremism & Lessons for P/CVE. https://home-affairs.ec.europa.eu/networks/radicalisation-awareness-network-ran/publications/gamification-violent-extremism-lessons-pcve-2021_en.

RAN (2021b). Extremists' Use of Gaming (adjacent) Platforms – Insights Regarding Primary and Secondary Prevention Measures. https://home-affairs. ec.europa.eu/networks/radicalisation-awareness-network-ran/publications/ extremists-use-gaming-adjacent-platforms-insights-regarding-primary-and-secondary-prevention_en.

RAN (2022). Countering the Misuse of Gaming-Related Content & Spaces: Inspiring Practices and Opportunities for Cooperation with Tech Companies. https://home-affairs.ec.europa.eu/whats-new/publications/countering-misuse-gaming-related-content-spaces-inspiring-practices-and-opportunities-cooperation_en.

Reicher, F. & Lippe, F. (2019). *Jamal al-Khatib – Mein Weg!* Online-Campaigning als Methode der Politischen Bildung. *e-beratungsjournal.net*, 15(1), article 4.

Schlegel, L. (2021). The Role of Gamification in Radicalization Processes. modusIzad Working Paper 1/2021. https://modus-zad.de/wp-content/uploads/2021/01/ modus-working-paper-12021.pdf.

Schlegel, L. (2022). Playing Against Radicalization: Why Extremists Are Gaming and how P/CVE Can Leverage the Positive Effects of Video Games to Prevent Radicalization. https://www.scenor.at/_files/ugd/ff9c7a_9f5f3687937b4f3384 e2b0a7eac8c33f.pdf.

Schlegel, L. & Amarasingam, A. (2022). Examining the Intersection Between Gaming and Violent Extremism. *UNOCT Action Research.* https://www.un. org/counterterrorism/sites/www.un.org.counterterrorism/files/221005_ research_launch_on_gaming_ve.pdf.

CONCLUDING THOUGHTS

Rachel Kowert and Linda Schlegel

The use of digital gaming spaces by extremist actors is of growing interest to a wide range of stakeholders. Governments are interested in how these spaces are being utilized to radicalize, mobilize, fundraise, and recruit. Parents are interested in what ideologies or propaganda their children may be exposed to while playing games. Tech companies want to understand how extremists exploit their platforms and actors working on preventing and/or countering (violent) extremism (P/CVE) want to understand how to curb extremists' influence in digital gaming spaces and use gaming for prevention efforts. Researchers are interested in all of the above.

As a growing area of interest and expertise, the last few years have brought significant strides in understanding the landscape of extremism in games. This book is the culmination of that progress, summarizes the current state of knowledge, and brings together a range of topics and perspectives from world-leading experts on gaming and extremism. It opened by exploring the unique technological features and cultures that created an amenable space within games, to better understand the past and present debates about the uses and effects of games as well as to provide an overview of what games are, how they are made, and how they are used (Chapter 1). This was followed by a theoretical overview of how extremists use gaming and game-related content, which integrates our knowledge on the use of gaming by extremists into existing theories of radicalization and introduces several aspects of extremist exploitation that are further developed throughout the volume, including typologies, gamification, and social and identity dynamics (Chapter 2).

DOI: 10.4324/9781003388371-12

Following this, there was a deeper exploration of the specific ways that games and gaming spaces have been, and currently are being, used for the propagation of extremist ideology. This included an examination of bespoke games and game modifications produced by extremists (Chapter 3), the documented methods of recruitment through digital games (Chapter 4), the role of gaming (-adjacent) platforms (Chapter 5), the prevalence of extremist content and users' experience with such content in digital gaming spaces (Chapter 6), the use of gaming aesthetics and cultural references to propagandize (Chapter 7), and the use of game mechanics to "gamify" radicalization, digital extremist activity, and offline violence (Chapter 8). Understanding the many facets of this landscape is important to gain a deeper insight into the manifold ways extremists seek to use gaming and to best inform the development of effective countermeasures.

The book concluded with two chapters exploring countermeasures and prevention efforts responding to extremist activity in gaming spaces (Chapters 9 and 10). Over the last few years, an increasing amount of insights on counter-extremism efforts in tech has been generated, which can also be applied and adapted to gaming spaces. This includes discussions around safety-by-design as well as more advanced interventions – although new challenges, such as the rise of the metaverse, are on the horizon and will require even further innovation and technical sophistication in counter-extremism measures. These efforts should be viewed as separate yet related to P/CVE projects driven largely by civil society actors seeking to address extremist activity in gaming spaces through positive intervention and prevention measures. In both areas, more diverse efforts, bold trial-and-error testing, and creative ideas are needed to understand more about and develop the best approaches against extremism in digital gaming spaces.

Research on gaming and extremism is still in its infancy. It is constantly evolving, being redefined, challenged, and further developed. Hence, this book provides an overview of our *current* understanding of games and extremism and has created a foundation of knowledge from which to build from to better understand how and why extremists are uniquely using games as well as the most effective measures that tech and civil society can combat these efforts. Nevertheless, it should be viewed as a snapshot of a young and highly dynamic field of research, which will evolve tremendously over the coming years as our knowledge on the potential nexus on gaming and extremism continues to grow.

In addition, we should be careful not to securitize gaming as such. Hence, we must conclude this volume with one final caveat: It is of the utmost importance to remember that gaming in and of itself is neither the sole cause nor the driver of radicalization. Millions of individuals around the world enjoy gaming and use gaming (-adjacent) platforms without ever encountering or being drawn into extremist activity. There is also no direct causal link between gaming and violence. As the American Psychological Association put it after its review of over two decades of research efforts on gaming and violence, attributing violent behavior to video games is "not scientifically sound" (APA, 2020, p. 1). Hence, there is also no direct causal link between gaming and (violent) extremism or terrorist attacks. The material contained within this book should be considered in context of this and the contents within it in no way suggest that the authors or editors assume that gaming *causes* radicalization or extremism in any shape or form. Rather, extremists are present in gaming spaces and seek to leverage gaming. This should not be ignored but needs to be critically discussed, researched, and reviewed with the appropriate degree of nuance.

While this volume provides a collection of shared knowledge to build upon, there remain many unknowns still left to explore around digital games and extremism. This is a new and constantly evolving field and we hope this book serves as a foundation for future studies to generate new insights and expand our knowledge base further. Some directions future research could take include (but are certainly not limited to):

- Delineating how and why not only right-wing extremists but extremists from other ideological backgrounds (e.g., jihadism, left-wing extremism, incels) are using gaming-related content and spaces for their ends as well as examining whether the apparent prevalence of right-wing extremism in digital gaming spaces is evidence of right-wing individuals being especially drawn to gaming.
- Dig deeper into hitherto underexplored gaming spaces, including real-time communication via voice- and text-based in-game chats and closed groups on gaming (-adjacent) platforms to address our blind spots and study extremist activity in these realms.
- Generating a better understanding of the digital extremist ecosystem and the role gaming spaces play within this ecosystem – not only to draw individuals towards or keep already radicalized individuals interested in extremism, but for internal communication, attack planning, vetting, financing, and other activities related to extremism.
- Outline how known drivers and contextual factors of radicalization (Vergani *et al.*, 2020), e.g., age, gender, family background, socialization, feeling of (non-) belonging, and social identities, may interact and converge with gaming-related activities and understand how (if at all) process of radicalization begin and evolve in digital gaming spaces. While much of the current literature focuses on individuals who already display support for extremist organizations and narratives, we know

much less about the processes by which this support has come about, the role of in digital gaming spaces in radicalization, and how (if at all) such processes can be detected early on, for instance by analyzing changes in communication style.

- Test, analyze, and evaluate not only technical or mechanics-based counter-extremism efforts but also proactive gaming-related P/CVE intervention and prevention measures to explore the positive impact videogames, gaming communities, gaming-related content, and digital gaming spaces can have in mitigating the impact of extremist activity and propaganda.
- Better understand the processes of in-game radicalization and pathways to out-of-game mobilization of terroristic and violent activity and the roles that in-game and game-adjacent spaces play in these processes.

References

APA (2020). APA Resolution on Violent Video Games. https://www.apa.org/about/policy/resolution-violent-video-games.pdf.

Vergani, M., Iqbal, M., Ilbahar, E., & Barton, G. (2020). The Three Ps of Radicalization: Push, Pull and Personal. A Systematic Scoping Review of the Scientific Evidence about Radicalization Into Violent Extremism. *Studies in Conflict & Terrorism*, 43(10).

INDEX

Entries in **bold** denote tables; entries in *italics* denote figures; entries followed by 'n' denote notes.

Printed and bound by CPI Group (UK) Ltd, Croydon, CR0 4YY
08/06/2025
01897008-0003